Story Hour

Story Hour

55 Preschool Programs for Public Libraries

by
JERI KLADDER

McFarland & Company, Inc., Publishers
Jefferson, North Carolina, and London

British Library Cataloguing-in-Publication data are available

Library of Congress Cataloguing-in-Publication Data

Kladder, Jeri, 1947–
    Story hour : 55 preschool programs for public libraries / by Jeri
Kladder.
        p. cm.
    Includes bibliographical references and index.
    ISBN 0-7864-0065-X (lib. bdg. : 50# alk. paper) ∞
    1. Storytelling—United States.   2. Public libraries—United
States—Services to preschool children.   3. Children's stories—
Bibliography.   4. Children—United States—Books and reading.
I. Title.
Z718.3.K58   1995
027.62′51′0973—dc20
                                                    94-42093
                                                    CIP

Manufactured in the United States of America

McFarland & Company, Inc., Publishers
    Box 611, Jefferson, North Carolina 28640

To Ron,
who afforded me the time to write,
gave me the courage to try,
and prompted the discipline to finish

Table of Contents

Acknowledgments

I wish to acknowledge all of the children, their parents and nursery school teachers at the Dayton View Library (Dayton, Ohio) for being such eager and active participants and excellent extenders of my preschool story hour programs. So much of what I have done in the way of planning preschool story hours is a direct result of their enthusiasm, curiosity, and sense of adventure.

Credit must be given, also, to friends and mentors of my professional life: Carolyn Field and Helen Mullen of the Free Library of Philadelphia; Charlotte Leonard and Letitia Wilson of the Dayton and Montgomery County Public Library; and Beverly J. Moody, branch manager of Dayton View Library, who allowed me great freedom to provide my own style of children's programming.

The children's librarians I have worked with over the years at the Free Library of Philadelphia (Philadelphia, Pennsylvania), the Dayton and Montgomery County Public Library (Dayton, Ohio) and the Columbus Metropolitan Library (Columbus, Ohio) have provided much appreciated creative support. My special thanks to Phyllis Pflomm, children's librarian, who wrote and shared her own tell-and-draw stories when she could not find enough in printed sources; and to Melanie Myers, whose enthusiasm for poetry promoted my own experimentation with using it with preschoolers.

Children's librarians everywhere owe a debt of gratitude to Carolyn W. Lima and John A. Lima for their *A to Zoo: Subject Access to Children's Picture Books* (R. R. Bowker, now in its fourth edition). This guide has provided countless additions to many story hours and has saved untold numbers of hours of searching for "just one more story" to round out a program.

Despite the ideas exchanged over the years with many creative professionals, any errors or oddities in the final programs as presented here are solely mine.

Jeri Kladder
Columbus, Ohio
January 1995

Introduction

As a former third grade teacher, former elementary and junior high school librarian, and current public library children's librarian, my mission has always been to get books into the hands of children as often and as felicitously as possible. My story hours have always been literature-based and my themes open-ended, encouraging children to explore each topic further.

Preschool story time at a public library may be the first time preschool children are exposed to a formal group experience and also may be the first opportunity for preschoolers to see reading and books outside of the family context. My goals are:

- to make the preschool story hour fun, exciting, and enriching;
- to lead children to a love of reading and books and an excitement about the process of reading;
- to open preschool children's eyes and minds to new ways of perceiving the world and to encourage a creative spark to explore beyond the immediate story.
- to model book sharing ideas and behaviors for parents, teachers and other care givers observing my preschool story hour programs.

I have found using the theme idea for a four to eight week series of 30–45 minute programs to be most satisfying. From week to week you can with a series:

- build on the children's knowledge of the theme material and the relatedness of the topics within the theme;
- build on the children's growing attention span as their experience allows them to be more attentive for longer periods of time;
- build on the children's growing sophistication by using more complex stories and varying presentation styles;
- build on the children's growing familiarity and ease within the story hour setting, calling for more participation in the stories and discussion of the topics;

- build on the children's growing sense of responsibility to carry the theme from week to week, to explore further and share their discoveries, and to remember to prepare for their own participation in upcoming programs.

In the public library setting I usually vary my preschool story hours with picture book stories; filmstrips, 16mm films, and videocassettes; traditional storytelling; song, dance, and music; poetry; fingerplays and participation stories; simple craft activities; and lots of talking and sharing. The previous week's topic is reviewed briefly if the children have explored further and wish to share their additional experiences or information.

The story hour usually ends with a book talk of related titles. The children are encouraged to explore the current topic further, sometimes with a simple activity, recipe, or poem they can take home. And, of course, they are reminded to share their library story hour experiences with parents, brothers and sisters, friends, babysitters, etc.

At the conclusion of each session the coming week's topic is announced and previewed to reinforce the theme and relatedness of the topics and to encourage the children to anticipate the program and, perhaps, bring in a picture or object, or wear something appropriate to the topic.

Unlike many children's librarians who use age categories to restrict preschool story time attendance, I encourage parents and day care providers to bring children of all ages from birth to kindergarten age. The home or day care setting usually is not restricted to children of the same age so children are often accustomed to accommodating the interest, behavior, and abilities of different ages.

Flexibility is the key to a successful multi-age group program so that all children benefit in some say, even if not all in the same way. Knowing your audience and the adults who bring them helps maintain enough order to accomplish something during your story hour programs despite broad age differences.

I have found that the range of behavior and readiness for story hour to be nearly as great amongst a random group of 3–4 year olds as it is of a group of 2–5 year olds. The more mature children often set the tone of the story hour and provide a good example of participation, attentiveness, and divergent thinking for the less experienced children. More mature children also enjoy the role of mentor to younger children who need encouragement, attention or understanding.

The presence of the younger children often fosters patience and a sense of responsibility in the older children. And younger children often make unusual and valuable connections between their experiences and the topic under discussion.

My preschool story hour sessions usually run for 30–45 minutes, depending upon how involved we get, how long the children are capable of sitting, and how much creative energy the topic is able to engender on any given day.

Theme

I have collected eight preschool story hour series themes of from four to eight topics each plus some individual seasonal and holiday story presentation ideas. The stories, activities, themes and topics have brought me and my preschool audience enjoyment, satisfaction, and springboards to further study.

Topic

My *modus operandi* is to prepare much more material than I can possibly use during one 30–45 minute session because dealing with preschool children calls for maximum flexibility. If a pair of cardinals are building a nest outside of my window the spring day I am telling bird stories, I might skip part of my prepared program to take advantage of the opportunity to sharpen the children's observational skills and share information about the why's and how's and whatever's of being a bird — including finding and sharing a simple nonfiction book to show how library books can provide information as well as stories.

Likewise, on a rainy day when irritations are magnified and no one wants to sit still for any reason, I will use a lot of active fingerplays, participation stories and music, saving the lengthier, more demanding stories for another time when the atmosphere is more conducive to close attention.

If I schedule three or four or five presentations of the same program to different groups of preschoolers I will pick and choose from the materials gathered to make each presentation a fresh program, responsive to the unique characteristics of each group of children.

Name Tag

I try to have a name tag suggestive of the topic — some simple construction paper shape. Given my lack of artistic abilities, we often have a lively discussion about just what the name tag shape is supposed to represent. Children or their accompanying adult are encouraged to print the child's name on the tag to free me for greeting arrivals and ushering them to the story hour area. I prefer to use adhesive tape for affixing name tags instead of pins, which can be dangerous, or string, which can be a tangled aggravation to handle in quantity. And children love to take charge of taping on their own name tag.

I was surprised to find out that the children often save their weekly name tags to decorate the refrigerator door at home and as a memory aid for telling others about their story hour. So name tags do act as extensions to the children's story hour experience. They are also simple and inexpensive to make. A valuable timesaver and fun method of creating name tag shapes in quantity is our library's recently acquired Ellison Letter Machine.* The number of available shapes keeps growing.

Stories

I have included the stories under each topic with which we have had the most fun and which have been most successful. Taken together they make a nicely rounded presentation. Occasionally I have added some helpful suggestions about introducing the stories or have offered an interesting approach to the telling.

Like any other storyteller, I have my own favorite stories that I repeat freely when the theme and topic are appropriate. You may have already discovered that children enjoy hearing their old favorites in a new context. You may use the same story in different versions or presentation styles:

- Read the picture book story aloud, sharing the illustrations with the children. Do be careful to know the story well enough that you can hold the illustrations open so the children can see them while you tell the story.
- Tell the story without the book. Be careful, some picture book stories are very dependent upon the illustrations to relate important information about the characters, setting, or plot and must be presented—text and illustration together. With effort you may be able to incorporate that necessary visual information into an illustration-free narrative without bogging down the tale.
- Have the children retell the story for you while you show the illustrations or manipulate flannel board shapes.
- Show a filmstrip, film, or videocassette version of the story.

*The Ellison Letter Machine is available from Ellison Educational Equipment, Inc.; P.O. Box 8209; Newport Beach, California 92658-8209.

- So many single edition fairy tales are available in several versions by different illustrators. Share other illustrations of the tale and compare illustrative styles or detail differences.
- Act out the story with children supplying their own dialog to relate the story.
- Make or provide simple puppets or masks for the children to use in re-telling or re-enacting the story.

I have also included under separate headings story retellings in other formats: Tell & Draw, Flannel Board, String, Cut & Tell, etc.

Additional Titles

I have tried not to overuse any of the stories, limiting repetition of individual titles as a primary story or as an additional title. The Author Index and the Title Index will help you locate the specific programs in which your favorite stories are repeated. The additional titles are provided for the variety and flexibility required for all program situations presented to preschool children. Annotations and helpful hints for using the stories are included when I have felt I have discovered a successful (or novel) idea.

Filmstrips, 16mm Films & Videocassettes

I realize that filmstrips (fs), films (16mm), and videocassette recordings (VHS) of children's book stories are not always readily available to librarians and teachers planning preschool age programs. But they have become an integral part of my preschool story hours and their inclusion may prompt others to try them too. Also, I have included them because they may give focus to future acquisitions. The titles listed in non-book media versions have been used for preschool story times and are tried and proven to be satisfactory additions to the preschool story hour experience.

Poetry, Songs, Music

I include additional formats for presenting literature to children and to provide that necessary change of pace preschoolers need. The stories may be the central part of each story hour but poetry, song, dance and music can add sparkle to the program, draw in a child whose attention is wandering, and indelibly stamp the program topic into the minds of your young audience. Rhythm and rhyme are essential elements to human speech, to learning to verbalize and learning to read; and they are fun to hear and feel and move to. (The symbol A/C is used to indicate audiocassettes.)

Activities

The activities presented here are meant to reinforce the child's understanding of the program topic and to extend that understanding beyond the information already presented. I am a firm believer in giving the children an assignment for follow-up investigation. I join in on their enthusiasm when they tell me something new they have learned, or when they remember the announced topic the following week. But I would never make a preschooler feel inadequate for not remembering, or not having been present for last week's program.

Because I encourage the adults, parents, babysitters and preschool teachers to sit in on my programs, they know the ground we have covered as a group and can carry on with further exploration, investigation and discussion after the story hour is over. The adults also gain insights about their young charges when they observe their child's behavior in a group and the child's response to a different adult authority figure.

My interest is not so much in giving the child a souvenir of the story time such as take home items or name tags. Rather, I want to give the child a sense of choice and or mastery over his or her acquisition of new experiences and new knowledge.

Professional Resources

Many educators and knowledgeable librarians have written extensively and effectively on the theory and philosophy of programming for preschool story hours and on the developmental stages of children in relation to the reading process. You will find bibliographic references appended in the Professional Resources Bibliography.

My purpose here is to provide some packaged programs from which you will be able to pick and choose what is best for you as a storyteller, children's librarian or preschool teacher to present in your particular setting with your particular audience. I hope my method of making story connections and shaping story hour themes and topics will prompt you to generate ideas of your own for getting preschoolers and books together. To that end I hope you freely add and annotate your own ideas, successes, and story additions so the book may keep pace with your own programming for preschoolers.

Yes, I am advocating writing in this book! Your great idea or alteration of one of mine will be lost if you do not record it while it is still fresh in your mind and you are still excited and inspired by it. And, of course, marginal notes tell you what you have used and helps you to avoid falling into the habit of doing the same lesson plan over and over and over, boring yourself and the children.

I also record the dates of the programs as I use them. This gives me a good idea of how current the story list is when I decide it is time to try something new with a particular program theme and topic. I am also constantly making new connections among books from several different themes. Dating the titles as I use them helps me determine when it is time to use an old story in a new context.

If you have a successful idea for preschool story hours of your own I would be interested in hearing from you. Full credit will be given to ideas you pass on to me if used in future editions of this book.

Two last pieces of advice:

    1. Plan your programs while surrounded by the picture books on your shelves. Make piles of them, sort and resort, set aside books just begging to be included in the earliest possible story hour program. Planning from your desk, an easy chair in front of the television, or the front seat of a car on a long trip is much less successful than actually having the books to handle as you go along.

    2. Enjoy! Fun and enthusiasm are contagious. The children and their parents and other caregivers will catch it from you. Your relationship with the children and their accompanying grown-ups has the potential for developing into a true symbiotic relationship as your story hour offerings prompt children's suggestions and ideas for future programs.

Barnyard Animals

The design of the *Barnyard Animals* theme is to present life in a barnyard, realistically and imaginatively. You will be providing information about farms and barnyard animals as well as including the animals in fictionalized situations. Identifying real animals and their distinctive characteristics (the sounds they make, their habits, how they raise their young, etc.) and separating reality from fantasy are two of the goals you hope to achieve. You also want to be entertaining and to provide a comfortable nonthreatening introduction to reading and books.

Because each animal is separate and distinct, the story programs can be used individually. However, if you are using the entire *Barnyard Animals* series you should be conscious of the lengthening attention span, increasing sophistication and more responsive sense of humor the children are developing and take advantage of longer, more complex stories and discussions as the series progresses.

As always, have lots of related titles available for browsing and taking home. Many new and wonderful nonfiction books are being published each year specifically for this very young crowd, so don't forget nonfiction when you are collecting picture book titles for your story hour display.

Be sure to book talk some of the extra titles each week. You want the children to be interested enough in the story hour topic to pursue new information or stories on their own. Feed their natural curiosity by encouraging additional exploration of the topic before they leave and then give the children an opportunity to talk about what they have subsequently learned at the beginning of the following session.

An on-going activity could be to make a flash card of the animal-of-the-day for those interested in learning to read. Simple animal shapes, perhaps the same ones used for your name tags could be passed out at the end of each story time with a 3″ × 5″ index card upon which to glue it and the word or animal sound typed or printed in large letters on a separate sheet to be glued to the opposite side. At the end of the series the children will have a set of flash cards for all of the barnyard animals you have talked about. At the start of each session you could review the words and pictures of preceding animals. (The Ellison Letter Machine is very useful for a variety of animals and shapes if you have access to one. Also small, inexpensive note pads often come in animal shapes.)

I am a firm believer in making hand-outs self-service. I explain the hand-out and demonstrate any assembly required, especially if it involves glue, scissors, markers or any other potential mess or hazard. I display examples of each stage of construction as well.

Children are invited to come up and collect the pieces necessary for the project after they have taken care of their floor cushion and selected the display books they want to take home. I feel we accomplish several objectives with this method.

1. The children are given a pattern that doesn't vary from session to session, thus giving them a framework of acceptable behavior and expectations.

2. The children are given responsibilities to live up to: putting things away, taking pride of ownership of their library surroundings and a feeling of group effort for a common goal.

3. The children are given a series of complex instructions that, through repetition and watching others, they are able to follow, giving them a feeling of accomplishment and mastery over their surroundings and behavior.

4. The children are learning the courtesy of taking only what is needed, keeping the piles of supplies neat for each other and waiting their turn.

5. Enough time has elapsed between my instructions and their construction of the item that the children will be less tied to instructions and will be freer to interpret them as creatively and differently as they wish. It is fun to have the children bring back the craft item they have worked on at home for us to marvel at their ingenuity and acknowledge their pride in a job well done.

Ducks & Geese

Name Tags
Small yellow and white duck shapes;
A decorated goose egg shape.

Filmstrips, 16mm Films & Videocassettes
The Story About Ping, Flack. (10 min. fs/16mm/VHS).
Make Way for Ducklings, McCloskey. (11 min. fs/16mm/VHS).

Stories
The Chick and the Duckling, Ginsburg. A humorous game of follow the leader until the chick decides that swimming is not for him.

Duckat, Gordon. A duck thinks that it is a cat despite a little girl's attempts to convince it otherwise.

Make Way for Ducklings, McCloskey. In the interest of anatomical accuracy Robert McCloskey bought some baby ducks and let them loose in his apartment for several weeks so he could sketch their natural behavior.

Rechenka's Eggs, Polacco. A good Easter story or introduction to a Russian background.

Solo Plus One, Scamell. A cat accidentally becomes a duckling's mother for a while.

Have You Seen My Duckling?, Tafuri. Counting with a twist, the idea that one duckling is missing will encourage the children to study the simple illustrations to find it. Introduce the concept of one less and one more. (Caldecott Honor)

Fingerplay
from *Hand Rhymes*, Brown: "Quack! Quack! Quack!"

Poetry
from *Read-Aloud Rhymes for the Very Young*, Prelutsky: "Quack, Quack!," Seuss

Songs
from *Gonna Sing My Head Off*, Krull: "Go Tell Aunt Rhody"
from *The Silly Songbook*, Nelson: "Be Kind to Your Web-Footed Friends"

Five Little Ducks, Raffi. (Also in *The 2nd Raffi Songbook* and on A/C *Raffi: Rise and Shine*, Raffi.)

from *Raffi Singable Songbook*, Raffi: "Six Little Ducks" (Also on A/C *More Singable Songs*, Raffi.)

Additional Titles

The Ugly Duckling: A Tale from Hans Christian Andersen, Andersen; illustrated by Lorinda Bryan Cauley. A sophisticated story for sensitive, more experienced listeners.

The Wounded Duck, Barnhart. Adrienne Adams' haunting illustrations and the sadness of the tale are very powerful for very young or very sensitive children.

Agatha's Feather Bed: Not Just Another Wild Goose Story, Deedy. Droll humor and puns aren't for everyone but the story of how Agatha knit wool coats for some goose-pimply geese is hard to resist.

The Little Duck, Dunn. Charming full-color photographs of a baby duck.

The Story About Ping, Flack. There is so much information here — diving cormorants, Chinese houseboat families, the custom of painting eyes on Yangtze River boats. . . . The story holds up well to repeated tellings.

Wood Duck Baby, Freschet. Natural history at its very best for young children.

Seven Diving Ducks, Friskey. The children will enjoy counting the ducks on each page.

Ducks Don't Get Wet, Goldin. Find out more information about the habits and behavior of ducks.

The Day the Goose Got Loose, Lindbergh. Humorous, active illustrations spill onto the page margins.

Samson Svenson's Baby, Moore. A touch of humor and kindheartedness.

One Duck, Another Duck, Pomerantz. Illustrations by Aruego & Dewey in a fun counting book.

Three Ducks Went Wandering, Roy.

Farmer Schulz's Ducks, Thiele. An Australian farm.

The Hunter and His Dog, Wildsmith. The anti-hunting message is strong. Be sure you know your audience.

Activities

▶Expand upon the information about China in *The Story About Ping*. Show photos of houseboats, cormorants, the Yangtze River, etc.

▶Make a 10-duck parade of child volunteers as in *Have You Seen My Duckling?* and count the ducklings. "Hide" one duckling at a time behind a "bush" and count those hidden and not hidden to demonstrate the idea of one more and one less.

►Make large (5″ × 8″ or larger) flash cards for the cheer:

> Give me a Q!
> Give me a U!
> Give me an A!
> Give me a C!
> Give me a K!
> What does it spell?
> QUACK!!!

►Hand out 3″ × 5″ cards, small duck silhouettes and "QUACK!" and or "Duck" typed on a small piece of paper for the children to glue together into a flash card. You might want to include ducks and point out that adding the squiggly letter "s" often makes more than one of something. Then invite the children to think of other words in which adding the "s" sound and letter make many out of one.

Chickens

Name Tags
Little chick shapes or egg shapes;
A chick hatching from an egg.

Filmstrips, 16mm Films & Videocassettes
The Most Wonderful Egg in the World, Heine. (6 min. 16mm/VHS).
Rosie's Walk, Hutchins. (3 min. fs; 5 min. 16mm/VHS). Delightful musical accompaniment.

Stories
City Sounds, Brown. Amid all of the city sounds, a farmer hears his chicks hatching out of their eggs.
The Broody Hen, Dunrea. Silly rhymed verse tells how the broody hen can't seem to find a place to lay her eggs where they won't fall off and get broken.
Zinnia and Dot, Ernst. Funny while teaching a lesson.

The Little Red Hen, Galdone. Just the right mix of illustration and text, with ample opportunity for audience participation.

Little Peep, Kent. A new baby chick puts the cocky rooster in his place when the sun comes up without the rooster crowing.

The Proud Rooster and the Fox, Threadgall. Fox outwits rooster by making him crow so much that he gets hoarse.

Fingerplay

from *Clap Your Hands: Finger Rhymes,* Hayes: "Chook, Chook, Chook-Chook-Chook"

Poetry

from *Read-Aloud Rhymes for the Very Young,* Prelutsky: "Five Little Chickens," Anonymous; "A Little Talk," Anonymous

Songs

from *The Silly Songbook,* Nelson: "Oh, I Had a Silly Chicken"

Old MacDonald Had a Farm, illustrated versions by Tracey Campbell Pearson, Lorinda Bryan Cauley, Glen Rounds and others.

Additional Titles

The Little Red Hen, Barton. Very simple text and illustrations for toddler-aged groups.

A Chick Hatches, Cole. Photographs clearly and accurately document the development and hatching of a baby chick.

Chanticleer and the Fox, Cooney; illustrated by Barbara Cooney. (Caldecott Award)

Henny Penny, Galdone. The *Chicken Licken* story reillustrated.

Little Tuppen, Galdone. Rollicking humor in this funny cumulative tale.

Good Morning Chick, Ginsburg. A chick hatches "like this," learns to eat worms "like this," is scared by a cat "like this" . . .

Rosie's Walk, Hutchins. Rosie doesn't seem to be the least bit aware of the inept fox stalking her. Almost wordless.

Wolf's Chicken Stew, Kasza. An interesting twist to the traditional wolf-eats-chicken tale.

Chicken Little, Kellogg. Another fun version with lots of illustrative detail.

How the Rooster Saved the Day, Lobel. The barnyard rooster foils a burglar by stalling him until the sun rises so everyone can see him. Sound effects and participation possibilities.

The Story of Chicken Licken, Ormerod. The traditional tale done in play form by school children. The mischief of a baby in the audience creeping out of his bassinet and joining the performance, and the silhouettes of audience members as they snooze, visit, and shush a toddler trying to tell them about the missing baby, all make a wonderful lap book to share.

The Little Hen and the Giant, Polushkin. This mother hen won't put up with a giant stealing her eggs. She wants to protect her babies.

Egg to Chick, Selsam. A simple, well done science book for those interested in learning more.

The Chicken Book, Williams. Warm, inviting illustrations.

The Little Red Hen; An Old Story, Zemach. Compare her illustrations to other versions.

Activities

▶ Using poster pictures or simple paper plate masks for the characters, have the children act out *Chicken Licken* as you narrate.

▶ As you explain the steps in making a flash card for Chicken, you may also want to make separate ones for Hen and Rooster incorporating the spelling of the animal sounds such as Peep!, Cluck!, and Cock-A-Doodle-Doo. Point out that the longest sounding noise is represented by the longest looking set of letters. These are all observations leading children to their first independent reading discoveries.

Pigs

Name Tags

Pink, brown, tan, black & white pig shapes;
A large pink letter "P";
Piggie snouts.

Filmstrips, 16mm Films & Videocassettes

The Three Little Pigs, Galdone. (fs)
The Pigs' Wedding, Heine. (8 min. fs; 7 min. 16mm/VHS)
The Three Little Pigs, Marshall. (9 min. fs; 8 min. 16mm/VHS)

Stories

Piggybook, Browne. Bad habits turn a normal loving family into a bunch of pigs—literally.

Mud Baths for Everyone, Cazet. Great fun! Won't you join in?

The Amazing Pig: An Old Hungarian Tale, Galdone. A peasant's son wins the hand of the beautiful princess when he outwits the king with tales about his amazing pig.

A Treeful of Pigs, Lobel. The lazy farmer finally keeps his promise to help when his little pigs disappear and he realizes how much he misses them.

Three Little Pigs and the Big Bad Wolf, Rounds. A great version for telling to groups. A toss-up between this version and Margot Zemach's.

The True Story of the Three Little Pigs, Scieszka. A revisionist version told from the wolf's point of view. Works well after a more traditional version.

Fingerplays

from *Finger Rhymes,* Brown: "Five Little Pigs"
from *The Story Vine,* Pellowski: "The Pigs"
Piggies, Wood

Poetry

This Little Pig-A-Wig and Other Rhymes About Pigs, Blegvad.
selections from *The Book of Piggericks: Pig Limericks,* Lobel.
from *Bill Martin Jr.'s Treasure Chest of Poetry,* Martin: "Pig Tale," "I Had a Little Pig."
The Piggy in the Puddle, Pomerantz. A delightful tongue twister of a pig story.
from *Read-Aloud Rhymes for the Very Young,* Prelutsky: "Mary Middling," Fyleman.

Songs

from *Sing a Song of Popcorn,* DeRegniers: "A Pig Tale," Reeves
from *Special Delivery,* Penner: (A/C) "The Old Sow Song," Silly; bears much practice and repeating till you can get it right.
from *Raffi: Everything Grows,* Raffi: (A/C) "Eight Piggies in a Row"
from *Sing A To Z,* Sharon, Lois & Bram: (A/C) "Susannah's a Funny Old Man," another version of "The Old Sow Song."

Additional Titles

Mrs. Simkin's Bed, Allen.
Hanna's Hog, Aylesworth.
Poinsettia and the Firefighters, Bond. A reassuring story about night frights and the fire fighters who are on duty 24 hours a day.
Perfect Pigs: An Introduction to Manners, Brown. Parents will appreciate this one.

Pigs in Hiding, Dubanevich. They're everywhere if you look closely — even in the wallpaper design. Illustrations are too small and detailed for group sharing.

Three Little Pigs, Galdone. The traditional tale told simply and with large illustrations for group sharing.

Oink, Geisert. Wordless except for the word 'Oink!" but said in so many different tones of voice and meanings.

The Pigs' Wedding, Heine. The pigs have a grand old time at the wedding until the rain washes off their painted finery.

Pig Pig Grows Up, McPhail. Pig Pig learns to do things for himself and give his mother a rest.

Pig Pig Rides. McPhail.

Garth Pig and the Ice Cream Lady, Rayner.

The Three Little Wolves and the Big Bad Pig, Trivizas. A fine, fun reversal of the traditional tale.

Piggins, Yolen. The perfect butler, even if he is a pig.

The Three Little Pigs: An Old Story, Zemach. A wonderfully tellable version, not too wordy for preschoolers.

Activities

▶Make simple paper plate pig masks, or ice cream stick puppets. You wear a wolf mask or use a stick puppet and prompt the children with wolf lines so they can act out the pigs' roles in *The Three Little Pigs*.

▶All wear simple piggie noses made out of pink construction paper (a simple rough-cut circle 1″–1.5″ in diameter with 2 nostrils colored in) during the program. A piece of double-stick tape will hold them in place.

▶Hand out supplies for making Pig flash cards. You might include Pig, Pigs, Piggy, Piggies or Oink! A good opportunity to explain what an exclamation point means in writing. Many picture book texts include exclamation points. If children know what they are and what they do, maybe they will try to spot them in the text as they are being read to.

Cows, Horses & Donkeys

Name Tags

A horse shoe shape;
A milk pail.

Filmstrips, 16mm Films & Videocassettes

Ferdinand the Bull, Leaf. (8 min. 16mm) (Walt Disney version)
Sylvester and the Magic Pebble, Steig. (10 min. 16mm/VHS) (Caldecott Medal)

Stories

No Milk!, Ericksson. The humor escalates as the city boy's frustration increases. Great for audience participation.
When Bluebell Sang, Ernst. Despite stardom, Bluebell longs to be back on the farm with her friends.
Cowboy Dreams, Khalsa. A little girl wants a horse so much she thinks, dreams and plays cowboy all the time. Includes several cowboy songs to sing.
The Story of Ferdinand, Leaf. The world's most beloved little bull.
White Dynamite & Curly Kidd, Martin. Lyrical rodeo action.
Sylvester and the Magic Pebble, Steig. Possibly a little on the longish side for young or inexperienced listeners. (Caldecott Medal)

Poetry

from *Talking Like the Rain*, Kennedy: "Purple Cow," Burgess.

Songs

She'll Be Comin' Round the Mountain, Quackenbush.
from *Sharon, Lois & Bram's Mother Goose Songs*: "My Pony Boy."
Erie Canal, Spier. (Also available in *Gonna Sing My Head Off!*, Krull.)
from *If You're Happy and You Know It*, Weiss: "Tingalayo" (Also on A/C *One Light, One Sun*, Raffi.)

Additional Titles

The Gift of the Sacred Dog, Goble.
The Girl Who Loved Wild Horses, Goble. (Caldecott Award)
Bonny's Big Day, Herriot.
Under the Lemon Tree, Hurd.
Pecos Bill: A Tall Tale, Kellogg. Should be shared in rip roaring tall tale style to match the illustrations.
Charlie Drives the Stage, Kimmel. On the long side for sharing with groups but a great story one on one for little girls looking for an interesting female role model a little out of the ordinary.
Four Dollars and Fifty Cents, Kimmel. A cowboy is almost buried alive in a clever ploy to trick his creditors out of the money owed.
Black and White, Macaulay. Great fun for those who are ready to figure out the 4-part story.

Cowboys, Rounds. Full of character.
One Cowboy: A Cowpuncher's Counting Book, Scott. A counting book
    showing ranch life.
Daisy, Wildsmith. The grass always seems greener on the other side of
    the fence.
Sky Dogs, Yolen. A Blackfoot legend recounting the origin of He-Who-
    Loves-Horses.

Activities
►Make your own magic pebble by painting a small, round pebble
with red nail polish. Pass it around for each child to make a wish.
►Hand out supplies for making Cow, Horse and Donkey flash
cards.

Sheep & Goats

Name Tags
A white cotton ball affixed to a colorful card;
A yellow sock with argyle markings to color.

Filmstrips, 16mm Films & Videocassettes
The Three Billy Goats Gruff, Asbjornsen. Illustrated by Marcia Brown. (4
    min. fs; 6 min. VHS)
Charlie Needs a Cloak, DePaola. (6 min. fs; 8 min. 16mm/VHS)

Stories
Ida and the Wool Smugglers, Alderson. The rhythmic text invites physical
    and oral participation.
Emma's Lamb, Lewis. Engaging story full of lots of different farm animals
    and the lost lamb Emma plays with and cares for.
Speak Up, Blanche, McCully. Try to help children overcome shyness
    about speaking up in a group by asking simple questions and taking
    volunteers to answer.
Three Billy Goats Gruff, Rounds. Delightful retelling and illustrations.
Sheep Out to Eat, Shaw. Another hilarious misadventure.
Argyle, Wallace. Now you know where Argyle socks come from. Try to
    bring in a pair to show.

Songs

from *Eye Winker, Tom Tinker, Chin Chopper,* Glazer: "The Barnyard Song" ("and the cat goes Fiddle-I-Fee").

Mary Had a Little Lamb, Hale. (Illustrated by Tomi DePaola or photographed by Bruce McMillan).

from *The Silly Songbook,* Nelson: "Old Hogan's Goat." Make this a call-and-response song.

from *Fred Penner's Place,* Penner: (A/C) "Mairzy Doats" (Also on A/C *Sing A to Z,* Sharon, Lois & Bram).

from *The Raffi Singable Songbook,* Raffi: "Baa, Baa, Black Sheep" (Also on A/C *Raffi: Singable Songs for the Very Young,* Raffi).

Additional Titles

Borreguita and the Coyote: A Tale from Ayutla, Mexico, Aardema. Tell with gusto and expression, with a Spanish-flavored accent if you can manage it.

The Goat in the Rug, Blood. The process from shearing to finished Navajo rug, while Geraldine re-grows enough wool to start another one.

Charlie Needs a Cloak, DePaola. Shows the process of making clothing, from sheep to cloak, simply and with humor.

The Little Goat, Dunn. A photo-essay.

Little Bo-Peep, Galdone. Large, colorful illustrations work well with a group.

The Three Billy Goats Gruff, Galdone. This makes a wonderful mitt or finger puppet story. Also try the version by Janet Stevens.

When Sheep Cannot Sleep, Kitamura.

Gregory, the Terrible Eater, Sharmat. Perpetuates the myth that goats will eat anything.

Sheep in a Jeep, Shaw. More hilarious antics, and tongue-twister text, fun for beginning readers.

Sheep in a Shop, Shaw.

Sheep on a Ship, Shaw.

Goat's Trail, Wildsmith.

Activities

▶Provide supplies for making flash cards for Sheep, Goat, Lamb, Kid, and Baa-aaa or Maa-aaa.

▶Bring in lamb's wool, sheep's wool, and mohair (from goats) for the children to feel the difference. Different wools are available at fabric stores and knitting shops. Maybe someone you know knits and could provide you with samples. Samples of raw wool may be obtained sometimes from exhibitors at county or state fairs.

Barns & Farms & All the Animals

Name Tags
A simple red barn shape;
A simple hay wagon shape;
An old straw hat shape.

Filmstrips, 16mm Films & Videocassettes
The Little Red Hen, Galdone. (8 min. fs/VHS)

Stories
Big Red Barn, Brown, Margaret Wise. New illustrations of an old classic
   show animal life in a barn from morning to night.
The Big Sneeze, Brown, Ruth. Chain reaction storytelling.
Going to Sleep on the Farm, Lewison. Realistic scenes of a farm shutting
   down for the night help a child settle peacefully.
The Cow That Went Oink, Most. Silly fun with animals sounds.
Spots, Feathers and Curly Tails, Tafuri. A simple guessing game with an
   animal part on one page and the whole animal pictures on the verso.
Farmer Duck, Waddell. "How goes the work?" the farmer asks. The poor
   duck can only answer "Quack!" Great fun to tell, with lots of expressive quacks.

Fingerplay
from *Party Rhymes*, Brown. "The Farmer in the Dell."

Songs
from *Gonna Sing My Head Off!*, Krull: "Barnyard Song (or, I Had a Cat)"
from *The Silly Songbook*, Nelson: "Turkey in the Straw"
from *The Raffi Singable Songbook*, Raffi: "Cluck, Cluck Red Hen" (Also
   on A/C *The Corner Grocery Store*, Raffi) As an extension activity pull
   a variety of farm animal puppets out of a bag and have children help
   make sounds, name animals and the product they give.
from *The 2nd Raffi Songbook*, Raffi: "Down on Grandpa's Farm" (Also on
   A/C *One Light, One Sun*, Raffi)
Skip to My Lou, Westcott. The best, most fun version around. Just begs
   to be sung again and again.
There's a Hole in My Bucket, Westcott.

Additional Titles

Farmer's Alphabet, Azarian. Beautiful woodcut illustrations of antique farm implements could prompt discussion.

The Scarebird, Fleischman.

Farming, Gibbons. A nonfiction book worth sharing for its information and identification of tools and procedures.

Georgia Music, Griffith. Sequel to *Grandaddy's Place*.

Grandaddy's Place, Griffith. Tall tale telling.

Moses the Kitten, Herriot.

Harvest Song, Hirschi. A grandmother and a little girl on an early 20th century farm.

Brown Cow Farm: A Counting Book, Ipcar.

Benjamin's Barn, Lindbergh. A flight of fancy with Susan Jeffers illustrations soaring from cows to pterodactyls and back.

Farm Boy's Year, McPhail. A little long for story times but great, informational diary entries, one per month.

Barn Dance, Martin. Jouncing rhythm just begs to be read aloud.

Who Took the Farmer's Hat?, Nodset. The farmer hunts all over for his old brown hat the wind has swept away.

The Barn, Schoenherr.

Activities

►Run through the flash cards to see how many of the words the children can "read."

►Describe each animal individually and ask the children to identify the animal described. If you have a large turn-over week to week, you may need to have photographs or toy animals to prompt the correct response for each description.

The Caldecott Medal

The purpose of this series is to:

    1. Make children aware of the Caldecott Medal as an award for excellence in children's book illustrating.

    2. To introduce the concept of artistic style and different media used in children's book illustrating, leading the children to more critical enjoyment of children's books.

    3. To make children aware of the artistic process in illustrating children's books.

    4. To show children a possible way of expressing their own creative, artistic, imaginative ideas.

    5. To introduce a quality standard for picture books by which children can learn to measure other books.

    6. To make children aware of the real people behind the children's books they enjoy.

    7. To help the children realize that traditional folk tales come in a variety of linguistic and illustrative interpretations.

    8. To enjoy good stories and illustrations.

If you have the facilities to do so you may want to make up a printed bookmark listing titles illustrated by the featured illustrator each week with a replica of the Caldecott Medal or a photo of the illustrator.

Or you may print a bookmark with select Caldecott Medal and Honor titles appropriate for your preschool audience that can be used for the entire series. A complete Caldecott Medal list is available in quantity at a nominal fee through the Children's Book Council or the American Library Association catalog.

The Award with Some Winners & Honors

Name Tag

Create your own version of the Caldecott Medal and glue it onto an index card-sized name tag leaving room for each child's name. Gold foil replicas of the Caldecott Medal are available through the ALA catalog at a nominal cost.

Filmstrips, 16mm Films & Videocassettes

Shadow, Brown. (9 mins. fs) (Caldecott Medal)

Drummer Hoff, Emberley. (4 min. fs; 6 min. 16mm/VHS) (Caldecott Medal)

The Biggest Bear, Ward. (7 min. fs) (Caldecott Medal)

Stories

Shadow, Cendrars. Illustrated by Marcia Brown. A rather spooky African story about shadows. The creation of the illustrations, the block print effect on tissue paper plus the cut out silhouettes are impressive and easy to demonstrate to children. (Caldecott Medal)

Drummer Hoff, Emberley. Children will enjoy participating in the telling of this cumulative tale. Ed Emberley's uncomplicated block print illustration technique is easy to demonstrate with a simple rubber stamp and stamp pad. (Caldecott Medal)

A Story, a Story: An African Tale, Haley. This Ashanti version of the origin of all stories makes a nice beginning to any series. The block print method of illustrating is easy to demonstrate and for the children to try. (Caldecott Medal)

Anansi the Spider: A Tale from the Ashanti, McDermott. The making of the cut paper collage illustrations in bright bold colors and simple geometric designs will be easy to demonstrate to preschoolers. (Caldecott Honor)

Additional Titles

Madeline, Bemelmans. The illustrations can be demonstrated by using bold black marker to draw a simple figure and then coloring it in with colored markers or actually painting in watercolors. (Caldecott Honor)

Dick Whittington and His Cat, Brown. Illustrated by Marcia Brown. Bold wood cut illustrations. (Caldecott Honor)

The Girl Who Loved Wild Horses, Goble. A Native American tale of a girl who loves horses so much she becomes one. Strikingly bold colors outlined in black. (Caldecott Medal)

Cinderella; or, The Glass Slipper, Perrault. Illustrated by Marcia Brown. Thin wispy watercolor wash illustrations. (Caldecott Medal)

Glorious Flight: Across the Channel with Louis Bleriot, July 25, 1909, Provensen. Louis Bleriot's famous experiments with flight in France and the effect they had on his family. Won the Caldecott Medal the year after the Provensen's *A Visit to William Blake's Inn: Poems for Innocent and Experienced Travelers,* written by Nancy Willard, was named a Caldecott Honor and a Newbery Medal winner.

Baboushka and the Three Kings, Robbins. Eloquent wood cut illustrations in simple peasant-like style. (Caldecott Medal)

Owl Moon, Yolen. John Schoenherr had been devoting himself to museum art and didn't want to illustrate children's books any longer. But he was sent the manuscript anyway, and he liked it. He lives on a New Jersey farm appropriate for the illustrations. He even had friends who would go owling so he could sketch them. Lucky for us he decided to do the illustrations. (Caldecott Medal)

Hey, Al, Yorinks. Arthur Yorinks and Richard Egielski met for the first time in an elevator when they were both on their way to see Maurice Sendak who had taught both of them in children's literature classes. Sendak suggested that they should team up to do a book. Note the startling shift from dull, drab to glorious tropical color and the changed end-paper color. (Caldecott Medal)

Activities

►Cover a whole table top with rolled craft paper. Demonstrate linoleum and wood block printing and let the children make prints with all kinds of stamps and various colored stamp pads. Let the children move around and place their designs in several areas. This will give them the feel for creating in the wood block print style.

►You can also add to the rubber stamp "painting." Demonstrate Gerald McDermott's cut paper collage style and let the children glue or paste simple shapes of construction paper, wall paper, cloth, etc., for a collage effect. Print each child's name somewhere on the paper to give artistic credit. Hang the creation if you have space.

Stephen Gammell

Name Tag

Photocopy a picture of the illustrator and glue it onto an index card-sized name tag leaving enough room for the child's name.

Filmstrips, 16mm Films & Videocassettes

A Regular Rolling Noah, Lyon. (7:22 min. fs)
The Relatives Came, Rylant. (8 min. fs) (Caldecott Honor)

Stories

Song and Dance Man, Ackerman. Gammell explains that every illustration starts out as a blank sheet of paper. Every element in the illustration is the result of decisions. The plaid shirt became too difficult to draw in each illustration, so he decided to have the boy take it off — end of problem. (Caldecott Medal)

Old Black Fly, Aylesworth. A can't resist, bouncy rhyme follows a dirty, disgusting fly alphabetically through the family's food, hair, clean clothes, etc. The illustrations more than capture the feel of flies crawling on your food . . . and the SWAT! at the end is richly rewarding. Note Gammell's cryptic message about his art in this one.

Old Henry, Blos. Gammell is very attached to old things, and has a very solitary personality very much like Old Henry. He has coat hooks on walls all over his house to hang things on.

Will's Mammoth, Martin. An illustrated version of a story that storyteller Rafe Martin has used in his storytelling concerts for years. Will looks very much like the youngest boy in *Song and Dance Man.*

Monster Mama, Rosenberg. The illustrations convey the idea of the ominous Monster Mama, tickling the reader's imagination into overdrive.

The Relatives Came, Rylant. Stephen Gammell includes himself, his father (the barber) and several relatives in the illustrations making another author's story partly autobiographical for the illustrator. Note the use of colored pencil instead of more sophisticated-looking oils or watercolors. He also has a quirky sense of humor. Did you notice granny sucking her thumb in her sleep? (Caldecott Honor)

Poetry

selections from *Halloween Poems*, Livingston. The illustrations in shaded pencil are appropriately gruesome.

selections from *Thanksgiving Poems*, Livingston.

selections from *Dancing Teepees: Poems of American Indian Youth*, Sneve. Native American poems, prayers and chants.

Additional Titles

Airmail to the Moon, Birdseye. That's where whoever stole Oreo's tooth is going to be sent when she finds the culprit.

The Best Way to Ripton, Davis. Don't ask for directions, it'll take all day.

Git Along, Old Scudder, Gammell.

Once Upon MacDonald's Farm, Gammell. Is he really going to try to run his farm with circus animals?

The Old Banjo, Hasely.

Wing-A-Ding, Hoopes. The Wing-A-Ding gets caught in the tree and no amount of badgering will get it down.

Come a Tide, Lyon. The big flood and everybody helps everybody else. Good cadence for telling aloud.

A Regular Rolling Noah, Lyon. A boy accompanies all of the livestock and possessions of a farm family as they move by train across Canada to a new farm.

The Wing Shop, Woodruff. Illustrations very much in the style of his *Wing-A-Ding*.

Activities

►Talk about the colored pencil and soft pencil shaped techniques and have the children try their hand at using the materials on a picture to take home. Don't expect great art; you are giving experience in a particular medium. Success is in understanding that colored pencils make a different kind of mark than paint, that blunt lead pencils can make shadowy kinds of marks.

►Demonstrate Gammell's paint dribbling and spattering techniques as in *Old Black Fly*, Aylesworth.

Trina Schart Hyman

Name Tag
Photocopy a picture of the illustrator and glue it to an index card-sized name tag leaving enough room for the child's name.

Filmstrips, 16mm Films & Videocassettes
Saint George and the Dragon, Hodges. (12 min. fs/VHS) (Caldecott Medal)
Little Red Riding Hood, Hyman. (13 min. fs) (Caldecott Honor)

Stories
The Fortune-Tellers, Alexander (Cameroon). Watch for Hyman's grandson in the illustrations. A photo on the back flap will help identify him.
Swan Lake, Fonteyn. The story of the ballet.
Snow White, Grimm. Notice the use of decorative borders. She does a great deal of research on flora and fauna to get the proper time period, decorative elements and sense of place.
Saint George and the Dragon: A Golden Legend, Hodges. Authors and illustrators almost never collaborate on a story but these two hit it off so well that Hyman regularly called Margaret Hodges to check her ideas for the illustrations. Mr. and Mrs. Hodges appear as the old couple in the illustration on the back jacket cover. (Caldecott Medal)
Little Red Riding Hood, Hyman. Trina loves cats and puts pictures of her cats in almost every illustration. She loved the story as a child and her mother even made her a red cape and hood to wear. (Caldecott Honor)

Music
Swan Lake, any version of the ballet music.

Poetry
selections from *Cat Poems*, Livingston. Notice that Hyman's cats have made it into the illustrations once again. Specific cats can be identified from book to book.
selections from *Christmas Poems*, Livingston. Bold red and green on white paper and with black ink are in keeping with the theme. The borders and frames are recognizable Hyman style.

Additional Titles

The Man Who Loved Books, Fritz.

Why Don't You Get a Horse, Sam Adams?, Fritz. Author and illustrator make Sam Adams a real person, not just an historic personage.

Will You Sign Here, John Hancock?, Fritz. Again the winning author/illustrator team make an historic figure real flesh and blood.

On to Widecomb Fair, Gauch.

Sleeping Beauty, Grimm.

Tight Times, Hazen. One of the few picture book stories about unemployment and a family's money problems.

The Kitchen Knight: A Tale of King Arthur, Hodges. Sir Gawain proves himself and is knighted by Sir Lancelot of King Arthur's Knights of the Round Table. Again Margaret Hodges and her husband are included in the illustrations.

Self Portrait: Trina Schart Hyman, Hyman. An honest, revealing self portrait with information young children can relate to.

Herschel and the Hanukkah Goblins, Kimmel. Herschel frees the synagogue of Goblins so the village people can celebrate Hanukkah. (Caldecott Honor)

Rapunzel, Rogasky.

The Water of Life: A Tale from the Brothers Grimm, Rogasky.

Activities

►Compare Hyman's art work with Galdone's and Morris' *Little Red Riding Hood.*

►Compare Hyman's *Snow White* and *Rapunzel* with others illustrated by Burkert Iwasaki and Hague or Heyer respectively.

►See if you can spot the same cats from book to book.

►Have the children imagine themselves as swans and dance to the music. Perhaps, after sharing the story, each child could physically feel an interesting character to dance.

Ezra Jack Keats

Name Tag

Photocopy a picture of the illustrator and glue it to an index card-sized name tag leaving enough room for the child's name.

Filmstrips, 16mm Films & Videocassettes

Apt. 3, Keats. (8 min. fs/16mm/VHS)
Goggles, Keats. (6 min. fs/16mm/VHS)
Whistle for Willie, Keats. (5 min. fs; 6 min. 16mm/VHS)

Stories

Jennie's Hat, Keats. Jennie wants a beautiful hat for spring. Her bird
    friends help her decorate her plain one.
John Henry: An American Legend, Keats. A robust retelling of the story
    about the legendary steel driving man.
The Little Drummer Boy, Keats. In this book the art is all watercolor
    wash, no collage.
Peter's Chair, Keats. Keats usually writes about and illustrates common
    everyday problems of children.
The Snowy Day, Keats. Keats used torn paper and pieces of cloth to make
    this collage illustration. (Caldecott Medal)
Whistle for Willie, Keats. When did you first learn to whistle? How would
    you explain to someone else how to whistle?

Song

Over in the Meadow, Wadsworth. The well known song nicely illus-
    trated.

Additional Titles

Apt. 3, Keats.
Dreams, Keats.
Goggles, Keats. (Caldecott Honor)
Hi, Cat! Keats.
Kitten for a Day, Keats. A confused puppy thinks he is a kitten and plays
    with a batch of kittens all day. (Almost wordless.)
A Letter to Amy, Keats.
Louie, Keats.
Maggie and the Pirate, Keats.
My Dog Is Lost, Keats.
Pet Show!, Keats. A unique solution to the problem of not being able to
    find his cat in time for the pet show.
Regards to the Man in the Moon, Keats.
Skates, Keats. (Wordless.)
The Trip, Keats.

Activities

▶ Bring in scraps of fabric, ribbon, lace and let each child decorate a
spring hat. Upside-down paper plates attached with string work well. The

boys can make a spring hat for their mother if they aren't into wearing hats themselves.

►Make a torn paper and fabric scrap collage.

Anita Lobel

Name Tag

Photocopy a picture of the illustrator and glue it to an index card-sized name tag leaving enough room for the child's name.

Filmstrips, 16mm Films & Videocassettes

On Market Street, Lobel, Arnold. (12:30 min. fs) (Caldecott Honor)

Stories

Alison's Zinnia, Anita Lobel. An Alphabet book of flowers that leads you along and then full circle.

How the Rooster Saved the Day, Arnold Lobel. Anita Lobel illustrated many of her husband's texts. She uses fine ink line and watercolors with lots of detail.

On Market Street, Arnold Lobel. Anita wanted a text for an alphabet book. Arnold complained about her preparations for the letter "R—Ribbons" because she had ribbons scattered all over their apartment. Notice, for the letter "T—Toys" that Anita has put Frog and Toad hand puppets in the illustration in honor of Arnold's successful Frog and Toad stories. (Caldecott Honor)

The Rose in My Garden, Arnold Lobel. Arnold wanted to write a book that Anita could illustrate by putting in all the different kinds of flowers that she loves.

A Treeful of Pigs, Arnold Lobel. Notice the flowers everywhere. The lazy farmer has a mustache just like Arnold's. Do you suppose she really thinks that Arnold is lazy and she works hard?

Poetry

The Night Before Christmas, Moore. A Victorian version. Compare this with versions by Michael Hague, Tomie DePaola, or James Marshall.

Songs

selections from *Singing Bee! A Collection of Favorite Children's Songs*, Hart.

Additional Titles

The Wisest Man in the World: A Legend of Ancient Israel, Elkin.
Princess Furball, Huck. A longer story for experienced listeners or a good bedtime read-aloud for parents.
The Dwarf Giant, Anita Lobel.
King Rooster, Queen Hen, Anita Lobel.
The Pancake, Anita Lobel. Another version of the familiar Gingerbread Boy story.
The Straw Maid, Anita Lobel.
Troll Music, Anita Lobal.
Indian Summer, Monjo.
Little John, Orgel.
Clever Kate, Shub. An easy-to-read chapter book. Parents can try this one with children ready for longer titles but that still need some illustration.
A New Coat for Anna, Ziefert. Knowing that Anita spent time in a World War II concentration camp gives this story deeper meaning.

Activities

►Hand out a letter of the alphabet to each child. Have the whole group help the child name something that starts with that letter sound. This can be frustrating if your children don't know letter sounds yet. Be patient and accepting. Make it a game to take home and assemble a scrap book of as many items as they wish, starting with the letter you have given them. A good start to a whole alphabet scrap book parents can keep going at home.

►Bring in common objects or point out common objects in the room and have the children guess what letter they start with or match letters with objects.

►Make a letter person—head, hands, feet as in the illustrations in *On Market Street*. Invite the children to take the picture home and complete it with cut and paste pictures of things with the same initial letter.

Arnold Lobel

Name Tag

Photocopy a picture of the illustrator and glue it to an index card-sized
name tag leaving enough room for the child's name.

Filmstrips, 16mm Films & Videocassettes

from *Fables,* Lobel: "The Hen and the Apple Tree" (fs)
from *Frog and Toad Together,* Lobel: "Spring" (5:40 min. fs)

Stories

Days with Frog and Toad, Lobel. A series of stories about two very
different but very good friends. (Easy reader format.)
from *Fables,* Lobel: "The Bear and the Crow." A bear is fooled by a crow
into making a real spectacle of himself as he dresses to go into town.
This is a fun one to act out yourself or have enough supplies so all
of the children can dress in a silly manner. (Caldecott Medal)
   "The Hen and the Apple Tree." This works well with puppets.
Make a tree disguise for your wolf by gathering a length of green net
at the top, glueing on some red felt apples and placing it on your
villain's head. The fact that the children can "see through" the
disguise makes the story funnier. (Caldecott Medal)
Ming Lo Moves the Mountain, Lobel. When the book was nearly finished
Arnold wanted to know how a child would like it. So he showed the
pictures and told the story to a friend's 3-year-old. For days after that
the child was walking—backward—all over the house with his eyes
shut so he, too, could do the Dance of the Moving Mountain.
Bear All Year, Ziefert. Arnold Lobel's animals are always very human, very
gentle. He uses some ink line drawings and lots of watercolor paint.

Poetry

selections from *The Book of Piggericks: Pig Limericks,* Lobel. See how Arnold Lobel puts himself at the beginning and the end of the book.
He often includes himself in his illustrations. Watch for the glasses
and the mustache.
selections from *The Random House Book of Mother Goose,* Lobel.
selections from *Whiskers & Rhymes,* Lobel.
selections from *The Random House Book of Poetry for Children,* Pre-

lutsky. All kinds of fun rhymes with Lobel's expressive illustrations
to enjoy.

selections from *Tyrannosaurus Was a Beast*, Prelutsky. Dinosaur poems.

Song

from *Kidding Around with Greg & Steve:* "The Hokey Pokey" (A/C). Since
you are up anyway doing the Dance of the Moving Mountain, how
about doing another dance to get the wiggles out.

Additional Titles

As I Was Crossing Boston Common, Farber.
Frog and Toad All Year, Lobel. (Easy reader format.)
Frog and Toad Are Friends, Lobel. (Easy reader format.) (Caldecott
    Honor)
Frog and Toad Together, Lobel. (Easy reader format.)
Holiday for Mr. Muster, Lobel.
The Man Who Took the Indoors Out, Lobel.
Mouse Soup, Lobel. Four stories that keep one mouse out of the soup pot.
    (Easy reader format.)
Mouse Tales, Lobel. (Easy reader format.)
On Market Street, Lobel; illustrated by his wife Anita. Listed as a reminder
    of the husband/wife collaboration. Compare their styles. (Caldecott
    Honor)
Owl at Home, Lobel. (Easy reader format.)
The Rose in My Garden, Lobel; illustrated by his wife Anita. Listed as a
    reminder of the husband/wife collaboration.
Uncle Elephant, Lobel. (Easy reader format.)
Zoo for Mister Muster, Lobel. Since he can't keep his zoo animal friends
    in his home, Mr. Muster becomes a zoo keeper so he can be with
    them every day.
Circus!, Prelutsky.
Bear Gets Dressed, Ziefert. Simple toddler activities in this series, small
    for small hands to hold.
Bear Goes Shopping, Ziefert.
Bear's Busy Morning, Ziefert.

Activities

▶Make a Frog/Toad stick puppet using popsicle sticks, a frog/toad
head shape using green for Frog and brown for Toad. Glue the two faces
back to back with the stick in between. Talk about the differences in the
two characters. Have the children hold Frog face forward for Frog dialog,

and hold Toad face forward when Toad speaks as you read a short story from one of the Frog and Toad books.

▶Invite the children to act out *The Bear and the Crow* with paper bag shoes, sheets, and pots. Improvise easier props if you wish.

Maurice Sendak

Name Tag
Photocopy a picture of the illustrator and glue it to an index card-sized name tag leaving enough room for the child's name.

Filmstrips, 16mm Films & Videocassettes
In the Night Kitchen, Sendak. (6 min. fs/16mm/VHS) (Caldecott Honor)
Where the Wild Things Are, Sendak. (5 min. fs/8 min. 16mm/VHS) (Caldecott Medal)

Stories
What Do You Say, Dear?, Joslin. A lesson in funny stories about the polite response in silly situations.
Alligators All Around: An Alphabet, Sendak.
In the Night Kitchen, Sendak. (Caldecott Honor)
One Was Johnny: A Counting Book, Sendak.
Outside Over There, Sendak. A little girl must rescue her baby sister from the goblins who stole her from her cradle and left a goblin baby in her place. (Caldecott Honor)
Where the Wild Things Are, Sendak. Sendak's most famous story about Max, who defies his mother and is sent to bed without his supper. (Caldecott Medal)

Poetry
selections from *I Saw Esau: The Schoolchild's Pocket Book,* Opie.
Chicken Soup with Rice: A Book of Months, Sendak.

Additional Titles
Lullabies and Night Songs, Engvick.
Dear Mili, Grimm.
A Hole Is to Dig: A First Book of First Definitions, Krauss. Not for every group but fun to play with.
Father Bear Comes Home, Minarik. (Easy reader format.)

A Kiss for Little Bear, Minarik. (Easy reader format.)
Little Bear, Minarik. A series about Little Bear and his family. (Easy
    reader format.)
Little Bear's Friend, Minarik. (Easy reader format.)
Little Bear's Visit, Minarik. (Easy reader format.)
No Fighting, No Biting, Minarik.
Higglety Pigglety Pop; or, There Must Be More to Life, Sendak.
Maurice Sendak's Really Rosie, Sendak.
Pierre: A Cautionary Tale in Five Chapters and a Prologue, Sendak.
Seven Little Monsters, Sendak.
The Sign on Rosie's Door, Sendak. "If you want to know a secret, knock
    three times."
Mr. Rabbit and the Lovely Present, Zolotow. (Caldecott Honor)

Activity

▶ Have the children put on their imaginary wolf suits and provide
Wild Thing sound effects to the story.

Chris Van Allsburg

Nearly every children's book Van Allsburg has published has won
awards for excellence. Note the studied sculptured, rounded shapes that
seem solid enough to hold.

Name Tag

Photocopy a picture of the illustrator and glue it to an index card-sized
    name tag leaving enough room for the child's name.

Filmstrips, 16mm Films & Videocassettes

The Garden of Abdul Gasazi, Van Allsburg. (8 min. VHS) (Caldecott
    Honor)
Polar Express, Van Allsburg. (12 min. fs) (Caldecott Medal)

Stories

The Garden of Abdul Gasazi, Van Allsburg. Did his dog really disappear
    with his hat or was it just a dream? (Caldecott Honor)
Jumanji, Van Allsburg. A weird board game that wrecks havoc in the
    house. (Caldecott Medal)

Polar Express, Van Allsburg. A Christmas story for those who still truly believe. A silver bell passed around at the end for each child to hold and reaffirm that they still believe in Christmas makes a memorable finish to the story. (Caldecott Medal)

Two Bad Ants, Van Allsburg. The unusual perspectives from an ant's-eye-view are worth sharing. The abstract text may need to be repeated after the children begin to understand the ant-style references to sugar grains, coffee, etc.

The Widow's Broom, Van Allsburg. A good lesson in tolerance without being obvious.

Additional Titles

Ben's Dream, Van Allsburg. Black and white architectural scenes. Have the children try to guess where the illustrator was standing to get the perspective of the buildings shown.

Just a Dream, Van Allsburg. A heavy environmental message.

The Mysteries of Harris Burdick, Van Allsburg. Story titles, bizarre illustrations and mysterious captions entice the children to make up stories to go with them. Best used as a take home title for the children to share with a parent. The eerie illustrations may be frightening to sensitive children. Making up a story about them with the support of a comforting, encouraging adult will give the children a sense of mastery over any fears the illustrations engender.

The Stranger, Van Allsburg. He might be Jack Frost.

The Wreck of the Zephyr, Van Allsburg. A strange story of ships that sail through the air, told by an old sailor.

The Wretched Stone, Van Allsburg. For more sophisticated children who may be able to understand the references.

The Z Was Zapped: A Play in Twenty-Six Acts, Van Allsburg. A very weird alphabet book.

Activities

▶Point out the dog in *The Garden of Abdul Gasazi*. See if the children can spot the same dog in Van Allsburg's other stories. He's a pull toy in *Jumanji*, a hand puppet on the bed post in *Polar Express*. The dog is even found in the illustrations of *Black and White*, the Caldecott Medal winner written and illustrated by David Macaulay, Chris Van Allsburg's very good friend.

▶Make a simple game board as in *Jumanji* and ask the children to imagine events for which you draw a symbol in each of the squares.

Colors

Some children already know their colors when they come to pre-school story time. If they do, this will be excellent reinforcement. The theme encourages children to be more perceptive to colors in unusual places. Depending upon the age or sophistication of your participants, you may explore emotions prompted by particular colors as in Mary O'Neill's *Hailstones and Halibut Bones: Adventures in Color;* or learn the meaning of hue, tone, shade; or experiment with color mixing using food coloring or overlapping colored plastic sheets.

At the beginning of each session help the children identify the featured color in clothing, in items spotted around the room, etc. At the end of each session, ask the children to bring in or wear next week's featured color. It is amazing how many children remember from one week to the next. You are reinforcing responsibility, memory, participation, and the color itself—in all its hues, as well as encouraging follow-up activities.

Activity: An *easy,* interesting and fun on-going activity: cover the four sides of a small table with plain white poster board (or improvise with a sturdy appliance box). Sketch in windows, doors, and other features to make it look like a small house. Each week after the stories and other story time activities are finished hand out crayons or large washable markers of the featured color and let the children "paint" the library house as in Peter Spier's *Oh, Were They Ever Happy!* Print each child's name in a prominent spot on the house so they can proudly show it off to parents and others on subsequent visits to the library.

Additional Title Display: Tilt and fasten A-frame roof pieces of poster board with masking tape to the top of the box or table, leaving enough room for a small ledge to display color books. I even made a simple pennant with the Spier book title on one side and the story hour program name and logo on the other to fly above the house.

Take some action photos of the painting in progress for your library's photo album. Children and parents love to browse through photo albums and see themselves. And photo albums make ready resource material for publicizing future events, accompanying a feature newspaper article, or presenting library programs and services to parent and teacher groups.

The display of books and the painted house drew a lot of attention and was left up for the entire seven weeks of the preschool story hour series. The books in the display were constantly changing as I added all sorts of arts/crafts books, picture books, poetry and nonfiction featuring subjects of the appropriate color-of-the-week.

Caution: Place an old sheet under the box or the legs of the table; spread it out flat during painting, shove it underneath, out of the way, when not in use. I've found this far more satisfactory for protecting the floor than paper which tears, rustles, wrinkles, and disintegrates over a seven week period. And sheets fold or stuff out of the way so much better than paper does.

Caution #2: I have *never* had reports of children painting or drawing on walls at home after these programs. But, to be safe, *make sure* the parents know about the project so they can reinforce their own rules about crayons, paints and colored markers at home; and stress to the children that we would *never* do something like paint or draw anywhere but on paper without first checking with Mom or Dad or the sitter.

Activity: Another interesting, on-going activity is building a rainbow, color by color each week. Pencil in a large rainbow on shelf paper. Provide appropriately-colored torn-paper scraps for the children to glue to the proper band in the rainbow each week. (You can get rid of all of those paper scraps left over from other projects.)

The colors of the primary rainbow appear from outside to inside—red, orange, yellow, green, blue, indigo and violet (here use purple). Sometimes there is a fainter reflection or secondary rainbow in reverse order above the primary rainbow but don't go into that with preschoolers unless you are questioned about it. Display your "in progress" rainbow on a wall between programs.

Red

Name Tags

A simple small red puppy shape;
Red flowers;
Red hats;
Simple red shapes.

Filmstrips, 16mm Films & Videocassettes

Clifford the Small Red Puppy, Norman Bridwell. (5:02 min. fs)
Oh, Were They Ever Happy!, Spier. (4 min. fs)

Stories

Charlie Needs a Cloak, DePaola. How the wool is shorn, carded, spun, dyed, woven, cut and sewed to make a red cloak which Charlie's favorite sheep starts nibbling on.
The Lion and the Little Red Bird, Kleven. Incorporates all of the colors but have children spot the Little Red Bird in each page. I ask the children to tell me "in words" rather than all rushing up to point to the bird on each page. This reinforces language skills and prevents chaos.
The Story of Ferdinand, Leaf. A red scarf made into a bull fighter's cape is an effective story prop.
Red Riding Hood, Marshall. You may want to point out some of the humorous touches in Marshall's illustrations.
Oh, Were They Ever Happy!, Spier. Saturday, when the babysitter doesn't show up, the children decide to paint the house. They use all the paint they can find—in every color of the rainbow. This is the jumping off point for your seven-week project.
Red Is Best, Stinson. One little girl's attachment to her favorite color.

Poetry

from *Hailstones and Halibut Bones: Adventures in Color,* O'Neill: "What Is Red?"

Songs

from *The Raffi Everything Grows Songbook,* Raffi: "Mary Wore Her Red Dress" (hat, shoes, gloves, . . .)

from *Pockets: Songs for Little People,* Wise: (A/C) "I Love to Color" (5:04 min.). A rather lengthy song but fun. Demonstrating the various colors he sings about using "smelly" markers is great fun. He keeps coming back to "puce" so be sure to have an example of that as well as green, brown, red, etc.

Additional Titles

Clifford the Big Red Dog, Bridwell.

Clifford's Good Deeds, Bridwell.

My Red Umbrella, Bright. A little girl's red umbrella grows big enough for all the animals who need shelter.

Red Light, Green Light, Brown. Newly reissued with wonderfully reproduced illustrations.

Red Riding Hood, DeRegniers. The well-known story in verse form. Compare Edward Gorey's illustrations with other versions.

Is It Red, Is It Yellow, Is It Blue? An Adventure in Color, Hoban. This clearly photographed series of everyday articles in the three primary colors of the title encourages observation of colors and shapes in the things we see around us.

I Dance in My Red Pajamas, Hurd. Jenny relates the joys of visiting her grandparents.

The Red Baloon, Lammorisse. An escaped balloon fantasy.

Red Pandas: A Natural History, MacClintock. Share photographs and information about these endangered relatives to the Giant Panda. I brought in my stuffed red panda for children to see. World Wildlife Fund-sponsored stuffed animals and puppets are quite realistic, good for introducing animals to preschoolers who haven't had the benefit of a zoo nearby.

The Red Carpet: An Old Story, Malone. A runaway carpet has adventures in rhyme.

Little Red Riding Hood Rebus Book, Morris. Explain the function of the rebus illustrations so the children can help read the story.

Who Said Red?, Serfozo. More than just a color identification book, Narahashi's illustrations hide many small animals and figures in the scenery, building a child's observational skills.

Little Red Hen, Zemach. A good version to use or display for take-home.

New Coat for Anna, Ziefert. Anna needs a new coat which is nearly impossible to obtain in post–World War II Eastern Europe. But Anna's mother finds a way through work and barter.

Activities

►Introduce the house painting project. Paint the house red.

►Introduce the rainbow project. Add red torn-paper scraps to the first color band. Some instruction about the order of the colors may be necessary. You may even want to put red X's on the proper band for the children to paste onto.

►Dip cotton balls into red food coloring and water to demonstrate the dying process after telling *Charlie Needs a Cloak*. You can also twist out a thread from the cotton ball to show spinning of wool into yarn before dying.

►Put lots of titles on display for the week: any books with red on the cover, or about red objects, or about colors in general will do. You might even have the children round up books for the display and tell you why each is appropriate—red on the cover, red clothing on a character, etc.

Orange

Name Tags

A round orange, pumpkin;
An orange flower.

Filmstrips, 16mm Films & Videocassettes

A Rainbow of My Own, Freeman. (5 min. VHS)

Stories

The Gunniwolf, Harper. A little girl strays into the jungle to pick orange, pink and white flowers and is caught by the Gunniwolf.

The Vanishing Pumpkin, Johnston. A 700-year-old woman and an 800-year-old man set off to find their pumpkin, snitched from their garden on Halloween night.

The Big Orange Thing, Juhl.

Mousekin's Golden House, Miller. Mousekin finds an abandoned jack-o-lantern and converts it into a cozy winter home.

Pumpkin, Pumpkin, Titherington. Jamie is very proud of the pumpkin he grows from seeds he saved from last year's pumpkin.

Cut-and-Tell Story

from *Paper Stories*, Stangl: "The Little Orange House"

Poetry

from *Hailstones and Halibut Bones: Adventures in Color*, O'Neill: "What Is Orange?"

Songs

Mary Wore Her Red Dress, and Henry Wore His Green Sneakers, Peek. Ask children to stand up one at a time with an item of clothing and we all sing his or her name, the color and an item of clothing he or she is wearing. For large groups have all children wearing red shoes, blue shirt, etc., stand up at the same time. Be sure to include everyone in the naming. Here's where the name tags help with being able to call out the children's names.

from *10 Carrot Diamond: Songs and Stories*, Diamond: "10 Crunchy Carrots" (A/C)

Additional Titles

The Thirteen Days of Halloween, Green. A funny take-off on *The Twelve Days of Christmas*.

Roger in Charge!, Gretz. Just because he is left in charge doesn't mean Roger is allowed to be bossy. Roger appears in rather orange hue. Children may be asked to guess why Roger is included in the *Orange* program.

Orange Is a Color, Lerner.

The Great Pumpkin Switch, McDonald. Probaby too long and wordy for story hour but great for more advanced listeners one on one.

What Was It Before It Was Orange Juice?, Moncure. How orange juice is produced for our breakfast table.

Big Orange Splot, Pinkwater.

Activities

►Paint the house orange.

►Add orange to your rainbow.

►Decorate an orange with cloves to make a spicy pomander and explain its purpose.

►Pass out a snack of carrots for everyone.

►Collect appropriate orange books for the color display.

Yellow

Name Tags

A torn paper Little Yellow;
A simple yellow hat;
A chick;
A yellow leaf.

Filmstrips, 16mm Films & Videocassettes

Little Blue and Little Yellow, Leo Lionni. (10 min. 16mm)

Stories

Wild, Wild Sunflower Child, Anna, Carlstrom. Bright and soft yellows glowingly portray a small child's delight in the outdoors in summer.

Quiet! There's a Canary in the Library, Freeman. A small yellow canary starts a flood of animal visitors to the library, some not so well-behaved.

Here a Chick, There a Chick, McMillan. Learning simple direction words with photographs of real baby chicks.

Curious George, Rey. The man in the yellow hat finds a curious little monkey in the jungle and brings him home to live in his house.

Hide and Seek in the Yellow House, Rose. A mother cat frantically looks for her kitten who is playfully hiding from her.

The Lemon Drop Jar, Widman. Yellow lemon drops in a glass jar on the windowsill chase away the winter blues and recall cheery memories.

Poetry

from *Hailstones and Halibut Bones: Adventures in Color,* O'Neill: "What Is Yellow?"

from *Read-Aloud Rhymes for the Very Young,* Prelutsky: "Yellow Butter," Hoberman. Teach the children the poem by saying it several times between stories; add clapping, finger snapping, etc., for percussion and physical involvement to aid remembering — and for fun!

Song

from *Sidewalk Shuffle,* Beech: "Rainbow Colors"

Additional Titles

Yellow, Yellow, Asch.

The Yellow Boat, Hillert.

Little Blue and Little Yellow, Lionni. Two colors become friends and visit each other's homes. When they hug too tight they blend into a green that neither set of parents recognize.

The Yellow House, Morrison.

Curious George Flies a Kite, Rey. Curious George and the "Man with the yellow hat" appear in several original Curious George stories by Rey and many additional stories as part of an animated video series.

Curious George Gets a Medal, Rey.

Curious George Goes to the Circus, Rey.

Curious George Goes to the Hospital, Rey.

Curious George Learns the Alphabet, Rey.

Curious George Rides a Bike, Rey.

Curious George Takes a Job, Rey.

Curious George Visits the Zoo, Rey.

Yellow and Pink, Steig.

Marmalade's Yellow Leaf, Wheeler. A cat chases a yellow leaf as fall arrives.

Hellow Yellow, Wolff.

Activities

►Paint the house yellow.

►Add yellow to your rainbow.

►In the fall, bring in different shaped leaves of yellows, oranges, reds, etc., for the children to see, feel, talk about.

►Pass around a real lemon to touch, smell, and see. Demonstrate how to make lemonade by pricking the lemon, squeezing the juice out, adding water and sugar. Then serve lemonade as an after-story treat.

►Collect yellow books for the color display.

Green

Name Tags

Any simple green shape—pea, green egg, green turtle, etc.

Filmstrips, 16mm Films & Videocassettes

Dr. Seuss: Green Eggs and Ham, Seuss. (9 min. 16mm)

Stories

The Princess and the Pea, Andersen. Illustrated by Paul Galdone. Pass around dried peas to illustrate how uncomfortable they would be to sleep on.

The Aminal, Balian. An exaggerated gossip tale about a friendly little, harmless little, green little turtle. Have a small stuffed or ceramic turtle in a lunch bag to illustrate your story. Remind the children how small the bag was that Patrick put his Aminal into.

Jack and the Bean Tree, Haley. A version of *Jack and the Beanstalk*.

Tree of Birds, Meddaugh. Harry adopts a wounded Green Tufted Tropical and must face her friends who refuse to fly south without her.

The Lady with the Alligator Purse, Westcott. Bouncing rhythm and rhyme.

Poetry

selections from *Greens: Poetry*, Adoff. Several tempting selections.

from *Hailstones and Halibut Bones: Adventures in Color*, O'Neill: "What Is Green?"

Songs

from *And the Green Grass Grew All Around: Folk Poetry from Everyone*, Schwartz: "The Green Grass Grew All Around," Hoffmann.

from *The Sesame Street Song Book*, Raposo: "Bein' Green"

Additional Titles

Display simple frog and reptile nonfiction books.

Under the Green Willow, Coatsworth. Pond creatures gather under the green willow tree waiting to be fed.

Carrie Hepple's Garden, Craft. The fascinating overgrown garden of a supposed neighborhood witch harbors a hedgehog, among other things.

Green Says Go, Emberley. A rather sophisticated color book showing color mixing to make new, brighter, or darker colors.

The Owl and the Pussycat, Lear. "... went to sea in a beautiful pea green boat...." Compare different illustrated versions by Lorinda Bryan Cauley, Janet Stevens and Jan Brett.

Jack and the Beanstalk, Ross. Compare illustrations with other versions by Steven Kellogg, Paul Galdone and William Stobbs.

Where Is the Green Parrot?, Zacharias. Children will pore over the pictures trying to spot the elusive green parrot in each one.

Activities

►Mix blue and yellow food coloring to demonstrate how green is made.

►Paint the house green.

►Add green to your rainbow.

►How many green items can you see from where you are sitting? List them on a chalkboard or drawing pad in green. You will be demonstrating the connection between the word and its written representation.

►Pass around broccoli, cucumbers, green peppers, green leaves, etc., to show the many shades of green in nature.

►Ask the children to collect green books for your color display.

Blue

Name Tags

Round blueberry;

A blue balloon, write the children's names in felt tip marker and blow up after the program;

A scrap of blue fabric;

Small versions of Blue-Footed Booby feet.

Filmstrips, 16mm Films & Videocassettes

Blueberries for Sal, McCloskey. (9 min. fs/16mm/VHS) (Caldecott Honor)

Stories

Timmy Green's Blue Lake, Bergman. A sheet of plastic and a lively imagination make great fun.

The Blanket That Had to Go, Cooney. A little girl must part with her beloved blue blanket as she prepares for her first day of school.

I Want a Blue Banana, Dunbar. A little boy jokes with his mother in the grocery store by asking for strangely colored fruit.

Blue Balloon, Inkpen. Use a blue balloon to demonstrate some of the tricks mentioned.

Blueberries for Sal, McCloskey. A young bear meets a little girl in the blueberry patch. (Caldecott Honor)

The Old Red Rocking Chair, Root. An old red rocking chair is discarded because it doesn't go with the new blue chair. But it comes full circle.

Poetry

from *Hailstones and Halibut Bones: Adventures in Color*, O'Neill: "What Is Blue?"

Additional Titles

Legend of the Bluebonnet: An Old Tale of Texas, DePaola. The legend behind the profusion of flowers that cover the Texas hillside every spring because of a little girl's sacrifice to her people.

Irwin the Sock, Klein. A delightful story about a sock that ends in a pile of yarn at a concert. Winner of the Raintree Publish-A-Book Contest for young writers.

Blue Footed Booby: Bird of the Galapagos, Millhouse. These remarkable Galapagos Island birds truly have blue feet which they display to attract a mate. Share some of the fun information about them.

Blue Whales, Palmer. Learn about blue whales and begin consciousness of sea mammals.

Blue Bug and the Bullies, Poulet. Small Blue Bug learns how to deal with bullies.

Blue Bug Finds a Friend, Poulet. A simple, almost wordless book about finding friends.

Blue Bug Goes to School, Poulet. Simple going-to-school words give preschoolers a feeling of mastery over their new school situation.

Blue Bug Goes to the Library, Poulet.

Blue Bug to the Rescue, Poulet.

Blue Bug's Circus, Poulet.

Blue Bug's Surprise, Poulet.

Blue Bug's Vegetable Garden, Poulet.

Alice's Blue Cloth, Van Der Beek.

Activities

▶ Paint the house blue.

▶ Add blue to your rainbow.

▶ Measure off the length of a blue whale on the floor using children's bodies to show how many preschoolers equal the length of a whale.

▶ Tape blue construction paper feet to the children's shoes and have the children do the Blue-Footed Boobies' courting ritual, presenting their feet in various poses — good for balance, following spoken directions and learning right from left.

▶Have the children replenish your color display with blue books.

Purple

Name Tags

A purple shape of construction paper;
A Hobyah in purple;
A simple Purple People Eater with one eye, one horn and wings.
A purple crayon shape.

Filmstrips, 16mm Films & Videocassettes

Harold and the Purple Crayon, Johnson. (7 mins. fs; 8 min. 16mm/VHS)

Stories

The Purple Coat, Hest. Mama wants Gabrielle to get her usual navy blue coat but Gabrielle wants a purple one. Grandpa, their favorite tailor, solves the stand-off with a reversible coat.

My Very Own Octopus, Most. Black and white drawings set a stark stage for the bright purple octopus pal.

Emily's Bunch, Numeroff. Emily's great party costume — a bunch of purple grapes!

Love from Uncle Clyde, Parker. Care and feeding instructions for a gift from Uncle Clyde — a purple hippo.

The Last Time I Saw Harris, Remkiewicz. Harris the parrot knows all of the color flash cards except purple.

Max's Dragon Shirt, Wells. A trip to the department store with big sister Ruby for a new pair of pants results in Max getting his heart's desire, a green shirt with a purple dragon on it.

Fingerplay

Peanut Butter and Jelly: A Play Rhyme, Westcott. Go through the steps of making a peanut butter and jelly sandwich with rhythm, movement and fun. (Also set to music in *The Funny Songbook,* Nelson, as "The Peanut Butter Song.")

Poetry

from *Talking Like the Rain: A First Book of Poems*, Kennedy: "The Purple Cow," Burgess.

from *Hailstones and Halibut Bones: Adventures in Color*, O'Neill: "What Is Purple?"

from *Read-Aloud Rhymes for the Very Young*, Prelutsky: "Yellow Butter," Hoberman. Teach it to the children and have them repeat the poem, clapping to the rhythm. I've used simple picture flash cards to show the four items (yellow butter, purple jelly, red jam, black bread) to help children recite the poem when it gets going really fast.

Songs

from *Purple People Eater*, Bishop: "Purple People Eater" (A/C; or from your old 45 rpm record collection.)

from *Move Over, Mother Goose!*, Powell: (A/C) "Myrtle Picked a Purple Thistle"

Additional Titles

The Purple Turkey and Other Thanksgiving Riddles, Adler.
Skyfire, Asch.
Ed Emberley's Big Purple Drawing Book, Emberley.
Mr. Pine's Purple House, Kessler.
Purple Is Part of the Rainbow, Kowalczyk.
The Rosy Fat Magenta Radish, Wolf.

Activities

► Paint the house purple.
► Finish your rainbow with purple.
► Make peanut butter and grape jelly sandwich snacks on black bread.
► Add purple books to your color display.

Black & White

Name Tags

Black construction paper chalkboards to write the name on in white chalk;
A black pot shape.

Filmstrips, 16mm Films & Videocassettes

Oh, Were They Ever Happy!, Peter Spier. (4 min. fs) Use, perhaps, as a review of the theme.

Harry the Dirty Dog, Zion. (7:21 min. fs)

Stories

Popcorn, Asch. A Halloween party becomes an avalanche of popcorn when everyone brings the same favorite snack to the party.

Dylan's Day Out, Catalanotto. A bored Dalmatian escapes the confines of his house and gets involved in a hot soccer game between a team of penguins and a team of skunks with nuns officiating.

Marianna May & Nursey, DePaola. The solution to Marianna May's soiled white dresses is to dye them the colors of her activities.

Stopping by Woods on a Snowy Evening, Frost. Illustrated by Susan Jeffers. The beautifully detailed black and white ink illustrations have just a faint touch of color to add interest to the snowy scenes.

Poppy the Panda, Gackenbach. The panda can't sleep because he wants something special to wear like the other dolls and toys. Dressing a stuffed panda while telling the story works well to illustrate the story's humor.

The Magic Porridge Pot, Galdone. A small black pot makes delicious porridge when the proper magic words are spoken. Children enjoy supplying the forgotten words.

Poetry

from *Hailstones and Halibut Bones: Adventures in Color*, O'Neill: "What Is Black?" "What Is White?"

"Baa Baa Black Sheep," Mother Goose.

Songs

Mary Had a Little Lamb, Hale. (versions illustrated by Tomie DePaola or photographed by Bruce McMillan)

from *The Raffi Everything Grows Songbook*, Raffi: "Little White Duck" (Also on A/C *Raffi: Everything Grows*, Raffi.)

Additional Titles

Blackboard Bear, Alexander. A chalkboard drawing comes to life and won't go away.

Black Bear Baby, Freschet. Excellent natural history for preschoolers about a baby black bear.

The Three Kittens, Ginsberg. Black, white and gray when they start to play the three kittens get into flour and soot that turn them all white, then all black.

Cat Count, Lewin.

Black and White, Macaulay. Four stories running simultaneously interweave to hilarious results. Lots of playful humor for sophisticated readers but impossible to share in a group.

When Cats Dream, Pilkey. The cat's somber, quiet black and white life explodes into color and adventure when it sleeps.

White Snow, Bright Snow, Tresselt. Everyone prepares for a winter blizzard. (Caldecott medal)

Rabbits' Wedding, Williams. The wedding of a black rabbit and a white rabbit in Garth Williams soft illustrations.

Harry and the Lady Next Door, Zion.

Harry by the Sea, Zion. A terrible sea monster turns out to be Harry, covered in green seaweed to keep cool.

Harry the Dirty Dog, Zion. Harry is a small white dog with black spots until he runs off and gets so dirty no one can recognize him.

No Roses for Harry, Zion. Harry refuses to wear a flowered sweater knit for him.

Activities

►Paint the house black, glue white cotton snow on roof. Be sure to take a group photo of your finished house.

►Pop popcorn to take home. A hot air popper is very effective for showing how a little popcorn can get out of hand as in Asch's *Popcorn.*

►At the beginning of the program place sheets of black and white construction paper in a sunny place and have the children feel the difference in temperature at the end of the program.

►Collect black and white books for your book display.

Families

The idea is to focus on family membership, to identify relationship terms children have heard within their family, and to recognize and understand their feelings toward family members. Since every child is unique, he or she should not be made to feel inferior because his or her family make-up is different than another's. Here is where we celebrate diversity and try to help the child understand his or her own uniqueness and feel confident about it.

We are also trying to help a child sort out the meanings of common family terms such as aunt, uncle, cousin, and grandparent and to help the child realize that every person goes through the same growth stages. Their parents and grandparents were once children, possibly with brothers, sisters, new babies, cousins, aunts and uncles, parents and grandparents of their own. Also, one day many of these children will be parents and grandparents, aunts, uncles, etc.

I have combined topics in several instances (Moms & Dads; Grandmothers & Grandfathers; Brothers & Sisters & Babies). I didn't want children who may not live with both parents or who may not have brothers or sisters, either older or younger than themselves, to feel left out. Also, I try to avoid gender stereotyping when at all possible, to show that there are many different personality characteristics that cross gender lines. Children with mothers who work in non-traditional jobs outside the home or with fathers who do routine household chores are also represented in story.

An ongoing project could be to make a simple photo album of a few sheets of paper stapled together with a colored construction paper cover. Provide pages for Me, Mother, Father, Brother, Sister, Baby, Grandmother, Grandfather, Uncle, Aunt, Cousin, and perhaps even Babysitter. The children then can collect photographs or draw pictures of family members on their own and have someone help them to write in the names. Children that have followed through on the idea can share their photo albums with the group at subsequent story hour sessions.

You may also try creating a Family bulletin board and invite children to bring in family photographs or drawings of family members. Be sure that the photos are appropriately identified so they may be returned at the end of the Families program theme.

The action song "Skinnamarink" from Sharon, Lois & Bram's *One Elephant* might be a good theme song for the entire series with its "I Love You" message.

Families & Me

Name Tag
A mirror shape cut out of construction paper with a small oval of aluminum foil glued on as the mirror glass.

Filmstrips, 16mm Films & Videocassettes
I Like Me!, Carlson. (4 min. fs)

Stories
I Like Me!, Carlson. A young pig admires her finer points and shows her independence of character when alone.

The Patchwork Quilt, Flournoy. Tanya, Grandmother and Mother make a beautiful quilt from scraps of the family's old clothing, sharing their African-American family history as they work.

Chrysanthemum, Henkes. Chrysanthemum loves her name until she has trouble learning to write it and kids at school make fun of it.

I Go with My Family to Grandma's, Levinson. Five cousins and their families all travel by different methods on their way to visit their Brooklyn Grandma.

Chicken Sunday, Polacco. African American boys Stewart and Winston share their grandmother Eula Mae Walker with their neighbor, white Jewish Patricia, because her own babushka has died.

Smile, Ernest and Celestine, Vincent. Celestine is jealous when she discovers Ernest's old photo album with lots of pictures of him and other mouse children but none of her. Ernest solves the problem by having their picture taken together to add to the album. Now might be a good time to take photos of your story hour family for your library's photo album or family bulletin board display.

Fingerplays
from *Finger Rhymes*, Brown: "Clap Your Hands"
from *Clap Your Hands: Finger Rhymes*, Hayes: "How Many (People Live in Your House?)"

Poetry
from *Sing a Song of Popcorn: Every Child's Book of Poems*, De Regniers: "My Name Is...," Clarke

from *Read-Aloud Rhymes for the Very Young*, Prelutsky: "Ten Fingers,"
  Anonymous; "Jump or Jiggle," Beyer; "Hide-and-Seek Shadow,"
  Hillert; "Just Watch," Livingston; "Whistling," Prelutsky.
My Shadow, Stevenson; illustrated by Ted Rand.

Songs

from *Do Your Ears Hang Low?*, Glazer: "I Point to Myself" (top notcher,
  eyewinker, hornblower, etc.)
from *The Sesame Street Song Book*, Raposo: "Five People in My Family"

Additional Titles

The Terrible Thing That Happened at Our House, Blaine. Mother goes
  back to work and family routines change.
Poinsettia & Her Family, Bond. Poinsettia is a small pig fed up with too
  much family. (Easy reader format.)
Your Family, My Family, Drescher. Not all families are the same size and
  shape.
Christina Katerina and the Time She Quit the Family, Gauch. Unjustly ac-
  cused of just about everything, Christina Katerina changes her name
  to Agnes and quits the family on the spot.
Even If I Did Something Awful?, Hazen. A little boy seeks the reassurance
  of love from his mother.
Whose Mouse Are You?, Kraus. A small abandoned mouse rescues
  members of his family so he is no longer alone.
Family Pictures, Lomas Garza. The English/Spanish text describes grow-
  ing up in a Hispanic family in Texas.
The Relatives Came, Rylant. A huge assortment of relatives come to visit,
  filling up the house with hugs, kisses, laughter and good times.
I'm Terrific!, Sharmat. A small bear has a very good opinion of himself.
Spinky Sulks, Steig. Spinky is in a rotten mood so his parents just let him
  sulk until he gets over it.
Alexander and the Terrible, Horrible, No Good, Very Bad Day, Viorst.
  Well, maybe tomorrow will be better.
My Mama Needs Me, Walter. After the arrival of a new baby, Jason feels
  especially responsible to help his mother.
Something Special for Me, Williams. After helping to save for a big chair
  for everyone to sit and cuddle in, the little girl now gets to choose
  what she would like to buy with the money saved. Each idea seems
  perfect until it comes to actually paying out the money.
Tell Them My Name Is Amanda, Wold. A shy child learns to speak up.
Grandad Bill's Song, Yolen. A young boy asks various relatives and friends

about their feelings when Grandad Bill died. A beautiful story but perhaps a bit too intense and personal for group sharing.

Activities

▶Ask the children to draw a picture of their family or themselves. Have mirrors for them to use so they can check out eye and hair color, etc.

▶The week previous to this program, or for next program, ask the children to bring in pictures of themselves or their families to share.

▶Start the Family Photo Album idea explained in the introduction to the theme.

Moms & Dads

Name Tags

Construction paper cut into "MOM & DAD" or male & female head silhouettes;
Fake construction paper mustaches;
A bright red set of lips puckered into a kiss.

Filmstrips, 16mm Films & Videocassettes

My Mother Is the Most Beautiful Woman in the World, Reyher. (9 min. 16mm) (Caldecott Honor)
A Chair for My Mother, Williams. (8 min. fs) (Caldecott Honor)

Stories

Bread and Honey, Asch. Sam's mother loves the picture just the way it is. Makes a great Tell and Draw story.
My Mom Travels a Lot, Bauer. A little girl copes with her mother's frequent absences on business trips.
I'll See You When the Moon Is Full, Fowler. A boy's father helps him account for the passing of time until they are reunited by explaining the phases of the moon.
At the Crossroads, Isadora. South African children await their fathers' return to their village from work crews far away.
Five Minutes' Peace, Murphy. Mother can't get five minutes to herself, even in the bathtub.

Mother, Mother, I Want Another, Polushkin. No, not another mother, another good night kiss. Works well as a puppet story or with flannel board figures.

Owl Moon, Yolen. A little girl and her father go out owling late at night and share quiet moments together. (Caldecott Medal)

Poetry

selections from *Poems for Fathers,* Livingston.
selections from *Poems for Mothers,* Livingston.

Tell & Draw Story

Bread and Honey, Asch. A small bear makes a picture of his mother but friends insist he change so many features that it now looks a little like everybody else's mother. Easy to convert to Tell and Draw.

Additional Titles

Matthew and His Dad, Alda. Matthew and Daddy get along fine while Mommy is away on a business trip.

Just Like Daddy, Asch. A little bear wants to do everything just like Daddy until Mommy catches the biggest fish.

First Pink Light, Greenfield. A little girl falls asleep waiting for her Daddy who is due home at first pink light in the morning.

The Mommy Exchange, Hest. Every child wants to trade mommies with someone else at some time in their lives.

Daddy Makes the Best Spaghetti, Hines. A wonderfully close, happy father-son relationship.

A Mother for Choko, Kasza. A little bird seeks a mother and is finally adopted into a large family of assorted beings.

White Dynamite & Curly Kidd, Martin. Curly Kidd wants to grow up to be just like Daddy, a rodeo star. The fact that she is a girl doesn't stop her.

My Daddy's Mustache, Salus. Daddy can't shave off his mustache because then the elephants he keeps there wouldn't have anywhere to go.

Bea and Mr. Jones, Schwartz. Bea and her father exchange places for the day. She goes to his office, he goes to her school.

On Mother's Lap, Scott. Newly illustrated.

One More Thing, Dad, Thompson. Caleb packs ten items, one-by-one, to take on a picnic.

No Kiss for Mother, Ungerer. A little cat refuses to kiss mother because he is too old for that sort of thing.

Hazel's Amazing Mother, Wells. Hazel's mother always knows when her little girl needs her and arrives in the nick of time.

Only the Best, Zola. A new father searches for the best gift to give his new
son.

Activities

▶ If the program is timed around Mother's Day or Father's Day have
the children make greeting cards. You can photocopy a simple Mother's
Day or Father's Day message or poem onto colored paper and the
children can color a design or picture.

▶ Teach the children a simple poem from one of the Myra Cohn Livingston collections to share with their mothers or fathers.

▶ Before sharing *Only the Best,* elicit responses to the question
about what is the best gift a father or mother can give a new baby.

▶ Photocopy a nice picture frame design on colored paper and ask
the children to draw a picture of their mother or father as in *Bread and
Honey.*

Brothers & Sisters & Babies

Name Tags

Paper doll cutouts;
A construction paper pacifier shape, bib shape, or baby silhouette;
Shoe prints or clothing shapes of varying sizes.

Filmstrips, 16mm Films & Videocassettes

Peter's Chair, Keats. (4 min. fs; 6 min. 16mm/VHS)

Stories

Darcy and Gran Don't Like Babies, Cutler. Reassures older siblings that
    their ambivalent feelings about the new baby are ok; maybe deep
    down they love the baby, or maybe when the baby is older and more
    interesting they will.

Julius, the Baby of the World, Henkes. Everybody makes such a fuss about
    mouse baby Julius that his big sister is jealous, until a cousin makes
    a nasty comment about him.

You'll Soon Grow into Them, Titch, Hutchins. Titch outgrows his own
    clothing but his older brother's and sister's things are too big. All the
    while, Mom is quietly getting fatter and knitting baby items. Titch
    donates his own too-small things to the new baby.

Waiting for Hannah, Russo. Mother recounts preparations for the arrival of her new daughter.

A Lion for Lewis, Wells. Lewis, tired of playing only minor roles in his brother's and sister's "let's pretend" games, finds a lion costume that changes all that.

Stella & Roy, Wolff. Older sister Stella engages younger brother Roy in a tortoise and hare kind of race around the lake. Stella stops to look at everything "and Roy rolls right on by."

Fingerplay

from *Play Rhymes,* Brown: "John Brown's Baby"

Poetry

from *Tomie DePaola's Book of Poems,* DePaola: "Brothers," Hoberman.
selections from *Poems for Brothers, Poems for Sisters,* Livingston.
from *Read-Aloud Rhymes for the Very Young,* Prelutsky: "My Sister Laura," Milligan.

Additional Titles

The Baby's Catalogue, Ahlberg. A catalog of activities and objects in a baby's day.

Nobody Asked Me If I Wanted a Baby Sister, Alexander. Oliver tries to give away baby sister Bonnie.

When the New Baby Comes, I'm Moving Out, Alexander. Oliver feels hostile toward his pregnant mother until he is convinced that big brothers get special privileges.

The Purse, Caple. When her older sister calls her childish because she carries her money in an old Band-Aid box the little girl buys a purse, then has to earn money to put in it. But the sound of money in a purse isn't as satisfying as it was in the Band-Aid box.

Everett Anderson's Nine-Months-Long, Clifton. Nine months is a long time to wait for a new baby.

Jimmy Lee Did It, Cummings. A matter of passing off the blame.

She Come Bringing That Little Baby Girl, Greenfield. After eagerly awaiting the arrival of a new baby brother, Kevin is disappointed at the wrinkled, always crying baby sister his parents bring home.

A Baby Sister for Frances, Hoban. A little too wordy for group sharing, but little badger Frances' ability to cope with a new baby sister may comfort preschoolers faced with the same problem.

Much Bigger Than Martin, Kellogg. It's no fun being the smallest.

The Wild Baby, Lindgren. Wild Baby just can't sit still for a minute. His mother worries over him and loves him when he needs it.

New Baby, McCully. A wordless mouse story.
101 Things to Do with a Baby, Ormerod.
My Brother Never Feeds the Cat, Ruffins. We never learn until the very
    end that the reason the brother never helps with the chores is that
    he is still a baby.
Worse Than Willy!, Stevenson. The children just can't get the better of
    Grandpa when he starts telling about his awful little brother Willy.
I Think He Likes Me, Winthrop. Baby's first grin.

Activities

▶ Ask the children to talk about their brothers and sisters: how old
are they, do they play together, do the older ones have privileges the
younger ones don't, etc.
▶ Ask children to bring in their own or family member's baby pictures to share. Bring in some of your own as well. Make a bulletin board
display of baby pictures of famous people, staff members, attendees of
your story hour programs, etc.
▶ Have the children add to their family picture albums.

Grandparents

Name Tags

A construction paper mustache;
Old hat or various beach hat shapes;
Cookie shapes.

Filmstrips, 16mm Films & Videocassettes

My Grandson Lew, Zolotow. (13 min. 16mm)

Stories

Hotter Than a Hog Dog, Calmenson. Fun wordplay and one-upsmanship.
    Going to the beach is the only sensible action for this silly pair.
Bigmama's, Crews. Every summer the grandchildren visit Bigmama's old
    farm house for a glorious vacation.
Good as New!, Douglass. There isn't anything Grandpa can't fix, even a
    ruined teddy bear.
Grandpa's Face, Greenfield. A little girl is frightened by her grandfather's

rehearsal for a play until he reassures her he will never use his acting anger against her.

Waiting for Noah, Oppenheim. Grandma tells of the berry canes she pruned, the cookies she baked, etc., awaiting Noah's birth as she and Noah share berries and cookies in the kitchen together.

My Grandfather's Hat, Scheller. Jason inherits his grandfather's hat and wears it everywhere, just as Grandfather always did, to remember all of their good times together. Using a hat as a prop is most effective.

Fingerplay

from *Finger Rhymes,* Brown: "Grandma's Spectacles"

Poetry

from *Eats: Poems,* Adoff: "There Is a Place (with Grandma)"

Songs

from *Eye Winker, Tom Tinker, Chin Chopper,* Glazer: "Grandmother's Spectacles" (includes a grandfather verse too).

Jingle Bells, Kovalski. A rollicking ride through Central Park in a runaway horse-drawn sleigh.

The Wheels on the Bus, Kovalski. A rollicking picture book version of the ages old song. Great for singing along.

Additional Titles

How Georgina Drove the Car Very Carefully from Boston to New York, Bate. . . . to visit Grandma. A good opportunity to introduce maps.

Grandfather and I, Buckley. Reissued with new illustrations by Jan Ormerod.

Grandmother and I, Buckley.

The Trouble with Gran, Cole. This grandmother runs counter to the stereotype.

Nana Upstairs & Nana Downstairs, DePaola. Bed-ridden Nana Upstairs is 94 years old and Nana Downstairs her daughter busily keeps house.

Now One Foot, Now the Other, DePaola. A young boy teaches his grandfather how to walk again after a stroke, just as the grandfather once taught the boy how to walk.

Patrick and His Grandfather, Hayes. Patrick, a little bear, loves to go places with his piratical-looking grandfather.

Grandma's Wheelchair, Henriod. A young boy helps his Grandma reach things she can't reach from her wheelchair.

The Crack-of-Dawn Walkers, Hest. Sadie and her grandfather begin their
day with a walk to the bakery for onion rolls, to Fabio for cocoa, and
to the newspaper stand for the paper.

Grandpa's Song, Johnston. A little girl helps her once exuberant grandfather remember when he becomes forgetful.

Oma and Bobo, Schwartz. Alice's grandmother is not keen on the new
puppy Bobo but she is the only one who can make a success out of
Bobo at his obedience training.

"Could Be Worse!," Stevenson. There is just no topping Grandpa's tales
of outrageous events.

Kevin's Grandma, Williams. While the storyteller's grandmother does all
of the typical grandmother things, Kevin's grandmother is into Judo,
sky diving and peanut butter soup.

Music, Music for Everyone, Williams. The girls find a way to cheer Grandmother up and earn money besides.

My Grandson Lew, Zolotow. Six-year-old Lew, though only two when
Grandpa died, still remembers his nighttime comforting.

William's Doll, Zolotow. Only Grandma understands why William wants
a doll to play with.

Activities

▶Ask children to relate experiences with their grandfathers and
grandmothers, either together or separately.

▶Practice acting faces as in *Grandpa's Face.*

▶Add to the Family Picture Album started earlier.

▶Have the children think of the one item (like Grandfather's hat)
that most reminds them of one of their grandparents and draw a picture
of it. Then have them tell the group about it.

Aunts, Uncles & Cousins

Name Tags

A snapshot shape with small portrait drawn in;
Shapes of many different style hats.

Stories

My Three Uncles, Abalofia. The little girl can't tell her triplet uncles apart
until she starts studying them closely.

Aunt Nina and Her Nephews and Nieces, Brandenberg. Aunt Nina has such wonderful ideas for fun when all the cousins come over for a visit.

Uncle Willie and the Soup Kitchen, DiSalvo-Ryan. A young boy spends the day helping his uncle in the soup kitchen for the hungry and homeless.

A Weekend with Wendell, Henkes. Wendell is a holy terror when he comes to spend the weekend. But just as he is leaving his cousin realizes she is going to miss his action.

Aunt Flossie's Hats (and Crab Cakes Later), Howard. The girls just love to hear the stories that go with each of Aunt Flossie's many hats.

Her Majesty, Aunt Essie, Schwartz. Aunt Essie certainly acts like royalty.

Poetry

Auntie's Knitting a Baby, Simmie.

Additional Titles

Aunt Nina, Good Night, Brandenberg.

Aunt Nina's Visit, Brandenberg.

Mycca's Baby, Byers. A young Thai girl awaits the birth of her Aunt Rose's baby.

Just Us Women, Caines. A cross country car trip with her aunt, no timetable and no fixed routine is a special experience.

You Hold Me and I'll Hold You, Carson. When Helen's great-aunt dies, she and her father comfort each other at the funeral.

Li'l Sis and Uncle Willie: A Story Based on the Life and Paintings of William H. Johnson, Everett. A little African-American girl tells, from her rural North Carolina perspective, of her relationship with uncle/artist William H. Johnson, who gained prominence in Harlem and Europe between World War I and World War II.

Uncle Roland, the Perfect Guest, Green.

Fancy Aunt Jess, Hest. Becky admires her Aunt Jess who loves new clothes and doesn't mind talking about her old boyfriends.

My Great-Aunt Arizona, Houston.

Uncle Elephant, Lobel. The young nephew is reassured by his uncle while he awaits his parents' long-overdue arrival. (Easy reader format.)

A Visit to Amy-Clair, Mills. Rachel is jealous of all the attention older cousin Amy-Clair showers on younger sister Jessie until they find something all three can play.

A Birthday Basket for Tia, Mora. Cecilia gathers special memories into a 90th birthday basket surprise for her great-aunt.

Me and My Aunts, Newton.

Aunt Lulu, Pinkwater. Aunt Lulu is tired of being an Alaskan dog sled
    librarian so she moves her sled and her fourteen Huskies to Parsip-
    pany, New Jersey.
Harry Gets an Uncle, Porte-Thomas.

Activities

▶How many aunts, uncles and cousins can the children name?
Reintroduce the idea of a photo album including all sorts of relatives. Encourage the children to talk to their families about their immediate family members and relatives they see less often.

Babysitters

Name Tags

A comforting teddy bear shape;
A key shape;
A heart shape.

Filmstrips, 16mm Films & Videocassettes

Mr. & Mrs. Pig's Evening Out, Rayner. (9 min. fs)

Stories

Go and Hush the Baby, Byars. Will must get the baby settled for his nap
    before he can leave for his ball game.
An Evening at Alfie's, Hughes. Alfie is helpful when the inexperienced
    babysitter has troubles.
Mr. & Mrs. Pig's Evening Out, Rayner. The wolf poses as a babysitter to
    get at the little piggies but Garth Pig saves the day.
The Dog Who Had Kittens, Robertus. Furious at finding Eloise's kittens
    left untended, woeful basset hound, Baxter becomes their reliable
    babysitter.
The Lemonade Babysitter, Waggoner. Molly, convinced she no longer
    needs a babysitter, tries to tire out Mr. Herbert.
Jeremy Isn't Hungry, Williams. Preschooler Davey tries to help his rush-
    ing Mama by taking care of the crying baby. Unfortunately Davey
    can't read baby food jar labels yet and the ensuing chaos is hilarious.

Poetry

from *Bill Martin, Jr.'s Treasure Chest of Poetry*, Martin: "Catherine," Kuskin.

Additional Titles

The Good-Bye Painting, Berman. When the sitter announces she is leaving, a young boy is unhappy, knowing he will miss her.

Arthur Babysits, Brown. Those terrible Tibble twins!

Jerome the Baby-Sitter, Christelow.

What's Good for a Three-Year-Old?, Cole.

The Bravest Babysitter, Greenberg.

Babysitting for Benjamin, Gregory. What did they let themselves in for? An elderly couple babysits for a toddler-sized whirlwind.

Roger Takes Charge!, Gretz.

George the Babysitter, Hughes.

What Alvin Wanted, Keller. Alvin is inconsolable when Mother leaves without the traditional good-bye kiss.

Seven Kisses in a Row, MacLachlan. Aunt Evelyn and Uncle Elliott sit for Emma and Zachary as practice for when they become parents. This longer story might be a good transition for children ready to listen to longer chapter-at-a-time books at home.

Little Raccoon and No Trouble at All, Moore. The babies are really hard to keep up with, as Little Raccoon finds out.

Outside Over There, Sendak. Goblins steal the baby while big sister is supposed to be watching and they leave an ice baby in the cradle. (Caldecott Honor)

The Good-Bye Book, Viorst. A small boy tries to thwart his parents' going out plans.

Shy Charles, Wells. Despite Charles' shyness, he rises to the occasion when his babysitter falls down stairs and needs help.

Stanley & Rhoda, Wells.

Bear and Mrs. Duck, Winthrop. Bear is not at all convinced Mrs. Duck can care for him satisfactorily.

Activities

►Ask the children to suggest rules for babysitters and write up the list for them to see. Maybe they could suggest rules for themselves as well.

►Finish the Family Photo Album or bulletin board you have started. Perhaps leave a few extra pages at the end for family friends too.

A Feast of Stories

Some of the stories that stick in my mind most vividly from childhood are, in some way, related to food. I remember fancying pancakes and tiger butter after hearing *Little Black Sambo*. I remember wondering why *Goldilocks and the Three Bears* made such a big deal out of porridge, which sounded to me much like the then-detested oatmeal I was forced to eat on cold winter mornings. And I remember the popovers my mother made one hot summer afternoon after I had encountered them in *Little Women* for the first time.

You can have a lot of fun with the social aspects of food as well as the gastronomic. And you may get surprising responses from preschool children during some of your discussions. Everyone has favorite foods, foods they detest, foods that are traditional to their family and special occasions. You can celebrate diversity in a common element such as food without making children uncomfortable at their differentness.

My library situation is such that I never actually assemble recipes or try baking or cooking during the story hours, though many brave storytellers have done so successfully. Instead, I might bring in ingredients for the children to sample, or sniff-and-guess, or we might try making up recipes of our own and discuss whether they sound yummy. I might hand out recipes for the children to take home as a home extension of the story hour. Or, we might learn a song or poem together that they can then enjoy on their own.

Sometimes, just getting children to use their imaginations, to put their thoughts into words, to learn to carry on a discussion and stick to a topic are results enough for the story hour.

There is much more to food than eating it. There is enjoying the aroma of the ingredients, naming favorite or least liked foods, imagining the taste from description, learning about our body's nutritional needs, comparing like and different things, learning how to measure, deciding appropriate and inappropriate behaviors with foods (manners) and experiencing foods as they relate to plot and story.

Introduce the series by asking the children to name all of the food stories they can think of. If your group is unresponsive or inexperienced with children's stories try prompting them with "Did you know there is a book about *Green Eggs and Ham?* . . . or about a big bad wolf who eats grandmothers? . . . or soup with chicken feet in it?" Use as many examples as the group is willing to listen to, all the while book talking the stories you will be using in the coming weeks.

Outline the series so the children know one week will be about cookies and cakes, one about parties, etc. Indicate to them you will be asking them to think about foods for the entire series or maybe to bring in something food-related or to come prepared to participate in discussions. This is an especially good series to enlist the aid of the parents to carry through at home. A list of dates and topics to be covered will help them extend the topic you have just covered and to anticipate the one up-coming.

Growing Your Own Food

Name Tags
Construction paper vegetable or seed shapes;
A flower pot or watering can shape.

Filmstrips, 16mm Films & Videocassettes
The Little Red Hen, Galdone. (8 min. fs/VHS)
from *Frog and Toad Together*, Lobel: "The Garden" (VHS)

Stories
Eating the Alphabet: Fruits and Vegetables from A to Z, Ehlert. The
   glossary of fruits and vegetables at the end helps answer questions.
The Little Red Hen, Galdone. She has much more eager helpers when the
   cat, the dog and the mouse realize they don't get the goodies if they
   don't help with the chores.
Oxcart Man, Hall. The farm family grows or makes nearly everything they
   need in a yearly cycle that sees their produce and craft items sold
   to begin the cycle anew. (Caldecott Medal)
Growing Colors, McMillan. Fruits and vegetables of every color, lus-
   ciously photographed; with a glossary at the end.
This Year's Garden, Rylant. The yearly cycle of gardening is reviewed
   with the coming spring's preparation and planting. Have a variety of
   seed packets for the children to see.
The Turnip: An Old Russian Folktale, Morgan. A rollicking cumulative
   tale. Bring in a turnip, preferably with the top still on, so the children
   can feel, smell, and taste it.

Poetry
from *Eats: Poems*, Adoff: "After All the Digging"
Jamberry, Degen.
from *Clap Your Hands: Finger Rhymes*, Hayes: "Five Fat Peas"
from *Read-Aloud Rhymes for the Very Young*, Prelutsky: "Little Seeds,"
   Minarik.

Songs
from *Do Your Ears Hang Low?*, Glazer: "Can You Plant a Cabbage?" It
   is very effective to show some cabbage seeds then a whole head of
   cabbage. Peel and give out the leaves to feel, smell and taste.

from *The Silly Songbook*, Nelson: "I Like to Eat" (or "The Vowel Song")
Old MacDonald Had a Farm, Quackenbush. Includes many opportunities to make animal noises.
from *The 2nd Raffi Songbook*, Raffi: "In My Garden" (Also on A/C *One Light, One Sun*, Raffi)

Additional Titles

Your First Garden, Brown. A good basic guide for young people for starting a garden.
The Cock, the Mouse, and the Little Red Hen, Cauley.
Jamie O'Rourke and the Big Potato, DePaola. Hand out slices of raw potato to smell, feel and taste.
Growing Vegetable Soup, Ehlert. Simple bold graphics identify garden vegetables for the very youngest listeners.
Planting a Rainbow, Ehlert. A simple identification book of flowers in bright, bold graphic designs.
The Milk Makers, Gibbons. A simple explanation of how milk is produced.
Jack and the Bean Tree, Haley. An Appalachian version of *Jack and the Beanstalk*.
Titch, Hutchins. Titch's bigger brother and sister may have bigger tools and bigger jobs but young Titch has the tiny seed that grows a huge plant.
From Seed to Jack-O'-Lantern, Johnson.
The Carrot Seed, Krauss. One small seed grows one huge carrot after everyone else gives up on it.
A Treeful of Pigs, Lobel. The lazy farmer won't help his wife tend the pigs until they disappear like the snow in the spring.
How My Garden Grew, Rockwell. A very simple explanation of gardening and growing plants from seeds.
June 29, 1999, Wiesner. An eerie science project gets out of hand. Bring in *large* vegetables like whole heads of broccoli or huge rutabaga to share.
The Little Red Hen: An Old Story, Zemach. Another version to compare with Galdone's illustrations.
Happy Birthday, Grandpa!, Ziefert.

Activities

► Bring in different kinds of seeds for the children to look at. Identify the plant that comes from each seed.
► Cut open fruits and vegetables and show the children the seeds inside. Investigate cucumbers, tomatoes, apples, peaches, green peppers, etc.

▶If it is the appropriate time of year, talk about gardens the children are planting at home.

▶Plant carrot seeds in small styrofoam cups for the children to take home. Talk about watering, sunning, and general care.

Cooked in a Pot

Name Tags

A construction paper gray soup pot, tan wooden spoon, gray stone, or various vegetable cutouts;
A black soup cauldron shape using white crayon or chalk for the name.

Filmstrips, 16mm Films & Videocassettes

Stone Soup, Brown. (11 min. fs/16mm/VHS)
The Magic Porridge Pot, Galdone. (5:50 min. fs)
Goldilocks and the Three Bears, Marshall. (8 min. 16mm/VHS)

Stories

Mean Soup, Everitt. Tell carefully to control the intensity of the emotional reaction.
The Magic Porridge Pot, Galdone. Mother forgets the magic words to make the magic porridge pot stop and the village is flooded.
Lentil Soup, Lasker. His good wife tries everything to make lentil soup just like her mother-in-law and fails every time, until the day she gets so fed up she lets it burn.
Burgoo Stew, Patron. A contemporary version of *Stone Soup* with an Appalachian flavor.
Chicken Soup with Rice: A Book of Months, Sendak. Eating chicken soup with rice through the months of the year.
Wombat Stew, Vaughan. A stew with a decidedly Australian flavor and lots of rhythm and rhyme.

Fingerplay

Pease Porridge Hot: A Mother Goose Cookbook, Cauley. Teach the children how to play the clapping game. Pair the children by two's:

Pease   Porridge   hot,
(clap thighs, clap hands, clap partner's hands);
Pease   Porridge   cold,
(clap thighs, clap hands, clap partner's hands);
Pease   Porridge
(clap thighs, clap hands,)
in the   pot;
(clap right hands with partner, clap own hands)
Nine   days
(clap left hands with partner, clap own hands,)
old.
(clap partner's hands).

Poetry

from *Bill Martin, Jr.'s Treasure Chest of Poetry*, Martin: "Rhinoceros Stew," Luton.
from *The Three Bears Rhyme Book*, Yolen: "Porridge"

Song

from *The Silly Songbook*, Nelson: "Today Is Monday." A cumulative day-by-day menu song.

Additional Titles

Stone Soup: An Old Tale, Brown. Soldiers enter a town of very stingy people and show them how to make a delicious, economical soup out of stones—plus a few other things for flavor.
Possum Stew, Cushman. Yumm!
Strega Nona, DePaola. When Big Anthony uses Strega Nona's magic pasta pot he floods the whole village with pasta. On the longish side for telling.
Uncle Willie and the Soup Kitchen, DiSalvo-Ryan.
Chicken Stew, Firman.
Teddybear's Cookbook, Gretz.
Daddy Makes the Best Spaghetti, Hines. Have the children seen uncooked spaghetti before?
The Soup Bone, Johnston. Relish the repetitive alliteration.
Wolf's Chicken Stew, Kasza. Wolf's determination to fatten up a chicken for his stew backfires in a friendly way.
The Fat Cat: A Danish Folktale, Kent. The cat "ate the gruel, and the pot, and the old woman too. . .," cumulative.
Mouse Soup, Lobel. Four tales told by a mouse to keep himself out of the soup pot. (Easy reader format.)

Soup for Supper, Root. A hen and a giant make friends over a bowl of
vegetable soup with a great opportunity to sing about it.

Nail Soup, a Swedish Folk Tale, Zemach. A variant of the *Stone Soup* story.

Activities

▶ Ask the children to identify pictures of vegetables cut out of
advertisements or magazines. Place each picture in a soup pot and bring
out a picture or a can of vegetable soup.

▶ Or try the real thing, bring the ingredients for soup, show how
they are prepared, and serve small bowls of homemade vegetable soup.

▶ Hand out copies of a vegetable soup recipe for the children to take
home to make.

▶ Give each child a small soup stone of their own to take home to
remember the story of *Stone Soup.*

▶ Invite each child to tell what he or she would like to find in a
magic porridge pot.

▶ Make a construction paper magic pot with a ball of yarn inside.
Let each child pull off a length of "spaghetti" and make a wish.

▶ Have the children color their favorite food on a paper plate and
tell what it is.

▶ Ask the children what their favorite foods are when they are sick
in bed; or when they can have anything they want.

Yuck!

Name Tags

Small orange chicken feet;

Frog lollipops made with simple construction paper shapes and popsicle
sticks.

Filmstrips, 16mm Films & Videocassettes

Frog Goes to Dinner, Mayer. (12 min. 16mm)

I Know an Old Lady Who Swallowed a Fly, Westcott. (9:30 min. fs)

Stories

Old Black Fly, Aylesworth. An alphabet that really sets the tone for yucky
dining; inviting rhythm and rhyme.

No Peas for Nellie!, Demarest. There are lots of things Nellie would rather eat than her peas.

Watch Out for the Chicken Feet in Your Soup, DePaola. When Anthony takes Eugene to visit Grandma he cautions that she speaks funny and does weird things including putting chicken feet in the soup.

The Fat Cat: A Danish Folktale, Kent. The cat eats everyone he meets, until the woodcutter puts a stop to him. The repeated phrase and cumulative effect are very popular with or without the humorous illustrations. A good tale to tell without illustrations or props to accustom children to straight storytelling.

The Teeny Tiny Woman: An Old English Ghost Tale, Seuling. A tongue twister tale of a teeny tiny bone found in a teeny tiny church yard and taken home for a teeny tiny supper.

Gregory, the Terrible Eater, Sharmat. A little goat prefers to eat vegetables and fruits to tin cans and old clothes, much to the chagrin of his parents.

Poetry

Slugs, Greenberg. Undoubtedly the most disgusting, yuckiest picture book you'll ever find; all about the different uses and abuses of slugs. The children love it!

from *The Way to the Zoo: Poems About Animals*, Jackson: "Greedy Dog," Hurley.

from *Read-Aloud Rhymes for the Very Young*, Prelutsky: "The Meal," Kuskin.

Songs

from *Eye Winker, Tom Tinker, Chin Chopper*, Glazer: "I Know an Old Lady" (Also on A/C on *Special Delivery*, Penner.)

from *The Funny Songbook*, Nelson: "On Top of My Pizza"

I Know an Old Lady Who Swallowed a Fly, Westcott. Sing along as you show the illustrations to one of the many picture book versions. This story can be used as a regular element for the entire series.

Additional Titles

Green Wilma, Arnold. Wilma wakes up as a frog and has to eat bugs.

The Very Hungry Caterpillar, Carle. The very best counting, food listing, metamorphosis story ever created for early preschoolers. How does your tummy feel when you eat too much?

Golly Gump Swallowed a Fly, Cole. Another version of *I Know an Old Lady Who Swallowed a Fly*.

Fin M'Coul, the Giant of Knockmany Hill, DePaola. The greedy giant

Cucullin loses his teeth and his magic finger, the secret of his strength.

The Greedy Old Fat Man: An American Folk Tale, Galdone. The old man eats everyone he meets. A variant of Kent's *The Fat Cat.*

Bagdad Ate It, Green. But, then, he eats everything and anything.

Clive Eats Alligators, Lester.

Wide-Mouthed Frog, Schneider. A wide-mouthed frog asks many other animals, "What's the best food to feed my babies?"

Green Eggs & Ham, Seuss.

Yuck!, Stevenson.

Alexandra the Rock Eater: An Old Rumanian Tale Retold, Van Woerkum.

Activities

►Make or purchase an old lady/open stomach puppet and have the children hand you the items for her to swallow as they sing *I Know an Old Lady Who Swallowed a Fly.*

►Make frog lollipops using popsicle sticks, frog shapes and wide book tape.

Cookies, Cakes & Baking

Name Tags

A wedge from a very small paper plate or a cupcake paper;

A strip of construction paper in any shape that has been scented with vanilla, chocolate, or other cooking flavor (construction paper absorbs odors when placed in a covered container with a cotton ball soaked with an appropriate essence);

Round tan construction paper chocolate chip cookies (stored overnight in a sealed plastic bag with some chocolate flavoring or vanilla extract so they really smell like cookies);

A chef's hat shape;

Gingerbread men appropriately scented.

Filmstrips, 16mm Films & Videocassettes

The Gingerbread Boy, Galdone. (10 min. fs)

from *Frog and Toad Together,* Lobel: "Cookies" (VHS)

Stories

The Chocolate Chip Cookie Contest, Douglass. Everyone has an improvement to offer the boys in their cookie contest entry, but no time to help.

The Gingerbread Boy, Galdone. The traditional tale with large illustrations and cumulative rhythm for group sharing.

The Doorbell Rang, Hutchins. The more visitors, the fewer chocolate chip cookies per person—until Grandma arrives with a fresh batch. Good tension building to climax.

If You Give a Mouse a Cookie, Numeroff. One thing leads to another until the mouse asks for another glass of milk and another cookie to go with it.

Love from Aunt Betty, Parker. Aunt Betty sends a special secret recipe that explodes into a glorious birthday cake.

Chocolate Chip Cookies, Wagner. How to bake cookies, step-by-step.

Fingerplays

from *Party Rhymes,* Brown: "The Muffin Man"

from *Sharon, Lois & Bram's Mother Goose Songs,* Sharon, Lois & Bram: "One, One Cinnamon Bun"

Poetry

from *Sing a Song of Popcorn,* DeRegniers: "The Gingerbread Man," Barrett.

from *The Three Bears Rhyme Book,* Yolen: "Birthday"

Songs

Sing a Song of Sixpence, Pearson. According to *The Oxford Dictionary of Nursery Rhymes,* by Opie, there really was a 16th-century Italian cookbook that contained a recipe "to make pies so that birds may be alive in them and flie [sic] out when it is cut up."

from *The 2nd Raffi Songbook,* Raffi: "Biscuits in the Oven" (Also on A/C *Baby Beluga,* Raffi)

from *One Elephant,* Sharon, Lois & Bram: (A/C) "Who Stole the Cookies from the Cookie Jar?"

Additional Titles

Sand Cake, Asch. Creative play for Sam at the beach turns into a real cake baking experience.

Walter the Baker, Carle.

A Cake for Barney, Dunbar. He shares the cherries on top until there aren't any left.

Cakes and Miracles: A Purim Tale, Goldin. A late nineteenth century Eastern European tale complete with a recipe for *hamantashen.*

Sofie's Role, Heath. Sophie helps in her parents' bakery.

Carrot Cake, Hogrogian.

I Can Be a Baker, Lillegard.

Sam's Cookie, Lindgren. Wild Baby Sam loses his cookie to his dog.

from *Frog and Toad Together,* Lobel: "Cookies." Toad can't handle the temptation of all of those cookies. (Easy reader format.)

Grandfather's Cake, McPhail. The boys bring Grandfather a cake but sample it before they get it to him.

The Cake That Mack Ate, Robart. Patterned after *The House That Jack Built.*

Mother Goose Cookie & Candy Book, Rockwell. Recipes for parents and children together.

Mr. Cookie Baker, Wellington. Step-by-step cookie baking.

The High Rise Glorious Skittle Skat Roarious Sky Pie Angel Food Cake, Willard. A great read-aloud for those able to sit still for longer stories.

A Visit to the Bakery, Ziegler. A non-fiction introduction to bakeries.

Activities

▶ Use twelve stuffed felt cookies and twelve plates for *The Doorbell Rang* to visually demonstrate how more people means fewer cookies per person. The children like to play the parts of the visitors.

▶ Pass around covered containers of ingredients used in the *Chocolate Chip Cookie Contest* to see if the children can identify coconut, chocolate, peanut butter, raisins, etc., by aroma. If parents don't mind, you may offer a tiny packet of raisins, chocolate chips, etc., to sample.

▶ Bring in baking utensils and ask the children to identify them and explain how they are used. You get some really imaginative guesses for lesser known items. Some children see very little baking in this microwave age. Good vocabulary development and description practice.

Table Manners

Name Tag

Use small paper napkins or lacy doilies.

Filmstrips, 16mm Films & Videocassettes

The Goops, Burgess. (9 min. fs)
Alligators Are Awful (And They Have Terrible Manners, Too!), McPhail.
   (3:50 min. fs)

Stories

Piggybook, Browne. When mother gets fed up with her family's piggy
   ways and revolts, her family becomes truly revolting.
How My Parents Learned to Eat, Friedman. A Japanese-American child
   explains her parents' early timidity at eating together because of
   their cultural differences.
What Do You Say, Dear?, Joslin. Ridiculously funny situations call for
   proper responses—please, thank you, excuse me, etc. (Caldecott
   Honor)
Alligators Are Awful (And They Have Terrible Manners, Too!), McPhail.
What a Good Lunch, Watanabe. A young bear shows how eating soup,
   salad, and spaghetti are much easier if they are dumped onto the
   same plate and negotiated with the fingers.

Poetry

from *Eats: Poems*, Adoff: "I Am Learning (to Eat with Chopsticks)."
from *A Zooful of Animals*, Cole: "The Tiger," Lucie-Smith.
from *The Random House Book of Poetry for Children*, Prelutsky: "Table
   Manners," Burgess.
from *Read-Aloud Rhymes for the Very Young*, Prelutsky: "Yellow Butter,"
   Hoberman.

Songs

from *If You're Happy and You Know It — Sing Along with Bob #1*, McGrath.
   (A/C) "On Top of Spaghetti"
from *The Raffi Singable Songbook*, Raffi: "Aikendrum" (Also on A/C on
   Raffi: Singable Songs for the Very Young, Raffi.)
I Know an Old Lady Who Swallowed a Fly, Westcott.

Resource

*From Hand to Mouth: Or, How We Invented Knives, Forks, Spoons &
   Chopsticks, & The Table Manners to Go with Them*, Giblin. An amazing number of interesting tidbits you can share with children about
   eating utensils and the etiquette of using them.

Additional Titles

Manners, Aliki. Cartoon characters illustrate good and bad manners.
The Berenstain Bears Forget Their Manners, Berenstain.

Perfect Pigs: An Introduction to Manners, Brown. A cartoon strip format shows a variety of social situations. Proper and improper behavior is exhibited by a family of pigs.

I Can Read About Good Manners, Frost.

Dinner at Alberta's, Hoban. Arthur Crocodile's sister's new girlfriend seems to have a positive effect on *his* table manners.

What Do You Do, Dear?, Joslin. Amusing, outrageous situations and the polite response.

The Thingumajig Book of Manners, Keller.

The Day Jimmy's Boa Ate the Wash, Noble. A school field trip turns into chaos when the boa gets loose.

I Don't Want to Go, I Don't Know How to Act, Quackenbush.

Richard Scarry's Please and Thank You Book, Scarry.

If Everybody Did, Stover.

Activities

►Photocopy onto construction paper the outline of a placemat with a place setting—plate, glass, napkin, knife, fork and spoon. Provide cut out shapes of each of these items for the children to correctly glue down on their colored place mat. Show the children how a place setting is properly arranged when you want things especially nice for company. Some families don't stand on ceremony when it comes to setting the table for a meal and you don't want the children to feel embarrassed about their family's eating habits. You are just showing them another way to set the table.

►Introduce the use of chopsticks as in many Asian countries. Show pictures of children using chopsticks to eat. Let the children use the chopsticks and try to pick up simple pieces of paper wadded into balls or small paper-wrapped candies. Packages of chopsticks are available at larger supermarkets at a nominal cost.

Party Time, Company, Birthdays

Name Tags

Cupcake papers, shapes cut out of birthday wrapping paper, small paper doilies;

A self-stick bow with gift tag attached for the child's name;
A construction paper birthday crown or party hat.

Filmstrips, 16mm Films & Videocassettes

Mary Betty Lizzie McNutt's Birthday, Bond. (3:30 min. fs)
May I Bring a Friend?, DeRegniers. (7 min. fs)
Surprise Party, Hutchins. (6 min. fs)

Stories

Handtalk Birthday: A Number & Story Book in Sign Language, Charlip.
   A birthday party in sign language.
Alfie Gives a Hand, Hughes. Alfie overcomes his timidity at a party when
   he finds someone more timid than himself.
The Birthday Party, Oxenbury. Not all birthday gifts are easily given up
   and not all recipients are appropriately gracious.
The Big Sukkah, Schram. Berel has never seen so many relatives all in one
   place before.
King Bidgood's in the Bathtub, Wood. The king won't come out of the
   bathtub so his courtiers join him in it . . . until the page pulls the
   plug.
Company's Coming, Arthur Yorinks. Just what is the proper etiquette for
   entertaining beings from outerspace?

Fingerplays

from *Finger Rhymes*, Brown: "Ten Little Candles"
selections from *Party Rhymes*, Brown.

Poetry

selections from *Happy Birthday: Poems*, Hopkins.
selections from *Birthday Poems*, Livingston.
from *Read-Aloud Rhymes for the Very Young*, Prelutsky: "Five Years
   Old," Allen; "Birthdays," Hoberman.

Read-Aloud

from *Winnie-the-Pooh*, A. A. Milne: "Eeyore's Birthday"

Songs

from *Kidding Around with Greg & Steve*, Greg & Steve: "The Hokey
   Pokey." (Teach the children the dance. It is amazing how few
   children know this old party standby anymore.)
from *Gonna Sing My Head Off!*, Krull: "She'll Be Coming Round the
   Mountain." Put lots of movement into this one.

Mary Wore Her Red Dress, & Henry Wore His Green Sneakers, Peek. The pattern is simple enough for children to pick up. You may also sing about children in your audience and their clothing colors.

Additional Titles

May I Bring a Friend?, DeRegniers. The more the merrier at the Queen's tea party.

Happy Birthday!, Gibbons. Information about birthday celebrations for the very youngest.

Wilberforce Goes to a Party, Gordon. A small bear is invited to a party.

Happy Birthday, Sam, Hutchins. Grandpa's birthday present makes it possible for Sam to reach high places, even if a year older doesn't necessarily mean taller.

The 13th Clue, Jonas. Follow clever clues to the birthday party.

Fish Fry Tonight, Koller.

A Birthday Basket for Tia, Mora. Cecilia gathers special memories into a 90th birthday basket surprise for her great aunt.

Amelia Bedelia and the Surprise Shower, Parish. Maid Amelia Bedelia takes everything so literally. (Easy reader format.)

Love, from Uncle Clyde, Parker. What would you do if your uncle sent you a hippo for your birthday?

The Half-Birthday Party, Pomerantz. Everyone is invited to a half-birthday to which they must bring half of a present and tell the whole story about it.

Happy Birthday to Me, Rockwell. Simple family birthday party preparations.

Birthday Presents, Rylant.

The Foolish Frog, Seeger. The people down at the general store enjoy the song about a foolish frog so much they have a party with free strawberry pop and free soda crackers.

Max's Birthday, Wells.

Peabody, Wells. Beloved bear Peabody resents making way for a new birthday doll.

Activities

► Sing "Happy Birthday to You" to each other.

► Decorate a small paper plate with birthday candles for each child's age.

► Play "Pin the Tail on the Donkey" just like a real birthday party.

► Provide bubble solution for children to blow bubbles. A great, fun activity to celebrate any occasion.

Picnics

Name Tags

Simple picnic basket shape;
Red checked table cloth or oil cloth squares.

Filmstrips, 16mm Films & Videocassettes

Bear's Picnic, Berenstain. (5:40 min. fs)
The Picnic, McCully. (4 min. 16mm/VHS)
Ernest and Celestine's Picnic, Vincent. (5 min. fs)

Stories

Spot's First Picnic, Hill. Lift the flap and find what Spot finds.
The Giant Jam Sandwich, Lord. The residents of Itching Down prepare
  a picnic, a giant jam sandwich, to capture the four million wasps
  plaguing the town.
Picnic, McCully. A large mouse family loses one of the children on the
  way to a picnic. Have the children narrate this wordless story.
In My Garden, Maris. Half-page turns pull the reader further into the
  garden where a picnic is being enjoyed.
The Relatives Came, Rylant. When the relatives visit there is so much
  eating and talking they spill out of the house and into the yard.
Ernest and Celestine's Picnic, Vincent. Celestine pouts when rain cancels
  her picnic with Ernest.

Fingerplay

from *Clap Your Hands: Finger Rhymes,* Hayes: "Good Things to Eat"

Poetry

from *Read-Aloud Rhymes for the Very Young,* Prelutsky: "The Picnic,"
  Aldis; "Picnic Day," Field.

Songs

from *There's a Hippo in My Tub,* Murray: "The Teddy Bear's Picnic," Kennedy.
from *The Raffi Singable Songbook,* Raffi: "Going on a Picnic." (Also on A/C
  The Corner Grocery Store, Raffi.) Unpack picnic items from the picnic basket one by one and have the children fill in the blanks as they
  sing along.

Tell & Draw Story

from *Chalk in Hand: The Draw and Tell Book*, Pflomm: "A Picnic in the Park"

Additional Titles

Bears' Picnic, Berenstain. What they go through to get just the perfect picnic spot!

A Picnic, Hurrah!, Brandenburg.

The Picnic: A Frolic in Two Colors and Three Parts, Daugherty.

Picnic: How Do You Say It?, Dunham. Common picnic words in French, Spanish, Italian and English.

The Ants Go Marching, Freschet.

Wilberforce Goes on a Picnic, Gordon.

Antics: An Alphabetical Anthology, Hepworth. Rather sophisticated alphabet wordplay on the word and image of ants.

No Funny Business, Hurd.

Teddy Bear's Picnic, Kennedy. Several illustrated versions make for fun comparisons.

Who Goes There?, Lathrop.

Two Bad Ants, Van Allsburg. Ant antics from an ant's-eye-view.

The Picnic Basket, Wasmuth.

Picnic with Piggins, Yolen.

Activities

▶Bring in a relish tray of carrot and celery sticks, cheese cubes, olives, etc., spread a picnic blanket and share; even better if you can pull everything out of an old-fashioned wicker picnic basket. Be sure to hand out napkins first; show the children how to take what they want and place it on the napkin or paper plate.

▶Announce the theme a week ahead and invite the children to bring in a teddy bear or a favorite doll with whom to share their story time and picnic.

The Five Senses

In this series we introduce the five senses to preschool children and encourage them to experience things in a variety of ways—to smell, hear, feel, see, and taste life in its fullness. We will be giving children words to use to describe their experiences—an expanded vocabulary for them to communicate what they know and have learned.

This is also an opportunity to expose the children to the idea that not all people have the same abilities. That some people have hearing, vision or other disabilities and must learn how to compensate for them. Exploring sign language or other tools for compensating for vision or hearing disabilities expands children's ability to communicate and to understand others.

Taste

Name Tag

Ice cream cones with various "flavors" of ice cream. Sealing the construction paper shapes in plastic bags with cotton-ball food flavorings add a special extra to the name tag.

Filmstrips, 16mm Films & Videocassettes

The Great Big Enormous Turnip, Tolstoi. (fs)
Heckedy Peg, Wood. (10 min. fs)

Stories

Cloudy with a Chance of Meatballs, Barrett. People eat whatever the weather brings.
Lunch!, Fleming. On each page, a tiny part of the next lunchtime morsel pulls the reader along, trying to guess what the page turn will reveal. The last page shows our little mouse friend splattered with bits of the goodies he has eaten, offering a review of foods and colors.
Why the Sky Is Far Away: A Nigerian Folktale, Gerson. People used to be able to break off pieces of the sky to eat until they started wasting too much.
The Name of the Tree: A Bantu Folktale, Lottridge. Really belabor the lusciousness of the fruit and the dire hunger of the animals. A great story to tell with puppets.
Lambs for Dinner, Maestro. The lambs mistake Wolf's invitation to dinner. He just wants guests.
Heckedy Peg, Wood. The old witch steals the seven children and turns them into food. Mother must figure out which child is which in order to save them. What kind of food would you taste like if you were turned into food?

Flannel Board Story

from *The Flannel Board Storytelling Book,* Sierra: "Uwungelema." Another version of *The Name of the Tree* listed above. Really play up how delicious the unknown fruit is. Ask the children how they think the fruit tastes—maybe a little like. . . . The story works well with puppets too.

Poetry

selections from *Chocolate Dreams*, Adoff.
selections from *Egg Thoughts, and Other Frances Songs*, Hoban.
from *The Random House Book of Poetry for Children*, Prelutsky: "I Eat My Peas with Honey," Anonymous.

Songs

from *10 Carrot Diamond: Songs and Stories*, Diamond: (A/C) "10 Crunchy Carrots." The carrots sound so good, you should have carrots for the children to munch on afterward.
from *The Silly Songbook*, Nelson: "Found a Peanut." Pass out peanuts to everyone.
from *One Light, One Sun*, Raffi: (A/C) "Apples & Bananas."
from *Sharon, Lois & Bram's Mother Goose Songs*, Sharon, Lois & Bram: "If All the Rain Drops" ("were lemon drops and gum drops...").

Additional Stories

The Very Hungry Caterpillar, Carle. Especially useful for very young audiences.
I Want a Blue Banana, Dunbar. Imagine what the wrong colored fruits might taste like. Have some real fruits for the children to smell, feel and taste.
Bagdad Ate It, Green.
Bread and Jam for Frances, Hoban.
The Fat Cat: A Danish Folktale, Kent. Such a greedy cat. Hand out small colorful bandages so the children will remember the Cat's tummy bandage and be able to retell the story at home.
The Tasting Party, Moncure.
Snack Attack: A Tasty Pop-Up Book, Ruschak.
Green Eggs & Ham, Seuss. An old favorite children may be able to recite with you.
What a Good Lunch! Watanabe.
The Lemon Drop Jar, Widman. A great aunt shares her memories of other drab, dreary winter days and lemon drops as yellow and cheerful as the sun.

Activities

▶ Provide a selection of fresh fruit and vegetables. After the children have held and sniffed them, cut them into small pieces on paper plates for your audience to taste. Elicit taste words to describe the different tastes. Not only will the children be learning new vocabulary, but they may be learning new foods in their raw state, how properly to cut them up, the etiquette of eating them, etc. (One preschool mother told me after the program that her children were visiting from far Northeastern Canada and did not know fresh fruit and vegetables — only canned, dried or frozen. This was an eye-opening experience for them!)

▶Pass out lemon drops for the children to try. Does the taste and aroma remind them of sunshine? If you can find an ornately etched, stately-looking candy jar for them, all the better.

▶Discussion topic: What food or what taste does your family associate with . . .? Name a holiday, birthday, special event or occasion. Heighten the children's awareness of how foods and tastes can elicit memories.

Touch

Name Tag

Small green peas cut out of construction paper.

Filmstrips, 16mm Films & Videocassettes

Andy and the Lion, Daugherty. (7 min. fs; 10 min. 16mm/VHS) A thorn in the paw is a painful thing.

I Know an Old Lady Who Swallowed a Fly, Westcott. (9:30 min. fs) Encourage the children to sing along and wiggle appropriately when they get to the part in which the spider "wiggles and jiggles and tickles inside her."

Stories

The Princess and the Pea, Andersen. Illustrated by Paul Galdone.

Oh Lord, I Wish I Was a Buzzard, Greenberg. Imagine how hot it must be picking cotton all day.

Is It Rough? Is It Smooth? Is It Shiny?, Hoban.

Pretend You're a Cat, Marzollo. Have the children act out the animals to see if they can truly feel what it is like to be each of them.

The Blind Men and the Elephant: An Old Tale from the Land of India, Quigley. Works well as a storytelling riddle without the illustrations to give away the answer. Can the children guess what the animal is before all is revealed at the end?

Fingerplays

Five Little Monkeys Jumping on the Bed, Christelow.
We're Going on a Bear Hunt, Rosen. Feel the grasses swish against your
  legs, the mud clinging to your shoes, the solid bridge under your
  feet, the hard climb up the hill, the fear of the dark cave and the
  BEAR?
Piggies, Wood.

Poetry

The Piggy in the Puddle, Pomerantz. Doesn't the ooshy-squooshy mud
  feel heavenly? After the thorough, tactile enjoyment of wallowing in
  the mud, I usually have all of the children act out hosing each other
  off before settling back down for another story.
from *Read-Aloud Rhymes for the Very Young*, Prelutsky: "August Heat,"
  Anonymous.

Songs

from *Peter, Paul & Mommy*, Peter, Paul and Mary: (A/C) "Boa Constrictor," Silverstein.
from *The Corner Grocery Store*, Raffi: (A/C) "Pick a Bale of Cotton."
from *Late Last Night*, Scruggs: (A/C) "Ants in My Pants."

Additional Stories

Touching, Allington.
Turtle Tale, Asch.
Old Black Fly, Aylesworth. The illustrations make you feel just like a dirty
  old fly is crawling all over your food.
Waiting for Mama, De Regniers. All children know what it feels like to
  wait for a grown-up.
The Balancing Girl, Rabe. A good introduction to someone in a wheel-
  chair who has a special ability; focuses on her ability, not her
  disability.
Feel Better, Ernest!, Vincent.
On a Hot, Hot Day, Weiss. What can you do on a hot, hot day?
Albert's Toothache, Williams. How can a small turtle who doesn't even
  have teeth have a toothache?
"More! More! More!" Said the Baby: 3 Love Stories, Williams. The babies
  just love to be tossed, hugged and cuddled. (Caldecott Honor)
Seven Blind Mice, Young. Also a color story, with cardinal and ordinal
  numbers — and a moral to always explore the whole before drawing
  conclusions. (Caldecott Honor)

Activities

►Pass around dried peas so the children can feel just how uncomfortable sleeping on them would be ... and just how delicate the princess' skin was.

►Put small objects into a series of very large mittens. Mittens work well because they are readily available at seasonal sales, come in a variety of colors and patterns, and offer a snug fitting wrist band so the children can reach in but not see what is hidden inside.

Ask the children to stick their hand into the mitten and try to guess what is inside. Have the children trade mittens to see how many objects they can identify. After the children have had several tries, collect the mittens, stick your hands in and describe the feel of the objects. Ask the children what it is you are describing. Then pull the object out to show.

This expands the children's vocabularies, gives them a connection between descriptive words and the objects they have felt and helps them visualize an object from descriptive words.

Smell

Name Tag

Construction paper flowers (a cotton ball of cologne in a plastic bag overnight with the name tags leaves a very strong scent).

Filmstrips, 16mm Films & Videocassettes

The Story of Ferdinand, Leaf. (9 min. fs)

Stories

The Biggest Nose, Caple. Imagine what you could smell with a nose that size!

No More Baths, Cole. Jessie rebels at the very idea of a bath in the middle of the day.

The Story of Ferdinand, Leaf. Exaggerate the part when Ferdinand sits just quietly and (sniff) smells the flowers. The children will anticipate and sniff with you.

Alison's Zinnia, Anita Lobel. The alphabet and flower gifts come full circle.

The Rose in My Garden, Arnold Lobel. A take-off on *This Is the House That Jack Built.*

It Could Always Be Worse, Zemach. Did the peasant's house ever smell with all of those animals in it!

Poetry

from *A Zooful of Animals,* Cole: "Skunk," Hughes.

from *Read-Aloud Rhymes for the Very Young,* Prelutsky: "The Naughty Soap Song," Aldis; "Before the Bath," Marsh and Hilbert; "The Way They Scrub," Ross.

Songs

"I Like to Sniff . . . Pansies and Petunias" (a take-off on "Apples & Bananas" from A/C *One Light, One Sun,* Raffi). Try different alliterative flower names—Dandelions and Daffodils, Lilacs and Lady Slippers. If the children know flower names, they can suggest verses of their own.

from *The Silly Songbook,* Nelson: "John Brown's Baby." Be sure to get in a good "peee-yu!" when they rub the baby's chest with camphorated oil. Bring in some camphor-smelling substance to acquaint children with the smell.

Additional Stories

Arthur's Nose, Brown.

The Smelly Book, Cole.

Robert the Rose Horse, Heilbroner. Ahhh—Choo!

Julius, the Baby of the World, Henkes. Lilly thinks her new brother is smelly and slobbery and generally a big mistake.

Counting Wildflowers, McMillan. A small vase of flowers is a nice touch.

A Sniff in Time, Saunders.

Fritz and the Mess Fairy, Wells. Fritz, a skunk, is a master at creating terrible messes.

No Bath Tonight, Yolen.

Activities

►Pass around an assortment of smells for the children to guess—onion, chocolate, peanut butter, mentholated chest rub, etc.

►Make up a collection of smelly jars—baby food jars with cooking essences in them—for children to sniff and guess which are for dessert or for other kinds of foods.

►Bring a selection of flowers and have the children sniff the different fragrances. Be sure to include some that don't have a scent as well as some, like marigolds, that are less than flowery.

Hearing

Name Tags
Construction paper whistle shapes;
An egg shape with a crack in it;
Alphabet letter cutouts.

Filmstrips, 16mm Films & Videocassettes
Sing, Pierrot, Sing, DePaola. (6:40 min. fs)

Stories
Handtalk Zoo, Ancona. Introduces the hand signs for zoo animals. Great
    fun to try.
City Sounds, Brown. As a truck makes its way from farm to city the sounds
    overwhelm, then the chicks hatch.
How the Rooster Saved the Day, Lobel. The rooster plays hard of hearing
    to trick the robber into risking getting caught.
Polar Bear, Polar Bear, What Do You Hear?, Martin. A perfect oppor-
    tunity to share new words and act out different animals. Try using
    masks or stick puppets, or make flannel board figures for the story
    for variety.
Martha Speaks, Meddaugh. A dog becomes extremely conversant after
    eating a bowl of alphabet soup.
Charlie Parker Played Be-Bop, Raschka. Great sound words and a rhythm
    that begs to be sung.

Poetry
selections from *All Join In*, Blake. Boisterous refrains invite lively par-
    ticipation as they celebrate the joys of noise and mischief.

Songs
from *A Child's Celebration of Show Tunes:* "Whistle a Happy Tune,"
    Rodgers.
from *Fiedler's Favorites for Children*, Fiedler: "Whistle While You Work"
from *On the Move with Greg & Steve*, Greg & Steve: (A/C) "Scat Like
    That." The children can make up nonsense syllables to the music.
from *We All Live Together, Vol. 3*, Greg & Steve: (A/C) "If You're Happy
    and You Know It"

from *The Silly Songbook,* Nelson: "BINGO." Get softer and softer as you go through the verses. Using a mitt puppet or flannel board prop with removable letters helps children remember to eliminate letters at the appropriate verse. (Also on A/C *We All Live Together, Vol. 4,* Greg & Steve.)

Additional Titles

Noisy Nancy Nora, Gaeddert.
Hush Up!, Gage. A cumulative tale, lots of fun to tell.
I Hear, Isadora.
Whistle for Willie, Keats. Have the children try whistling for Willie too.
Silent Lotus, Lee. A deaf Cambodian girl trains as a Khmer court dancer.
Whoo-oo Is It?, McDonald. The noise heard is the owl chick cracking out of its shell.
Too Much Noise, McGovern. Great repetition of the sound words.
Crash! Bang! Boom!, Spier. Wonderful sound effects for participation.
Gobble, Growl, Grunt, Spier. Sounds to have fun with.
The Little Woman Wanted Noise, Teal.
Music, Music for Everyone, Williams. The accordion from *Something Special for Me* is put to good use for everyone's enjoyment.
Elbert's Bad Word, Wood. When Elbert uses a word he has learned everyone is horrified.
The Jade Stone: A Chinese Folktale, Yacowitz. A stone carver can only carve what he hears in the stone, angering the emperor.
It Could Always Be Worse, Zemach. Have the children make the noises from the story to add to the reality of the overcrowding.
If You Listen, Zolotow.

Activities

►Everyone try to whistle.
►Try to identify the sounds the children hear as they listen closely—traffic, siren, birds, heating system, water cooler, telephone ringing, etc. Tear paper, wad paper into a ball, ring a bell, etc., to make new sounds to identify.

Sight

Name Tag

Magnifying glass shapes or mirror shapes. A simple mirror can be made
by adhering a slightly smaller oval of food wrap foil onto a construction paper "mirror."

Filmstrips, 16mm Films & Videocassettes

Have You Seen My Duckling?, Tafuri. (4:50 min. fs) Have the children
"quack" when they spot the lost duckling in each picture. Stop the
narrative to have them "tell in words" where he is hiding. Great exercise in putting thoughts into words.

Stories

The Complete Story of the Three Blind Mice, Ivimey; illustrated by Paul
Galdone.
The Eyes of the Dragon, Leaf. The painter is forced to paint the eyes into
his dragon mural, thus bringing it dangerously to life.
Brown Bear, Brown Bear, What Do You See?, Martin. Bouncy call-and-
response rhymes reinforce colors and animal names.
When Cats Dream, Pilkey. From waking dull gray, black and white to
dream time surreal technicolor.
Hide and Seek in the Yellow House, Rose. When the children spot the kitten, have them tell you in words where it is. "Tell me in words" keeps
everyone from rushing up to point him out. It helps maintain control
while building verbal skills.
Seven Blind Mice, Young. A retelling of *The Blind Men and the Elephant*
with seven variously colored mice that explore the large animal
throughout the days of the week.

Poetry

from *Juba This and Juba That: Story Hour Stretches for Large or Small
Groups*, Tashjian: "My Eyes Can See"

Song

from *Kidding Around with Greg & Steve*, Greg & Steve: (A/C) "Copy
Cat"

Additional Titles

Mom Can't See Me, Alexander. A young child describes life with a blind mother and the clever methods she employs to cope. Maybe some ideas here to share with your preschoolers.

Guide Dog Puppy Grows Up, Arnold. Interesting information to book talk.

If at First You Do Not See, Brown. Pictures hidden within pictures.

See You Tomorrow, Charles, Cohen. The first grade class gets accustomed to their new, blind classmate.

What Do You See?, Domanska.

Look Again . . . & Again, & Again & Again Book, Gardener.

The Chinese Mirror, Ginsburg. A silly story of the misunderstandings brought about by a mirror, something the villagers have never seen before.

Cakes and Miracles: A Purim Tale, Goldin. Young, blind Hershel is able to help his mother during Purim with special talents developed because of his blindness.

Look Again!, Hoban. A die-cut square allows a small view of the next page in close-up photo. The verso then reveals a more normal view of the same common objects.

Take Another Look, Hoban. Close-up views through a die-cut page are followed by full-page photographs of everyday objects.

I See, Isadora. Simple concept book in soft pastels.

The Trek, Jonas. With a vivid imagination you can see all sorts of beasts in the bushes.

Apt. 3, Keats. A blind musician and two lonely boys become friends.

Where Can an Elephant Hide?, McPhail. A game of hide-and-seek is hard for the elephant.

Glasses: Who Needs 'Em?, Smith. When a young patient worries about looking like a dork, his outlandish optometrist lists all kinds of famous people who wear glasses.

Activities

►Bring in the items from *Look Again* (Hoban) and have the children look closely. Use a magnifying glass to look at common items.

►Photocopy simple eyeglass shapes onto construction paper or lightweight cardboard for the children to color and cut out.

►Have the children make a paper plate face of themselves and draw in the eyes correctly colored. They may add eye glasses if they wish.

►Show the children Braille books or dual Braille/printed books and explain how blind readers can read.

►Play "I Spy" as you describe items or clothing around the room for the children to identify. Another good exercise in matching words with their meanings and developing thinking skills.

Reptiles & Amphibians

Many children, even as young as preschoolers, have a strong curiosity about nature. Here you can encourage that interest by introducing *Reptiles & Amphibians* as groups of animals with similar characteristics as well as individual animals and their habitats. Using realistic books alongside fantasy and story should not be confusing. You can reinforce the difference between reality and fantasy and encourage children to make that distinction for themselves.

Incorporate nonfiction materials in your story times and book displays for circulation, provide information as well as story, and give your young audience members opportunities to relate their experiences with and questions about the topic of the day. If they stump you with a question you cannot answer (such as the difference between alligators and crocodiles), what better way to demonstrate the use of reference books than to look up the answer after the program?

An on-going project might be to make a swamp/pond/river mural for the children to add their own pictures they cut out from magazines or other printed sources and bring in.

Or you can make a flat, table-top swamp/pond/river habitat for the children to decorate with their pictures of frogs, snakes, lizards, crocodiles, etc.

If you have been contemplating adding animals to your library, a unit like this would be ideal for introducing the aquarium animals such as turtles, newts or snakes.

Frogs & Toads

Name Tag
A small greenish frog shape or a small brownish toad shape.

Filmstrips, 16mm Films & Videocassettes
A Boy, a Dog and a Frog, Mayer. (9 min. 16mm/VHS) Wordless.
The Foolish Frog, Seeger. (8 min. fs/16mm/VHS) Rollicking great fun!

Stories
Jump, Frog, Jump!, Kalan. The children can join in the chant as they warn
    the frog of imminent capture.
The Caterpillar and the Polliwog, Kent. The polliwog is so busy admiring
    the cocoon the caterpillar has spun that he doesn't notice his own
    change.
Pig Pig Goes to Camp, McPhail. . . . And makes lots of new friends. How
    would your mother like it if you brought all of your camp friends
    home to live—especially if they were all frogs?
Better Move On, Frog!, Maris. Can frog ever find a home for himself?
from *Just Enough to Make A Story: A Sourcebook for Storytelling,* Schim-
    mel: "The Frog Trap." Everyone will want to learn how to make a
    frog trap with their fingers.
Tuesday, Weisner. On Tuesday night at nearly 8:00 a strange
    phenomenon is documented in this wordless picture book—frogs on
    lily pads fly kamikaze fashion through the twilight town. (Caldecott
    Medal)

Poetry
from *A Zooful of Animals,* Cole: "Growing Up," Dennis. ("Little Tommy
    Tadpole . . .")
from *Read-Aloud Rhymes for the Very Young,* Prelutsky: "The Toad,"
    Coatsworth; "The Frog on the Log," Orleans.

Songs
Frog Went A-Courtin', Langstaff/Rojankovsky.
from *The Silly Songbook,* Nelson; "Mr. Frog Went A-Courtin'."
from *The Raffi Singable Songbook,* Raffi: "Five Little Frogs" (Also on A/C
    Raffi: Singable Songs for the Very Young.)

from *Sharon, Lois & Bram's Mother Goose Songs*, Sharon, Lois & Bram: "Five Speckled Frogs"

Additional Titles

The Princess and the Frog, Isadora. Luxurious, rich watercolor art.

The Mysterious Tadpole, Kellogg. That's one big baby frog! . . . or is it?

Days with Frog and Toad, Lobel. Gentle stories of friendship between two seemingly opposite personalities. (Easy reader format.)

Frog and Toad All Year, Lobel. (Easy reader format.)

Frog and Toad Are Friends, Lobel. (Easy reader format.) (Caldecott Honor)

Frog and Toad Together, Lobel. (Easy reader format.)

A Boy, a Dog, a Frog and a Friend, Mayer. (Wordless.)

A Boy, a Dog and a Frog, Mayer. (Wordless.)

Frog Goes to Dinner, Mayer. (Wordless.)

Frog on His Own, Mayer. (Wordless.)

Frog, Where Are You?, Mayer. (Wordless.)

One Frog Too Many, Mayer. (Wordless.)

The Frog Prince Continued . . . , Scieszka. The tongue-in-cheek humor of this one will make fans of the grown-ups reading to the younger ones. How well a younger one enjoys the story depends on how well his or her sense of humor is developed.

The Frog Prince, Tarcov.

The Princess and Froggie, Zemach. Tongue-in-cheek comedy with Zemach's droll illustrations.

Activities

►Teach the children how to make a modified frog trap. Preschooler's fingers usually aren't long enough or supple enough to manage Schimmel's version.

►Fold paper jumping frogs and have a hopping contest.

►Make a stick puppet with a popsicle stick sandwiched between a greenish frog face and a brownish toad face for the re-telling of Lobel's Frog and Toad stories.

►Explain your swamp/pond mural or table-top environment and invite the children to bring pictures of animals to add to it. Start the project with some pictures you have cut out for the occasion and have the children paste or glue frogs, toads and tadpoles onto the surface.

Snakes, Lizards & Chameleons

Name Tags
Shape of a lizard from *Lizard's Song*, Shannon;
Chameleons of many different colors.

Stories
Baby Rattlesnake, Ata. Young children will identify with this Chickasaw
    tale about a baby rattlesnake that teases once too often to be more
    like his elders before he is wise enough to handle the responsibility.
Furry, Keller. A little girl can't have furry pets because of family allergies
    so her brother buys her a chameleon.
Lizard's Song, Shannon. See extension activities below.
Crictor, Ungerer. Give each child his or her own pipe cleaner Crictor to
    shape into letters and numbers. Be sure all Crictors are put around
    wrists before moving on to the next story so they don't cause mis-
    chief.
Mouse Count, Walsh. Ten mice outsmart a hungry snake.
A Million Chameleons, Young. A visit to the zoo with bright colors too.

Poetry
from *The Way to the Zoo: Poems About Animals*, Jackson: "Boa Constric-
    tor," Silverstein (See recorded versions below.)

Songs
from *Hap Palmer's Sally the Swinging Snake*, Palmer: (A/C) "Sally the
    Swinging Snake." Give everyone a length of heavy green yarn so they
    can swing their snakes.
from *Peter, Paul & Mommy*, Peter, Paul & Mary: (A/C) "Boa Constrictor,"
    Silverstein. (Also on A/C *The Chenille Sisters 1-2-3 Kids*.)

String Story
from *The Story Vine: A Source Book of Unusual and Easy-to-Tell Stories
    from Around the World*, Pellowski: "Lizard and Snake" (New
    Guinea)

Additional Titles
Hide and Snake, Baker. A great challenge to find the snake in each
    picture.

A Snake Is Totally Tail, Barrett.
The Mixed-Up Chameleon, Carle. Illustrations updated from the 1974
   edition.
The Watersnake, Freschet. Natural history at its finest for preschoolers.
To Bathe a Boa, Kudrna. . . . especially when he doesn't want a bath.
Crafty Chameleon, Mwenye Hadithi.
The Day Jimmy's Boa Ate the Wash, Noble. Jimmy's pet boa gets away on
   a class trip to the farm and wreaks havoc.
Jimmy's Boa and the Big Splash Birthday Bash, Noble.
Jimmy's Boa Bounces Back, Noble.
Mrs. Peloki's Snake, Oppenheim. Dear Mrs. Peloki's second grade class
   battles a very snake-like mop string.
Python's Party, Wildsmith.

Activities
▶ Show the children a variety of animals (puppets, toys, or pictures)
and elicit from the children where each one lives. Then sing *Lizard's
Song* (Shannon) adding new verses for other animals.
▶ Add pictures to your swamp/pond mural or table-top environ-
ment. Provide extra pictures for those who forgot to bring any.

Alligators & Crocodiles

Name Tag
An alligator or crocodile shape is easy to make. Fold a small piece of
   paper (3″ × 5″) lenthwise, cut the folded edge in jagged teeth along
   ⅓ of the folded side. Open it back up and add an eye.

Stories
The Monkey and the Crocodile: A Jataka Tale from India, Galdone.
   Monkey outwits Crocodile to avoid becoming his dinner.
Mama Don't Allow: Starring Miles and the Swamp Band, Hurd. Rambunc-
   tious and fun as the band members try to avoid being the alligators'
   dinners.
Crocodile Beat, Jorgensen. A can't-sit-still sort of story. Invite hand clapping, finger snapping, toe tapping, etc. Stress the rhythm and beat
   as you tell it.

There's an Alligator Under My Bed, Mayer. And one little boy has a very
   clever method of getting rid of it.
Elizabeth and Larry, Sadler. Elizabeth and Larry are contented best
   friends until Larry is scorned by neighbors for being an alligator.

Fingerplay

Five Little Monkeys Sitting in a Tree, Christelow. A counting down rhyme
   that can be just as active as your group needs it to be.

Poetry

The Lady with the Alligator Purse, Westcott. The infectious rhythm and
   rhyme bears repeating.

Songs

Do Your Ears Hang Low?, Glazer: "The Crocodile" movements make this
   a participation song to get the wiggles out. (Also on A/C on *Singing
   'n Swinging,* Sharon, Lois & Bram as "The Smile on the Crocodile.")
from *Gonna Sing My Head Off!,* Krull: "Mama Don't Allow"
from *Sharon, Lois & Bram's Mother Goose Songs,* Sharon, Lois & Bram:
   "Tiny Tim." A musical version of *The Lady with the Alligator Purse.*

Additional Titles

A Crocodile's Tale: A Philippine Folk Story, Aruego.
Bill and Pete, DePaola. A crocodile named William and a plover named
   Pete form a strong friendship.
Bill and Pete Go Down the Nile, DePaola.
Spoonbill Swamp, Guiberson. A beautifully illustrated nonfiction picture
   book story of predator and prey—spoonbills and alligators.
Who Lives In . . . Alligator Swamp?, Hirschi. Excellent nonfiction for
   younger folk.
Alligators Are Awful! (and They Have Terrible Manners, Too!), McPhail.
There's a Crocodile Under My Bed!, Schubert.
Alligators All Around: An Alphabet, Sendak.
Monty, Stevenson.

Activities

►Talk about the differences between crocodiles and alligators.
Show several photographs of alligators and crocodiles and have the
children correctly label them.
►Add pictures of crocodiles and alligators to your mural or display
as well as any pictures the children bring in. If you see a pattern of inappropriate animals for the habitat, how about setting aside a corner for a zoo.

You can reinforce the swamp/pond habitat while allowing for individual contributions.

Turtles

Name Tag
Green turtle shapes.

Filmstrips, 16mm Films & Videocassettes
Tortoise and the Hare, Aesop/Stevens. (7:50 min. fs)
The Hare and the Tortoise, LaFontaine/Wildsmith. (4 min. fs)

Stories
The Aminal, Balian. Exaggeration makes a monster out of the small Aminal that Patrick caught.
Turtle Day, Florian. Relates a day in the life of a turtle in simple terms.
Box Turtle at Long Pond, George. A day in the life of a box turtle shows the pond microcosm as well.
I Can't Get My Turtle to Move, O'Donnell. He just sits there . . . great to get children to respond with the repeated line "I can't get my turtle to move!"
The Clever Turtle, Roche. An African version of Uncle Remus' Brer Rabbit in the briar patch tale. The repeated plea not to be thrown into the river will invite participation.
The Tortoise and the Hare: An Aesop Fable, Stevens. The hare goofs off and the tortoise outsmarts him.

Fingerplay
from *Finger Rhymes,* Brown: "There Was a Little Turtle"

Poetry
from *Read-Aloud Rhymes for the Very Young,* Prelutsky: "A Big Turtle," Anonymous; "The Little Turtle," Lindsey.
Turtle in July, Singer.

Songs
from *Eye Winker, Tom Tinker, Chin Chopper,* Glazer: "There Was a Little Turtle"

from *Sharon, Lois & Bram: In the Schoolyard*, Sharon, Lois & Bram: (A/C) "You Can't Make a Turtle Come Out"

Additional Titles

The Hare and the Tortoise, Aesop; illustrated by Paul Galdone. Compare the different illustrated versions.

Turtle Tale, Asch. Turtle can't decide whether it is best to keep his head out or in all day.

Scoots the Bog Turtle, Cutchins. (Nonfiction).

Dancing Turtle, Duff. The dancing turtle holds its audience spellbound until it dances right into the water and escapes. On the longish side for young audiences.

Turtle Pond, Freschet. A natural history study of turtles for the very young.

Lily Pad Pond, Lavies. (Nonfiction, photographs).

Let's Get Turtles, Selsam. An easy reading science book for beginning readers.

In the Middle of the Puddle, Thayer.

Albert's Toothache, Williams. How can a turtle who doesn't have any teeth complain of a toothache?

Activities

►Describe several animals you have introduced in your story hours bit by bit as in *The Aminal* and ask the children to guess which animal you are describing. If your group is very young, inexperienced, or if a large number of them have not been in your prior Reptile and Amphibian story times, line up photographs of the animals without identifying them to see if they can pick the correct animal with your description. Make your descriptions scientifically accurate.

►Add to your swamp/pond environment with pictures of your own and the children's.

Around the
World in Story

One of the purposes of this series of story hours is to acquaint children with the body of folklore that is part of their American heritage. But another purpose is to show children the common thread that runs through folk literature of all peoples while pointing up the delightful diversity in cultural interpretations and explanations of universal phenomenon.

Having a large map or globe handy to point out where we live, where the topic culture historically predominates, and the distance between "us" and "them" will perhaps be the child's first introduction to geography—the concept of where we are in relation to the first listeners to the stories we are about to hear.

Activity: A continuing project throughout the series might be to locate "us" on a bulletin board–sized map—city, state, country, continent. Mark it with a flag or some recognizable symbol that represents your location. If your library has a readily identifiable logo or mascot, use that to mark the spot.

To give your map extra meaning you may ask children to name places that they know about—places they have visited, places their grandparents live, etc., and mark them with small pins of the same color.

Each week thereafter, point out the country or continent of origin of the current week's stories and mark those with distinctive flags of appropriate color and design—such as a black spider for the Anansi stories from Africa, an Oriental dragon for Chinese stories, or a woolly llama for South America or Peru.

As a wrap-up to each story hour or as a wrap-up for the series, you may have the children explain the significance of the symbol on each of the pins. Granted, they are only four or five years old, but young children are amazing at remembering elements of stories they have enjoyed. Children also delight in making connections between ideas presented at different times.

107

You may extend this simple logo idea to other programs you present. After a particularly cohesive and well-received program ask the children what they would use as a representative symbol for the stories you have just told. Some children may suggest the name tag symbol you have provided. But you may also get some really surprising and fun answers. Just remember, the connection the child makes in his or her own mind is valid for him or her even though it may be something you had never considered. Be open-minded with their first attempts at thought along these lines.

This exercise helps the children learn to identify the main point of a story—something required to become a literate reader. Children are also encouraged to recognize character traits and, with help, human similarities and differences.

Any ethnic memorabilia you can introduce within the story hour will help children see (and remember) beyond the immediate story to the larger picture of culture. Just be careful you don't create stereotypes or caricatures of the people or culture you are trying to represent.

Do a little research. Shop in ethnic grocery stores or import shops for small but telling objects to share. Non-edible props and reminders can be used over and over again in a variety of contexts. Edible ones have the distinction of adding additional sensory messages (taste and smell) to those of sight, sound, and feel.

A simple greeting in the language of the cultural group in question might make a very nice opening and closing to your program. Intersperse your story with a few phrases in the language of the story's origin. Just be sure you are being as accurate as possible. Try out your accent on native speakers if possible, listen to a foreign language instruction tape and practice.

Try some ethnic folk music as the group enters or as they are putting away their cushions or cleaning up after a program. Many folk dances are easy enough to learn and give children an opportunity to get up and get the wiggles out without breaking the flow of the program's content.

Examples of simple art or craft projects that represent the culture under study are another way of immersing the children in the culture, of giving them one more cultural clue—a simple origami frog, a small piñata animal loaded with confetti and a piece of wrapped candy, button castanets, etc.

My preference for craft projects is to show the finished product and explain a little about its significance within the culture. Then I describe step-by-step how it is made and line the materials up in piles on a table. After the children have put away their cushions and made their selection of books to check out, they may come up to the table and select from each pile what they need. Then the children take the materials home to complete with parental supervision. Occasionally they proudly bring the finished product back the following week for me to admire.

I struck upon this combination of instructions and procedures quite accidentally after several years of program presentations to the preschool set. My goals and objectives and reasoning are as follows:

Time Management: First of all, I got really tired of putting down and picking up floor cushions every week. It just added to the preparation time for each program. And back-to-back programs really had me hustling. These kids seem to have a whole lot more energy than I do. Why not let them use it for something useful?

Pride of Ownership: Secondly, these kids seem to take pride in caring for their library. Why not let them take a certain amount of ownership for their story hour space? Surprisingly, this idea seems to carry over into the other areas of the library too! What a delight to see children picking up scrap paper off the floor and putting it in the waste basket. It makes the children really proud to be praised for this kind of behavior.

Creativity Is Individual: Thirdly, I don't do crafts well myself. Attempting to do the craft at the end of the program with all the children together, even with parents pitching in, was not very enjoyable for me or anyone else. I don't mind the children seeing my project turn out funny-looking but I felt that those who wanted to be painstaking were rushed and frustrated. Also, I found that children were unreasonably concerned with "am I doing it right?" and needed my approval at every step. Besides, they have been excited by all we have covered in the 30–45 minute program and are not necessarily ready to concentrate their energies on a craft project requiring small muscle coordination and precision.

Nose Count: If you count the craft pieces set out you will have some idea of how many children attended your program by simply counting how many pieces are left. I am notoriously bad at remembering to count attendance while the program is going on . . . and their little bodies are nigh on to impossible to count once they have dispersed to put their cushions away, pick out books and select craft pieces to take home. Counting craft supplies left is my fail-safe measure so I don't lose any statistics in the heat of the moment.

Following Instructions: The instructions I give are pretty routine from one program to the next. The children, with gentle reminders, are expected to:

1. Put away the cushions (this tidies the room);
2. Select books to check out (always have plenty to circulate, both stories and age-appropriate nonfiction);

3. Pick up craft project pieces (the crowd is more spread out now);

4. Remember how many pieces to pick up for the craft (and take only what they need, no waste. Surprisingly I have had very little problem with children taking handfuls when only one or two pieces are appropriate).

5. Using their own words, reiterate to their accompanying grown-up just what the craft is and the steps to its completion.

I am always right there to help, but it is amazing how well the children remember and help each other. And I have discovered that by removing the completion of the craft in time and location from where they first learned about it the children are able to interpret the craft to their liking and give free reign to their creativity.

Sequencing Skills: Although my projects are very simple, and I strive to make them as open to individual interpretation as possible, it is necessary to remember the steps to the assembly of the craft. The children will find out, perhaps by trial and error, that coloring an item before cutting it out is easier than after; that cutting something out is necessary before glueing it down, etc.

Verbal Skills: Even when parents are in the room during the program, which I heartily encourage, I have overheard the children describing to them in great detail, the steps to completing the craft and just how and when they are planning to work on it at home.

Follow-Up: It is always my hope that I give the children food for thought, a new way of looking at the world, a way of expanding upon the ground we have already covered that day in story and discussion. If the craft goes home to be completed, maybe the ideas of the day will go home to be worked on and thought about and expanded upon as well.

Modeling: By getting the parents involved in the craft and subsequent interest in the topic of the day, we are showing them a way of extending a book to make a story or concept more memorable. Story extending ideas we take for granted because we work with children and children's literature every day may not be so obvious to adults in different career paths. Watching the children's librarian may free the parents' own creativity for interacting with their child in a positive, interest-arousing way.

Time: Little bodies can sit through only so many minutes of story hour. Rather than beat a subject or story hour topic to death, give them something to take away with them to explore or finish at their leisure. They can come back to a topic again and again if you leave them wanting more.

Name tag idea: Photocopy a name tag sized globe with a simple outline of the continents to be used for each story time. Be sure to show the children on a map or globe the area of the world visited with each story hour.

Music and song: Try opening each program with "To Everyone in All the World" from *Raffi: Baby Beluga;* or "The World Is a Rainbow" from Greg & Steve's *We All Live Together Volume 2;* or "Big Beautiful Planet" or "He's Got the Whole World," both from *Raffi: Rise and Shine;* or "It's a Small World" from *Sharon, Lois & Bram: In the Schoolyard.*

Tell & Draw Story: from *Chalk in Hand: The Draw and Tell Book,* Pflomm: "A Trip Across the Ocean." This can be used to set the tone for each program in the series. Trace the route from home to your new destination. Review where you were the week before.

China

Name Tags

Use brightly colored index cards fastened on with a necklace-length
piece of contrasting yarn like the name tag you will be showing for
Tikki Tikki Tembo (Mosel) to demonstrate his *very long* name;
A kite shape complete with tail or guide string;
A Chinese dragon head shape *without* eyes.

Filmstrips, 16mm Films & Videocassettes

The Five Chinese Brothers, Bishop. (10 min. fs/16mm/VHS)
Tikki Tikki Tembo, Mosel. (8 min. fs; 9 min. 16mm/VHS)

Stories

The Eyes of the Dragon, Leaf. You may elicit information about dragons
from the children first, then describe the specific characteristics of
a Chinese dragon before the story. Maybe even have illustrations of
various styles of dragons to look at.

Ming Lo Moves the Mountain, Lobel. Audience response at the question
"Did the mountain move?" after each attempt brings peals of
laughter.

The Fourth Question: A Chinese Tale, Wang. Along the way to the Wise
Man of Kun-lun Mountain, poor but kindly Yee-Lee promises to ask
questions for those who helped him. Make a flannel figure or show
some small prop to represent each question Yee-Lee promises to ask
to reinforce how many promises he makes *vs.* the three questions he
is allowed to ask.

The Jade Stone: A Chinese Folktale, Yacowitz. The emperor gives a hum-
ble jade carver a stone to carve but the carver doesn't see the same
thing in the stone as the emperor does. A nice prop for this story
would be several pieces of raw, uncut stone for the children to imagine what carving is inside awaiting release — obtainable sometimes
at stone quarries or nature museum stores.

Why Rat Comes First: A Story of the Chinese Zodiac, Yen. Jade King
names the twelve years in the Chinese calendar cycle after the
twelve animal guests he invites to the palace. Try some creative
dramatics using masks for the different animals.

The Emperor and the Kite, Yolen. The youngest daughter of the emperor proves her worth when she cleverly uses her kite to fly food to her father and helps him escape from his tower prison. (Caldecott Honor)

Music

Try playing some recorded ethnic Chinese instrumental music for the beginning and ending of your program.

Poetry

from *Eric Carle's Dragons, Dragons and Other Creatures That Never Were*, Carle: "Chinese Dragon" (A Chinese Mother Goose Rhyme.)

selections from *Dragon Kites and Dragonflies: A Collection of Chinese Nursery Rhymes*, Demi.

selections from *High on a Hill: A Book of Chinese Riddles*, Young.

Additional Titles

The Artist and the Architect, Demi. The story is a delight but the sophistication of the plot may require some preparation. Use advisedly for experienced story hour attendees.

The Empty Pot, Demi. A good selection, especially if you are presenting this program in the spring.

The Magic Boat, Demi.

The Story About Ping, Flack. A lot of cultural information wrapped up in an appealing story.

The Voice of the Great Bell, Hodges. A moving story of a daughter's devotion to her father, a bell-maker for the emperor of China. For older listeners.

Yeh-Shen: A Cinderella Story from China, Louie. An elegantly told, sophisticated variant.

The Seven Chinese Brothers, Mahy. A variant of the *The Five Chinese Brothers* (Bishop), longer and more challenging.

Everyone Knows What a Dragon Looks Like, Williams. A good one to start with when discussing dragons. Make a list of dragon attributes as the children describe one to you.

Lon Po Po: A Red Riding Hood Story from China, Young. (Caldecott Medal)

The Great Adventures of Wo Ti, Zimelman. Wo Ti, the carp, saves himself and the other fish and birds at the Emperor's Summer Palace when Kitti Ho, a clever alley cat becomes resident.

Activities

▶Everyone should try doing "The Dance of the Moving Mountain" like Ming Lo to demonstrate that he was tricked into walking backward from the mountain instead of actually moving the mountain.

►Make brightly colored index cards with the separate syllables of Tikki Tikki Tembo-No Sa Rembo-Chari Bari Ruchi-Pip Peri Pembo. String them together with brightly colored yarn and have children learn to chant the name as it is unfurled. Be sure to make a card for Chang as well so the children can see the difference in length. Make the children's name tag similarly. Does anyone recognize the similarity?

►Booktalk *Lion Dancer: Ernie Wan's Chinese New Year,* Waters. Throw a decorative sheet over your young crowd. Stand at the head of the line with a "lion head" mask and do a lion dance, chanting "Gung Hay Fat Choy"—"Happy New Year to All," while Chinese music plays in the background. Pass out red "lucky money" or Chinese fortune cookies to everyone before they go home.

Great Britain & Ireland

Name Tags

Teeny tiny bone shapes large enough for a child's name;
A brown, lumpy potato shape;
A long green bean pod shape or dried bean shape.

Filmstrips, 16mm Films & Videocassettes

King of the Cats, Galdone. (6 min. fs; 5 min. 16mm/VHS)
Frog Went a-Courtin', Langstaff. (12 min. 16mm/VHS) An old Scottish ballad.

Stories

Teeny Tiny, Bennett. (England). A slightly scary English tale, fun to tell all in a rush.
Jamie O'Rourke and the Big Potato: An Irish Folktale, DePaola (Ireland). Jamie O'Rourke, the laziest man in all of Ireland, catches a leprechaun who outwits Jamie—or does he?
The Woman Who Flummoxed the Fairies: An Old Tale from Scotland, Forest (Scotland). Children delight in trying to help the baker outwit the greedy fairies and they learn a new word (flummox) in the process.
What's in Fox's Sack? An Old English Tale, Galdone (England). An old favorite. Do the children recognize the trickster from other tales? A gingerbread treat is ever-so-lovely after this one.

Jack and the Beanstalk, Kellogg (England). Who can resist his chaotic, highly detailed illustrations and sense of fun at the telling?

Clever Tom and the Leprechaun, Shute (Ireland). Start the program with a ribbon or piece of yarn tied around the finger of each child and yourself but don't tell them its significance. Let them make the connection between their bow and the one Tom ties around the leprechaun's treasure plant.

Flannel Board Story

from *Multicultural Folktales: Stories to Tell Young Children,* Sierra: "Lazy Jack" (England)

Music

Play some traditional bagpipe music for the children to listen to either before or after the program.

Poetry

from *When We Were Very Young,* Milne (England): "Buckingham Palace"; "Disobedience" (or "James James Morrison Morrison Weatherby George Dupree . . ."); "Hoppity." A great way to get rid of the wiggles while learning a line or two of English poetry. "Lines and Squares."

Songs

from *Gonna Sing My Head Off!,* Krull: "Fox Went Out on a Chilly Night"

Always Room for One More, Leodhas (Scotland). An old Scottish folk song, fun to sing and share.

London Bridge Is Falling Down!, Spier (England). Teach the children how to sing and play the game.

Additional Titles

Anno's Britain, Anno (Great Britain). Children see sights throughout Britain, from a medieval castle to a Beatles concert.

Leprechauns Never Lie, Balian (Ireland). The language of the story is delightful but the illustrations are too faint to share with a group. You'll need to tell this one.

Molly Whuppie, De La Mare (England). A plucky heroine with deliciously cadenced text, on the longish side but the "rule of three" keeps your audience with you.

Fin M'Coul, the Giant of Knockmanny Hill, DePaola (Scotland). Fin outwits Cucullin with help from his dear Oonaugh.

King of the Cats: A Ghost Story, Galdone (England).
Saint George and the Dragon: A Golden Legend, Hodges (England). For
those children who truly love dragon tales. (Caldecott Medal)
Wee Gillis, Leaf (England). A very old favorite but fun, especially if you
have a bagpiper to demonstrate the Highland bagpipes.
The Three Little Pigs: An Old Story, Zemach (England). The best oral interpretation of the traditional tale yet. Zemach's watercolors are a
delight.

Activities

►Plant small bean seeds in paper cups and watch them sprout over
the next couple of weeks as in *Jack and the Beanstalk.*

►Play *What's in Fox's Sack?* with a sackful of toys, puppets, and
other props from the various stories you use. Pass the cloth sack around
for people to stick their hand in and feel but not see. Then ask the
children to name the objects inside. They will be putting together sensory clues to identify objects.

►A variation on *What's in Fox's Sack?* could be to describe common
objects that might be in the sack and have the children guess what they
are. Make your descriptions vocabulary-enriching experiences.

►Bring in a very large baking potato and cut it into slices for the
children to taste. It is surprising how many children have never tasted
a raw potato in this age of prepackaging and microwave food preparation.

Native Americans

Name Tags

Bi-valve seashell shapes;
Buffalo head or horns;
A coiled rattlesnake with prominent rattles at the end of the tail;
A white bird feather.

Filmstrips, 16mm Films & Videocassettes

The Legend of the Bluebonnet, DePaola. (9 min. fs)
The Legend of the Indian Paintbrush, DePaola. (8:45 min. fs)

Stories

Very Last First Time, Andrews. For the first time a little girl of Northern Canada is trusted to go under the lake ice to collect mussels while the tide is out.

Iktomi and the Buffalo Skull: A Plains Indian Story, Goble. Iktomi sallies forth to impress the girls but gets his head stuck in a buffalo skull and floats down the river instead.

Mama, Do You Love Me?, Joose. The Inuit setting is an added dimension to this reassuring story of a mother's love.

How the Stars Fell into the Sky: A Navajo Legend, Oughton.

Raven's Light: A Myth from the People of the Northwest Coast, Shetterly. A lively retelling to share.

Moon Mother: A Native American Creation Tale, Young. A simple tale, beautifully illustrated.

Poetry

selections from *Thirteen Moons on Turtle's Back: A Native American Year of Moons*, Bruchac.

selections from *Dancing Teepees: Poems of American Indian Youth*, Sneve.

Songs

from *Simple Magic*, Brodey: (A/C) "Ya-Ho Na Ho-Ya." A simple call and response song, easy to follow along. When a woman in the Hopi tribe is having a baby, all the women of the tribe gather around outside of her teepee and sing this song to her—translated "Be strong as a bear."

Additional Titles

The Goat in the Rug, Blood. Sort of a *Charlie Needs a Cloak* from the Navajo tradition.

First Dog, Brett.

Northern Lullaby, Carlstrom. Lovely illustrations and calm, serene text.

The Legend of the Bluebonnet: An Old Tale of Texas, DePaola. The tale of a small girl, She-Who-Lives-Alone, and her sacrifice to help bring rain to the drought-ridden land; and the origin of the bluebonnet flower that grows wild in Texas.

The Legend of the Indian Paintbrush, DePaola.

Arctic Memories, Ekoomiak. Though the text is beyond preschoolers I wanted to point this title out especially because it is bilingual, written in English and Inuktitut. The exceptional artwork in applique technique shows traditional scenes and games.

Brother Eagle, Sister Sky: A Message from Chief Seattle, Jeffers.
The Land of Gray Wolf, Locker. Lovely oil paintings illustrate a poignant
  lesson in ecology and human rights.
Hiawatha, Longfellow. Illustrated by Susan Jeffers.
Knots on a Counting Rope, Martin. A young boy and his blind grandfather
  retell the story of the boy's birth.
The Rough-Face Girl, Martin. An Iroquois (?) version of the Cinderella
  story.
Dreamcatcher, Osofsky. Ed Young's illustrations.
The Story of Light, Roth. A stunningly illustrated story of how the animals
  acquired light.
The Story of Jumping Mouse: A Native American Legend, Steptoe. A sen-
  sitively told tale of a small mouse who sets off to see the world and
  gives of himself when he encounters others in greater need. (Caldecott Honor)
Sky Dogs, Yolen.

Activities

►Even if you don't use Osofsky's *Dreamcatcher,* describe a dreamcatcher and demonstrate how to make one using a plastic coffee can or
margarine tub lid with the center cut out to make a picture frame. Cut
wax paper circles to fit and collect brightly colored small leaves, flower
petals, fabric scraps, yarn or paper "confetti," etc. Arrange materials onto
a wax paper circle, top with a second wax paper circle and iron together.
Frame with the plastic top and hang in the window where the sun can
shine through.
    ►Make an outline of the Big Dipper or another constellation that
is prominent in your night sky during this particular time of year. Mark
the stars prominently and glue the paper onto a round oatmeal box top.
Show the children how to punch holes (carefully and with supervision)
for the stars. Place a lighted flashlight into the oatmeal box, replace the
lid and shine the Big Dipper onto the ceiling of the darkened room. Remind the children to look for that same pattern of stars in the night sky.
Also, remind them to turn off the flashlight after they are finished using
it to save the batteries.

Central & South America & Mexico

Name Tags
A big, round, yellow moon or cheese;
A tree shape;
A silver quarter moon shape for *Moon Rope;*
A kernel of corn.

Filmstrips, 16mm Films & Videocassettes
Arrow to the Sun, McDermott. (9 min. fs) On the longish side, and quite
  sophisticated graphically.

Stories
Borreguita and the Coyote: A Tale from Ayutla, Mexico, Aardema.
  Children enjoy chiming in with Coyote's howl each time his plans
  to eat the fat little lamb are thwarted. Add as many Spanish words
  and phrases as you feel comfortable.
Pedro & the Padre: A Tale from Jalisco, Mexico, Aardema. Lazy Pedro nar-
  rowly escapes a drowning. Use lots of expression and distinctive
  voices.
*The Rooster Who Went to His Uncle's Wedding: A Latin American
  Folktale*, Ada. This cumulative tale, similar to *The Old Woman and
  Her Pig*, makes a marvelous flannel board or prop and puppet story.
The Great Kapok Tree: A Tale of the Amazon Rainforest, Cherry (Brazil).
  A strong ecological message.
Tonight Is Carnaval, Dorros (Peru). A perfect lead-in to making *arpilleras*
  (wall hangings of cut and sewn cloth) for the library.
Moon Rope/Un Lazo a la Luna: A Peruvian Folktale, Ehlert. Fox and Mole
  try to climb to the moon on a woven grass rope.

Flannel Board Story
from *Multicultural Folktales: Stories to Tell Young Children*, Sierra: "The
  Goat in the Chili Patch" (Hispanic). The story appears in both English and Spanish to make it possible to introduce new Spanish words.

Music
from *Folk Dance Fun: Simple Folk Songs and Dances*, Stewart: "Mexican
  Hat Dance." Use the instructions below for making castanets or
  maracas to add a little rhythm to the dance.

Additional Stories

The Gold Coin, Ada (Central America). A little on the longish side for using with a group, but makes a good read-aloud from a lap.

Llama and the Great Flood: A Folktale from Peru, Alexander. Presents a
little-known culture, the similarities to Noah's flood are obvious.

Perez & Martina: A Puerto Rican Folktale, Belpre. A story of Seno-
rita Martina, a Spanish cockroach and Perez, the mouse she mar-
ries.

Abuela's Weave, Castaneda (Guatemala). Grandmother and granddaughter carry on the family tradition of weaving special items to sell
in the marketplace.

Abuela, Dorros. Actually, Rosalba's Spanish-speaking grandmother visits
her in New York. The liberal sprinkling of Spanish words makes for
an added treat.

Gilberto and the Wind, Ets (Mexico). A simple child-at-play sort of
story.

Amazon Boy, Lewin (Brazil). An environmental awareness story.

The Legend of El Dorado: A Latin American Tale, Van Laan. The Chibcha
Indian legend of how the treasure of El Dorado came to be.

The Rain Player, Wisniewski. A Mayan tale, powerfully illustrated but a
bit long and intense for group use.

Activities

►Make simple castanets by stringing small rubber bands through
the holes of large buttons. Tie the rubber bands in place and show
the children how to mount them on their fingers and thumbs. Click
away.

►Make simple maracas by decorating small white bags in bright
"Mexican" designs. Fill with a few dried beans and twist the bag opening
together to make a handle. Shake in time to the music.

►Make *arpilleras* (story cloth wall hangings) out of colored cloth
shapes of the different name tags you have used throughout the year
and have the children tell the occasions in which they were used or
the story hour themes they represent. You might even make the *arpilleras* part of an on-going decorative project, a different one for each
series of story hours, by adding name tag shapes at the start or end of
each program. At some point you might even want to stitch these separate *arpilleras* together to make a story quilt wall hanging of larger
size.

Africa

Name Tags

A simple calabash shape with geometric design;
Spots, either leopard colored or guinea hen colored;
Recognizable fruit shapes in odd colors, cut from construction paper that
has been sealed in plastic overnight with pineapple or banana flavoring for scent. Mix several flavors together to make a truly remarkable
magical fruit as in *The Name of the Tree* (Lottridge).

Filmstrips, 16mm Films & Videocassettes

Why Mosquitos Buzz in People's Ears, Aardema. (10 min. 16mm/VHS)
Not So Fast, Songololo, Daly. (8 min. 16mm/VHS)
A Story, a Story, Haley. (10 min. fs/16mm/VHS)

Stories

Traveling to Tondo: A Tale of the Nkundo of Zaire, Aardema. Storyteller
Verna Aardema uses hand gestures as well as repeated sound words
for each of the animals. Encourage the children to mimic your hand
gestures and enter into the rhythm of the tale's telling. Though the
story is long, the participation helps hold interest until the end.
A Story, a Story: An African Tale, Haley. The origin of all stories. A good
way to introduce the trickster tales of Africa. (Caldecott Medal)
How the Guinea Fowl Got Her Spots: A Swahili Tale of Friendship, Knutson. When Guinea Fowl twice saves her friend Cow from Lion, Cow
sprinkles milk over her to give her formerly all-black feathers some
white spots of disguise.
The Name of the Tree: A Bantu Folktale, Lottridge. I've told this story using animal puppets to great success. Or gather your group around
a low table and tell the story using toy animals and a homemade tree.
It also works well as a simple flannel story. (See *The Flannel Board
Storytelling Book* [Sierra] for another version of the tale titled
"Uwungelema.")
Anansi the Spider: A Tale from the Ashanti, McDermott. This makes a
wonderful flannel story, easy to remember for telling because each
character has an obvious talent you can incorporate into the flannel
figure.

Songs

from *Jambo and Other Call-&-Response Songs & Chants*, Jenkins. (A/C) "On Safari"; "Jambo"

from *Raffi: Baby Beluga:* (A/C) "Kumbaya"

String Story

from *The Story Vine: A Source Book of Unusual and Easy-to-Tell Stories from Around the World*, Pellowski: "The Mosquito." Use as an introduction to *Why Mosquitos Buzz in People's Ears*

Additional Stories

Bimwili & the Zimwi: A Tale from Zanzibar, Aardema. An evil ogre called a Zimwi kidnaps a little Swahili girl and forces her to become the voice inside a singing drum.

Bringing the Rain to Kapiti Plain: A Nandi Tale, Aardema. What grace and rhythm to this cumulative tale, similar to *The House That Jack Built*.

Oh, Kojo! How Could You! An Ashanti Tale, Aardema. You can't go wrong with Aardema's retellings.

Not So Fast Songololo, Daly. Songololo helps his elderly grandmother on a shopping expedition in a South African city.

Jambo Means Hello: Swahili Alphabet Book, Feelings. (Caldecott Honor)

Moja Means One: Swahili Counting Book, Feelings. (Caldecott Honor)

Darkness and the Butterfly, Grifalconi.

The Village of Round and Square Houses, Grifalconi. A grandmother explains why, in their village on the side of a volcano, the men live in square houses and the women live in round ones. (Caldecott Honor)

At the Crossroads, Isadora. Life in a South African village stops while children await the return of their fathers from the mines.

Over the Green Hills, Isadora. Zolani visits his Grandma in a rural black homeland of South Africa.

Masai and I, Kroll. The contrast between a Western, modernized city and East African scenes is well drawn and memorable.

Jafta's Father, Lewin. Everyday life in an African village.

Jafta's Mother, Lewin. Daily life in an African village.

Zomo the Rabbit: A Trickster Tale from West Africa, McDermott. Sky God tells Zomo the Rabbit that wisdom must be earned by performing three impossible tasks. Do children notice this is an Anansi story in disguise?

The Orphan Boy: A Maasai Story, Mollel. An orphan boy is welcomed into the drought-ridden compound and good fortune follows him.

Activities

►After telling *The Name of the Tree*, have the children make paper plate masks of their favorite African animal. (Pre-cut eye holes and holes for string to tie behind the head to keep them on.) Then they can act out the story with a little prompting from you. Encourage the children to use this idea with other stories they hear during story hours.

►Make up sounds and hand gestures for the way different animals move as in *Traveling to Tondo*.

Europe

Name Tags

A black cooking pot, write names in white chalk or crayon;
Flower shapes cut from construction paper that has been sealed in plastic with floral fragrance overnight so the children can "sit just quietly and smell the flowers" with Ferdinand;
A hot air balloon shape (this takes some time to make, best give it to volunteers to do).

Filmstrips, 16mm Films & Videocassettes

Strega Nona, DePaola. (9 min. 16mm/VHS)
Here Comes the Cat!, Vagin & Asch. (7 min. fs; 6 min. 16mm/VHS)

Stories

The Mitten: A Ukrainian Folktale, Brett (Ukraine). This works well with a stretchy mitten into which you can fit animal puppets or animal toys.
Trouble with Trolls, Brett (Scandinavian). There are lots of opportunities to join in the storytelling with repeated lines by the trolls. A wonderful opportunity also for creative dramatics.
The Three Billy Goats Gruff, Galdone (Norway). A perennial favorite for joining in. Don't forget to have several different illustrated versions for the children to compare.
Where's Our Mama?, Goode (France). A Paris gendarme helps two young children find their mama after getting separated in the train station.
Puss in Boots, Kirstein (France). Storytelling at its finest with dramatic illustrations and a perfectly realized cat-hero.

The Story About Ferdinand, Leaf (Spain). A delight, whether told or watched.

Flannel Board Story

from *Multicultural Folktales: Stories to Tell Young Children,* Sierra: "The Elegant Rooster" (Spain). Be sure to encourage your audience to join in on the repeats of this cumulative tale, especially the Spanish phrase "No quiero!" for "I don't want to!" A perfect occasion for a flannel story, with the patterns included.

Music

Teach the children a simple polka step and put on some polka music and dance, or just clap and toe-tap to the beat.

Play some rousing Russian music and do a modified Russian dance (arms crossed over chests, alternately pointing heels to the beat).

Play a classic minuet and have the children do a stately court dance.

Songs

from *The Corner Grocery Store,* Raffi: (A/C) "Frere Jacques"

from *The Raffi Singable Songbook,* Raffi: "There Came a Girl from France" (Also on A/C *The Corner Grocery Store.*)

Additional Titles

Bony-Legs, Cole (Russia). A new twist on the concept of witches for American children.

Snow-White and Rose-Red, Cooney (Germany).

Strega Nona, DePaola (Italy). A little long for sharing from the book, I prefer the film or filmstrip, but lots of fun as a lap sharing book.

Strega Nona's Magic Lesson, DePaola (Italy).

The Man Who Kept House, Hague (Norway).

Esteban and the Ghost, Hancock (Spain). Delightful sound effects.

One Fine Day, Hogrogian (Armenia). Fox loses his tail and must get it back again. (Caldecott Medal)

The Fool and the Fish: A Tale from Russia, Hort (Russia).

Bearhead: A Russian Folktale, Kimmel (Russia). Bearhead's slapstick approach to outwitting Madame Hexaba is perfect for experienced 4's and 5's.

Mirette on the High Wire, McCully (France). Mirette's daring feats of tightrope walking will probably be more impressive to preschoolers than Monsieur Bellini's recovery from his fear. (Caldecott Medal)

Hansel and Gretel, Marshall (Germany). Be sure to have other versions of this classic German tale available for comparison. Take time to point out the differences in Marshall's illustrations and general tone.

Here Comes the Cat!, Vagin & Asch (Russia). The title (the only words in the story) is repeated on nearly every page in both English and Russian.

Let the Celebration Begin!, Wild (Poland). A child helps the women in a concentration camp make toys to celebrate their liberation. A lovingly told story but best shared in a family setting unless you really know your audience.

New Coat for Anna, Ziefert. Anna needs a new coat which is nearly impossible to obtain in post–World War II Eastern Europe. But Anna's mother finds a way through work and barter.

Activities

►Ask each child to describe his or her mama for the gendarme.

►Provide a simple line outline of a woman and ask the children to color an accurate picture of their mother . . . hair, eyes, clothing, etc., so mama can be found.

►Give everyone a peaked green paper troll hat (folded paper) or long pointed ears to tie on and teach them their lines before telling *Trouble with Trolls* so the children feel the part. Carry it one step further and use a large stuffed dog or a dog puppet as a prop.

►Provide each child with a paper lunch bag. Have them select three billy goat patterns of different sizes and three popsicle sticks. Also have them select two troll eyes, a troll mouth, troll ears, troll hair, etc., you have cut out of appropriately colored construction paper. They place all of these materials into their paper bag to take home. They can make goat stick puppets and use the paper bag to make the troll paper bag puppet by gluing the face features on the outside. Then they can retell the story to their heart's delight.

This requires a lot of thinking and following directions. If you have samples of the stick puppets and troll bag puppet glued to a poster board the children can see how many of each piece to select. Don't make this the first activity of this type you do, be sure the children have had experience selecting materials for take-home crafts before and know the routine. Be on hand for help if they need it. This is a big accomplishment for children if they get it right. A simplified method for making the troll is to photocopy all face pieces on one sheet to take home, color and cut out. This limits the number of pieces the children must remember to pick up.

Coming to America

Name Tags

Small U.S. flags;

A ticket to the U.S. Blank tickets can be purchased in rolls at party supply stores, or make your own;

A passport with space for picture on one side and name on the other. You will have to explain the passport idea to preschoolers.

Filmstrips, 16mm Films & Videocassettes

Watch the Stars Come Out, Levinson. (7:41 min. fs)

Stories

Abuela, Dorros. The Spanish words are fun to share.

How My Parents Learned to Eat, Friedman. A little girl relates the embarrassment of her parents' first meeting. Father was a U.S. sailor. Mother was a young Japanese woman.

Sofie's Role, Heath. This is Sofie's debut helping at her family's busy Broadway German bakery.

How Pizza Came to Queens, Khalsa.

Happy Birthday, Grampie, Pearson (Sweden). A little girl makes a special birthday card for her blind grandfather, in his first language, Swedish.

Uncle Vova's Tree, Polacco. The family gathers to celebrate Christmas in the Russian tradition, remembering the tree Uncle Vova and his wife planted when they first arrived from Russia.

When Africa Was Home, Williams. A young boy misses life in Africa when his family returns to the U.S. An interesting concept that an American child feels more at home in another culture.

Fingerplay

Making Pizza:

> First you take the flour and mix it, mix it;
> Then you take the dough and twirl it, twirl it;
> Next you take the sauce and spread it, spread it;
> Take the pepperoni and place it, place it;
> Sprinkle it with cheese and bake it, bake it;

Cut it into pieces and share it, share it;
Boy, it sure is good, our pizza, pizza!

Poetry

from *Eats: Poems*, Adoff: "Momma Cooks" (with a Wok); "I Am Learning" ("to Eat with Chopsticks").

Songs

from *10 Carrot Diamond: Songs and Stories*, Diamond: (A/C) "I Am a Pizza"

from *If You're Happy and You Know It — Sing Along with Bob McGrath #1*, McGrath: (A/C) "On Top of Spaghetti" (Adapt the song to sing "On Top of a Pizza.")

from *The Corner Grocery Store*, Raffi: (A/C) "There Came a Girl from France"

Additional Titles

Peppe, the Lamplighter, Bartone. The concept of making a better life for your children is a lot for preschoolers to understand but I really like the child's determination to help by taking a job as lamplighter in New York City when his immigrant father loses his own job.

How Many Days to America? A Thanksgiving Story, Bunting. Refugees from a Caribbean island seek freedom in the U.S.

My Grandmother's Journey, Cech.

Coal Mine Peaches, Dionetti.

Watch the Stars Come Out, Levinson.

Family Pictures, Lomas Garza. Bilingual text.

Keeping Quilt, Polacco. Bring in a family quilt if you have one and briefly tell the children the "story" behind the different pieces.

Mrs. Katz and Tush, Polacco. A wonderful blend of Russian Jewish heritage with that of an African American child.

Thunder Cake, Polacco. Russian immigrant Baboushka calms her granddaughter's fears by baking a Thunder Cake during a thunder storm.

A Visit to Oma, Russo. Some children may have had experience meeting someone who doesn't speak their language, a difficult concept to get across but worth trying.

Tree of Cranes, Say. In this story a mother brings back to Japan a holiday custom she experienced on a visit to the U.S. Your audience sees American culture through the eyes of a Japanese child.

Klara's World, Winter.

Cornrows, Yarbrough. Describes how the hair style, symbolic in African culture, has been transported to the United States to symbolize African American pride. (Coretta Scott King Award — illustration)

Roses Sing on New Snow: A Delicious Tale, Yee. A young woman proves
her talents in a male-dominated Chinese family.

Activities

►Ball small pieces of paper into bite-sized morsels and have the
children practice picking them up with chopsticks. The balled paper pro-
vides nooks and crannies for the chopsticks to gain purchase, better than
slippery food. Paper-wrapped candies are okay if you don't mind giving
out sugar.

Chopsticks are inexpensively obtainable at most large supermarkets
and a package of 50 sets will last a long time.

►Make pizza on a round piece of dough-colored felt by gluing down
felt scraps of green pepper, tomato, pepperoni, mushrooms, etc., and a
yellow yarn shredded cheese.

►Make a special greeting card with raised letters to read with your
fingers. Provide a half sheet of paper folded over. On the inside you have
already photocopied the message "I (heart shape) YOU." Cut from heavy
construction paper the letters "I, Y, O, U" and the heart shape in a contrasting color.

The children select a card and the letters and shapes they will need
to complete the message. When the letters are glued down over the
printed message the result will be a greeting they can feel as well as see.
This helps children learn to recognize and match shapes as well as
remember and follow directions.

Holidays &
Seasonal Events

Celebrating holidays and seasonal events in the story hour setting is one way of helping preschool children relate their library and story hour experiences to other parts of their lives. We can give the children activities and literature that reinforce and extend their own family activities. At the same time we can take the enthusiasm generated by family preparations and rituals and channel it into language development activities during story time.

Lest we foster stereotypes or impose our own cultural and religious biases on children of different backgrounds, we should be especially observant and sensitive to the religious, ethnic and other influences in our preschool audience's lives. My plan of action has always been to recognize and celebrate the unique events important in each child's life while showing the children that other families and other peoples have equally fun and exciting traditions to celebrate and share.

Because I have always conducted story times in libraries within very diverse communities, I have usually planned my celebration programs around the natural world while including information, discussion and stories about specific religious or cultural events. For example, a December story hour may focus on the coming of winter while including a story on gift making or gift giving, an idea which encompasses both Christmas and Hanukkah.

I have included five all-purpose seasonal programs as examples of my approach and more specific Calendar/Holiday-related programs in the hopes you, the practicing children's librarian, will adopt and adapt my approach to suit your own audiences and your own favorite books.

Though these programs, of necessity, are not run in a series as the other theme series programs are, I have attempted to have a common thread of family celebration running through the five programs as an aid to me in feeling an over-arching theme to this planning series as well. Coming back to the same common thread during presentation of the five

129

programs spread out throughout the year will reinforce the concepts with your young audiences.

(I've tried to include lots of extra stories from which to choose, depending upon the exact time in each season you offer these programs.)

Winter

Name Tags
Snowman shapes, snowflake shapes, mitten shapes.

Filmstrips, 16mm Films & Videocassettes
The Snowy Day, Keats. (6 min. fs/16mm/VHS)
Ladybug, Ladybug, Winter Is Coming (9:30 min. 16mm/VHS)
Owl Moon, Jane Yolen. (8 min. fs/16mm/VHS)

Stories
Goodbye Geese, Carlstrom. Observe the annual phenomenon of geese heading south for the winter.
White Snow-Blue Feather, Downing. Talk about feeding birds in winter. Maybe some of your audience members already do set out bird feeders.
The Snowy Day, Keats. (Caldecott Medal)
Froggy Gets Dressed, London. Froggy is so forgetful when he dresses for playing outside in the snow. Put everything you have into this one to keep it from getting tedious and encourage the children to call out "Froggie...!" with you. Great fun if entered into with the proper amount of spirit and energy.
Snow Day, Maestro. A realistic look at what happens when a snowstorm clogs the city. Then I usually booktalk *Blizzard at the Zoo* (Bahr) for home sharing for those interested.
A Year of Birds, Wolff. How many birds do the children recognize? Which ones are native to your area?

Cut & Tell Story
from *Paper Stories*, Stangl: "Five Little Snowboys." I prefer to alter the idea to Snow People. But the outcome is amazing.
from *"Cut & Tell" Scissor Stories for Winter*, Warren: "Mr. Snowman's Ride"

Poetry
selections from *Snowy Day: Stories and Poems*, Bauer.
from *The Word Party*, Edwards: "Snow"
Stopping by Woods on a Snowy Evening, Frost. Illustrated by Susan Jeffers.

The Jacket I Wear in the Snow, Neitzel. A fun cumulative take-off of *The House That Jack Built*.
selections from *It's Snowing, It's Snowing!*, Prelutsky.

Songs

from *Sharon Lois & Bram's Mother Goose Songs*, Sharon, Lois & Bram: "If All the Rain Drops" ("were lemon drops and gum drops"...) An added verse I picked up somewhere... "If all the snowflakes were Hershey bars and milk shakes... I'd stand outside with my mouth open wide" ... then hum the next line with your head tipped back and your tongue sticking out to catch the raindrops or snowflakes.
from *"Cut & Tell" Scissor Stories for Winter*, Warren: "The Snowman." Sung to the tune of *The Muffin Man*.

Tell & Draw Story

from *Chalk in Hand: The Draw and Tell Book*, Pflomm: "The First Snow"

Additional Titles

Midnight Snowman, Bauer. The whole neighborhood joins in, even families newly arrived that have never seen snow before.
The Snowman, Briggs. This wordless story book reinforces story sequence and encourages the child to tell the story. A good one to show parents how to share a story interactively with their preschooler.
Katie and the Big Snow, Burton. On the longish side; works better as a film or filmstrip.
The Winter Bear, Craft. Illustrations a bit delicate and finely detailed for large group sharing.
Sleepy Bear, Dabcovich. A simple, yearly cycle in the life of a bear; for very young audiences.
A Walk on a Snowy Night, Delton. A nice family story.
The Walking Coat, DePaola. A coat big enough for two boys to wear at the same time yields chuckles. Lots of fun if you have a huge coat or sweater for children to try on. Such props are sometimes available at thrift shops or yard sales.
Happy Winter, Gundersheimer. The illustrations are really small for sharing with a group but the story works well as a lap story.
Up North in Winter, Hartley. Grandpa's life is saved by a dead fox he finds as he walks home across the frozen lake. The fox revives from Grandpa's body heat and is saved as well. On the longish side. For mature or experienced groups.

The Mystery of the Missing Red Mitten, Kellogg. A fun story but the format is a little small for group sharing.

First Snow, McCully. I've used McCully's wordless stories to model for parents the techniques for getting children to look at the pictures and tell what they see, to put the events into story form. Success depends upon the story sophistication of your audience. Wordless mouse story.

Grandma's Promise, Moore. Snuggling in during a winter snow storm.

Winter Barn, Parnall. I find Parnall's lyric text a little spare for my storytelling style. Try it for yourself, or display his books for circulation.

Brrr!, Stevenson. Stevenson's stories about Grandpa, Mary Ann and Louie don't work well with a group because of their cartoon panel format and bubble dialogue in addition to the narrative but they make wonderful stories for parents to share one on one.

White Snow, Bright Snow, Tresselt. Everyone prepares for a blizzard in his or her own fashion. (Caldecott Medal)

Groundhog Day

Stories

A Garden for a Groundhog, Balian.
It's Groundhog Day!, Kroll.

Cut & Tell Story

from *"Cut & Tell" Scissors Stories for Winter,* Warren: "Little Georgie Groundhog"

Valentine's Day

Stories

Four Valentines in a Rainstorm, Bond.
One Zillion Valentines, Modell.
Somebody Loves You, Mr. Hatch, Spinelli. A little wordy but can be judiciously shortened and still get the point across.
Valentine Foxes, Watson.

Activities

►Make snow people out of large and small marshmallows held together with toothpicks. Use markers to place features.

►Provide different sizes of white circles for the children to glue onto a paper plate (or colorful piece of construction paper) in the form of a snowman.

►Spread pinecones with peanut butter and roll in bird seed to make a bird feeder for the winter birds.

►Photocopy an unclothed Froggy on half a sheet of paper. On the other half, provide pants, coat, scarf, boots, mittens and hat for the children to cut out and dress Froggy.

Spring

Name Tags

Flowers cut from construction paper and scented. Use smelly markers
   for writing the children's names;
Decorated egg shapes;
Kite shapes;
Hat shapes.

Filmstrips, 16mm Films & Videocassettes

from *Frog and Toad Together,* Lobel: "The Garden" (VHS)
This Year's Garden, Rylant. (5:12 min. fs)

Stories

Bentley & Egg, Joyce. Though the illustrations are of the palest spring-
   time hues, the story works well with young listeners.
Mrs. Katz & Tush, Polacco. Mrs. Katz shares her Jewish background with
   young Larnel as they jointly care for a scrawny kitten without a tail.
The Sea-Breeze Hotel, Vaughan. The wind is so great that it spoils business
   until kite flying becomes the main attraction.
Max's Chocolate Chicken, Wells. Maybe Max doesn't enter into the spirit
   of the Easter egg hunt but he gets the prize nonetheless. (Caldecott
   Honor)
Mr. Rabbit and the Lovely Present, Zolotow. A little girl searches for just
   the right present for her mother, with the help of a wise white
   rabbit.

Fold & Tell Story

from *Just Enough to Make a Story: A Sourcebook for Storytelling*, Schimmel: "The Rain Hat." I usually make a big deal out of how boring it is when it rains all day long in the spring time, which leads right into the story.

Poetry

from *The Golden Treasury of Poetry*, Untermeyer: "In Just _____," cummings.

Songs

from *If You're Happy and You Know It: Sing Along with Bob #1*, McGrath: (A/C) "The Incey Wincey Spider"

from *Peter, Paul & Mommy*, Peter, Paul & Mary: (A/C) "It's Raining"

from *Raffi: Rise and Shine:* (A/C) "Ducks Like Rain"; "Row Row Row." Especially good for getting the wiggles out during excessively rainy weeks if you row along.

from *Sharon, Lois & Bram's Mother Goose Songs*, Sharon, Lois & Bram: "If All the Rain Drops" ("were lemon drops and gum drops"...). An added verse I picked up somewhere... "If all the snowflakes were Hershey bars and milk shakes ... I'd stand outside with my mouth open wide..." Hum the next line with your head tipped back and your tongue sticking out to catch the raindrops or snowflakes.

Tell & Draw Story

from *Chalk in Hand: The Draw and Tell Book*, Pflomm: "Really Spring"

Additional Stories

Four Stories for Four Seasons, DePaola.

Turtle Spring, Hoban.

First Comes Spring, Rockwell. Almost a picture dictionary of activities and clothing for the four seasons. Good for looking at again and again.

Spring Green, Selkowe.

The Selfish Giant, Wilde (illustrated by Lisbeth Zwerger). A little intense and lengthy for telling but one that parents might want to know about and use.

Really Spring?, Zion.

Wind & Kites

Stories

The Battle of Reuben Robin and Kite Uncle John, Calhoun. Perfect if you happen to have birds building nests close by. Save hair trimmings for bird nests.

The Wind Blew, Hutchins. Everything ends up topsy-turvy.

The Turnaround Wind, Lobel. Arnold Lobel's last picture book.

Curious George Flies a Kite, Rey. I've always found Curious George stories on the wordy side but some have had real success using them with preschoolers.

The Big Kite Contest, Ruthstrom.

St. Patrick's Day

Stories

Leprechauns Never Lie, Balian.

St. Patrick's Day in the Morning, Bunting.

Mary McClean and the St. Patrick's Day Parade, Kroll.

Passover

Stories

A Picture Book of Passover, Adler. More an informational book than a story, but useful for eliciting from Jewish children in the group what they know about and how they celebrate Passover in their families.

One Little Goat: A Passover Song, Had Gadya. A Passover story.

I Love Passover, Hirsch. A little boy describes family preparations for Passover.

Easter

Stories

Spot's First Easter, Hill. A lift-the-flap, very easy, toddler identification book.

Chicken Sunday, Polacco. Eula's two grandsons and their friend make decorated eggs to sell so they can buy Eula a beautiful Easter hat. A meaningful story that would work well right up to third grade children.

Rechenka's Eggs, Polacco. On the longish side but having some pysanky (decorated Ukrainian Eastern eggs) nestled in a basket of straw makes this a very effective story.

The Great Big Especially Beautiful Easter Egg, Stevenson. Another Grandpa, Mary Ann and Louis story.

April Fool's Day

Stories

Arthur's April Fool, Brown. Another popular Arthur the Aardvark story.

Look Out, It's April Fools' Day, Modell. Fun to share.

Fingerplay

Play "Simon Says" using instructions that get the wiggles out. When Simon asks for the impossible, you can shout "April Fool!" Have the children make up movements, too.

Mother's Day

Stories

The Mother's Day Mice, Bunting. What kinds of gifts would you get your mother if you were a mouse? Suggest other kinds of animals to get your preschoolers to put themselves in the shoes (paws?) of others to solve a problem.

Happy Mother's Day, Kroll.

Hazel's Amazing Mother, Wells. Elicit from your audience amazing things their own mothers (or fathers or care givers) do for them.

Activities

►Provide fabric, ribbon and lace scraps, brightly colored flowers and tissue paper, etc., for the children to decorate a bright spring hat for themselves or their mother. Use paper plates held on with ribbon as the base.

►Photocopy a large Easter egg shape onto pastel construction paper or copier paper and have the children decorate it with crayons or markers.

►Use large sheets of construction paper (18″ × 24″) cut into kite shapes. Have the children decorate their own "kite" to their liking with tissue paper scraps, markers, crayons, etc.

►Help the children to make simple rain hats out of newspaper with a little tape so they don't fall apart. Here is a good time to enlist the aid of the watching parents.

Summer

Name Tags

Sand pail or sand shovel shape;
Sunbursts or ice cube shapes;
Sunglasses or beach hat shapes.

Filmstrips, 16mm Films & Videocassettes

A Treeful of Pigs, Lobel. (fs)
The Relatives Came, Rylant. (8 min. fs/VHS)

Stories

Up North at the Cabin, Chall. The magic of summer in the north woods. Perhaps children can share experiences visiting grandparents.

Oh, Lord, I Wish I Was a Buzzard, Greenberg. I really like this story for its effective repetition (good for inviting audience participation) and its success at conveying the heat and hard work of picking cotton. You can throw your storytelling soul into telling this with or without using the illustrations. Follow up with a rousing rendition of the song "Pick a Bale of Cotton" listed below.

Grandpa and Bo, Henkes. A warm, intergenerational story but small pictures might make this a problem for some groups.

Harry by the Sea, Zion. Help! It's a green sea monster — or Harry covered with cooling seaweed.

The Summer Snowman, Zion. For those of you with the foresight, now is the time to pull out of your freezer the snowman or snowballs you stashed there last winter.

Summer Is . . . , Zolotow. Have the children make up their own responses to "Summer is. . . ."

Poetry

from *When We Were Very Young,* Milne: "Sand-Between-the-Toes."
from *Read-Aloud Rhymes for the Very Young,* Prelutsky: "In the Summer We Eat," Gay.

Songs

from *Gonna Sing My Head Off!*, Krull: "Take Me Out to the Ball Game." (Also on A/C *If You're Happy and You Know It: Sing Along with Bob #1*, McGrath.)

from *The Raffi Singable Songbook*, Raffi: "Mr. Sun." (Also on A/C *Raffi: Singable Songs for the Very Young*.); "Pick a Bale of Cotton." (Also on A/C *The Corner Grocery Store*, Raffi.)

There's a Hole in My Bucket, Stobbs (or Westcott). With a little coaching, the children will be able to sing this simple song along with you.

Additional Titles

Time of Wonder, McCloskey. A lovely mood piece for children familiar with exploring beaches. (Caldecott Medal)

For Rent, Martin. Best shared with parent and child because of the small, detailed pictures.

The Sea View Hotel, Stevenson.

The Field Beyond the Outfield, Teague. For children who might have a brother or sister in Little League.

Father's Day

Stories

A Perfect Father's Day, Bunting. What would you like to do to make your Father's Day perfect?

Happy Father's Day, Kroll.

Hooray for Father's Day, Sharmat.

Fourth of July

Stories

Mean Old Uncle Jack, Hines. Do any of the children have an uncle that teases like Uncle Jack does?

Fourth of July, Joose.

Henry's Fourth of July, Keller. A good story to help prepare children for the fireworks and the noise—to help allay fears.

Tell & Draw Story

from *Chalk in Hand: The Draw and Tell Book*, Pflomm: "Happy Birthday, USA!" Especially effective if you have a cake and candles and a July 4th parade during story time.

Activities

►Make red, white and blue streamers out of crêpe paper and march around the room to some rousing John Phillips Sousa tunes for a Fourth of July parade.

►Make "sparklers." Fold in half a few long, thin strips of colored tinsel (available at party supply stores) and place them into the end of a straw. Wedge the strands into the straw end by stuffing the end with a small coil of paper. The strands shoot up out of the straw just like a sparkler.

►Make Father's Day cards using construction paper folded into greeting card shape. Provide heart shapes or heart stickers for decoration.

►Make a large summer snowman cut-out of poster board for the children to cover with cotton balls. Give each child a sucker (as in *Oh Lord, I Wish I Was a Buzzard*) after all their hard work.

Fall

Name Tags

Brightly colored leaf shapes;
Orange pumpkin shapes with green stems. If you want, you can have the children put jack-o-lantern faces on them afterward.

Filmstrips, 16mm Films & Videocassettes

Arthur's Thanksgiving, Brown. (8:44 min. fs)
Farms in the Fall. (9 min. fs)
Mousekin's Golden House, Miller. (fs)

Stories

Oxcart Man, Hall. A story that reinforces the changing seasons as well as the process of making things from scratch to sell to buy necessities that can't be made. (Caldecott Medal)
The Ghost-Eye Tree, Martin. A hat as a prop works very effectively.
The Bear's Autumn, Tejima. You might explain how the woodcut illustrations were made.
Pumpkin, Pumpkin, Titherington. What fun to have some pumpkin seeds

for the children to compare to the real thing. Perhaps you could even cut open a pumpkin to show where the seeds come from.

Let's Build a Sukkah, Groner. If you have Jewish families in your community this is a perfect opportunity to explain the Jewish harvest festival and alert the children to watch for the structures as they drive past people's houses.

Poetry

selections from *Merrily Comes Our Harvest In: Poems for Thanksgiving*, Hopkins.

Songs

Over the River and Through the Woods, Child.

Tell & Draw Story

from *Chalk in Hand: The Draw and Tell Book*, Pflomm: "A Walk in the Woods";

"Tom Turkey." A simple Thanksgiving poem easy enough to teach the children how to draw.

Additional Stories

It's Rosh Hashanah!, Gellman.

The World's Birthday: A Rosh Hashanah Story, Goldin. Daniel wants to have a birthday party for the whole world.

The Great Pumpkin Switch, McDonald. Boys topple sister's prize-winning pumpkin off the porch and have to replace it.

Mousekin's Golden House, Miller. An abandoned pumpkin makes a perfect house for a field mouse.

Halloween

Filmstrips, 16mm Films & Videocassettes

The Halloween Performance, Bond. (3:30 min. fs)

Stories

A Dark, Dark Tale, Brown. A terrific "jump" story to make as scary as your audience is ready for. I have a small toy mouse that I spring out at the last minute. Then we talk about how it feels to be a little bit scared or pretend scared at the things we see at Halloween.

The Soup Bone, Johnston. Reads like a folktale when a little old lady finds a skeleton while innocently looking for a soup bone on Halloween.

Space Case, Marshall. Aliens are not thought funny-looking on Halloween night.

Picnic at Mudsock Meadow, Polacco. A Halloween party to end all Halloween parties with pumpkin-carving, pie-eating and seed-spitting contests.

It Hardly Seems Like Halloween, Rose. A good one for helping set fears to rest. The story can be turned into a really funny one with the right delivery.

The Big Pumpkin, Silverman. Great repetition and cumulative verse.

Cut & Tell Story

from *Paper Stories,* Stangl: "The Little Orange House." (Also available in *Highlights Magazine,* October, 1982.) A perennial favorite.

Fingerplay

from *Clap Your Hands: Finger Rhymes,* Hayes: "Three Little Pumpkins"

Poetry

selections from *Halloween Poems,* Livingston.
selections from *It's Halloween,* Prelutsky.
The Gobble-uns'll Git You Ef You Don't Watch Out, Riley. A classic. Try to get the children to chime in with the closing line of each verse.

Thanksgiving

Stories

Sometimes It's Turkey, Sometimes It's Feathers, Balian. The illustrations, with olive backgrounds, don't carry in a group setting at all well, but the story is so great I love to use it anyway. If I have been talking to the children about the making of children's books or how illustrators work I will point this out to the children and ask for comments.

A Turkey for Thanksgiving, Bunting. I'm beginning to wonder if anyone ever gets to eat turkey for Thanksgiving anymore.

One Tough Turkey: A Thanksgiving Story, Kroll. Solomon Turkey outwits pilgrim hunters who return home to eat squash. "Everyone just thinks they ate turkey."

Watch the Stars Come Out, Levinson. An immigrant Thanksgiving story that may need a little interpreting for preschoolers but the wonderful family feeling is worth the trouble.

Thanksgiving at Our House, Watson. Also includes some Thanksgiving
poems along with the large family preparation and celebration.
Turkey on the Loose!, Wickstrom. Watch out for silliness.

Poetry

selections from *Thanksgiving Poetry,* Livingston.
selections from *It's Thanksgiving,* Prelutsky.

Activities

►Photocopy a 1″ frame onto different colors of construction or
copier paper. Demonstrate how to cut out the center by folding two
sheets in half and cutting along the lines. Then make a leaf window picture by ironing brightly colored fall leaves between two sheets of wax
paper. Carefully paste the leaf picture between your two picture frame
pieces. Have the children select two wax paper pieces and two picture
frame pieces to take home. They can gather leaves on the way home.

►Cut out a variety of eye, nose and mouth shapes from black construction paper. Have the children select the appropriate pieces to glue
down on an orange paper plate to make their own jack-o'-lantern. Write
their names on the back but keep them to decorate your story hour space
until Halloween is over.

►Have the children repeat the ten-line verse of the tell & draw
story *Tom Turkey* (Pflomm). Help them draw their own turkeys by
repeating it again.

December & Year's End

Name Tags

A colorful stick-on package bow or ribbon;
A colorful streamer (curly ribbon works well) taped to the back of a star
shape;
A Christmas stocking shape, decorated present shape or use Christmas
gift tags;
A dreidel, a star of David, a gold coin.

Filmstrips, 16mm Films & Videocassettes

Charlie Needs a Cloak, DePaola. (6 min. fs; 8 min. 16mm/VHS)
Morris's Disappearing Bag, Wells. (5 min. fs/16mm/VHS)

Stories

Christmas at Long Pond, George. A search for the perfect Christmas tree brings father and son to close observation of nature.

The Nutcracker, Isadora. A really pared-down version of the tale. The illustrations are, nonetheless, frighteningly effective.

Round Robin, Kent. This reinforces the cycle of seasons quite nicely.

Socks for Supper, Kent. A funny story that can be told as a simple gift story if you have children in your group who don't celebrate Christmas.

Goodbye Old Year, Hello New Year, Modell. Two little boys want so much to celebrate the New Year.

Elijah's Angel: A Story for Chanukah and Christmas, Rosen. A Christian lay minister, barber and woodcarver and a small Jewish boy become friends, learning to respect each other's traditions and beliefs.

Songs

from *We All Live Together, Vol. 2,* Greg & Steve: "Months of the Year" (A/C)

Jingle Bells, Kovalski. Grandma and the girls are back in a rollicking, runaway sleigh ride through Central Park.

Tell & Draw Story

from *Chalk in Hand: The Draw and Tell Book,* Pflomm: "My Dreidel"; "Getting Ready for Christmas"

Additional Titles

The Nutcracker, Hoffman. Illustrated by Lisbeth Zwerger. Another beautifully illustrated version for comparison.

Little Bear's New Year's Party, Janice.

Christmas

Stories

The Clown of God, DePaola. (Caldecott Honor)

The Twelve Days of Christmas, Duntze. A puzzle to find all of the items repeated in each verse and in each illustration.

The Little Drummer Boy, Keats.

Baboushka and the Three Kings, Robbins. (Caldecott Medal)

Tree of Cranes, Say. A little Japanese boy learns about Christmas when his mother explains how it was celebrated when she visited America.

Polar Express, Van Allsburg. Full of wonder but on the longish side. (Caldecott Medal)

Max's Christmas, Wells.

Poetry

selections from *Christmas Poems*, Livingston.

The Night Before Christmas, Moore. Various illustrated editions by Michael Foreman, Tomie DePaola, Gyo Fujikawa, Anita Lobel, Tasha Tudor and Michael Hague (one of my favorites—a delightful pop-up version).

Songs

Away in the Manger: A Story of the Nativity, Nussbaumer.

The Twelve Days of Christmas, traditional. Various editions by Jan Brett, Brian Wildsmith, and Jack Kent.

We Wish You a Merry Christmas: A Traditional Christmas Carol, Pearson.

Hanukkah

Stories

Grandma's Latkes, Drucker. Molly learns how to make latkes while she learns about the meaning of Hanukkah.

Just Enough Is Plenty: A Hanukkah Tale, Goldin. A poor family welcomes a mysterious stranger to their Hanukkah celebration.

I Love Hanukkah, Hirsh. A small boy remembers only the candle lights from last year's Hanukkah so his grandfather tells him the story again. Many preschoolers will have only dim memories of a whole year ago so this strikes a chord with them.

The Chanukkah Guest, Kimmel. An old bear is mistaken for the rabbi and is given delicious potato latkes in celebration of Hanukkah.

Hanukkah Money, Shulevitz. This is a period piece that trades on nostalgia while explaining the Hanukkah traditions of potato pancakes and giving money to children.

Cut & Tell Story

from *"Cut & Tell" Scissors Stories for Winter*, Warren: "The Singing Dreidl." It makes a dreidl and a menorah.

Songs

from *If You're Happy and You Know It: Sing Along with Bob #1*, McGrath: (A/C) "Dreydel."

from *The Raffi Singable Storybook*, Raffi: "My Dreydel." (Also on A/C *Raffi: Singable Songs for the Very Young*.)

Activities

►Photocopy clock faces to be cut out and glued to a paper plate. Provide small brads and clock hands in two sizes with a hole punched in one end. Show the children how to take a long hand and a short hand and make a clock. Demonstrate what the clock will look like at midnight — the end of one day and the beginning of another, or the end of one year and the beginning of another.

►Make a miniature dreidel by poking a sturdy round toothpick through the center of a marshmallow. Teach the children how to spin the dreidel.

Bibliographies

Stories & Story Collections, Poetry & Song

Aardema, Verna. *Bimwili & the Zimwi: A Tale from Zanzibar*. Illustrated by Susan Meddaugh. Dial Books for Young Readers, 1985.

_____. *Borreguita and the Coyote: A Tale from Ayutla, Mexico*. Illustrated by Petra Mathers. Alfred A. Knopf, 1991.

_____. *Bringing the Rain to Kapiti Plain: A Nandi Tale*. Illustrated by Beatriz Vidal. Dial Books for Young Readers, 1981.

_____. *Oh, Kojo! How Could You! An Ashanti Tale*. Illustrated by Marc Tolon Brown. Dial Books for Young Readers, 1984.

_____. *Pedro & the Padre: A Tale from Jalisco, Mexico*. Illustrated by Friso Henstra. Dial Books for Young Readers, 1991.

_____. *Traveling to Tondo: A Tale of the Nkundo of Zaire*. Illustrated by Will Hillenbrand. Alfred A. Knopf, 1991.

_____. *Why Mosquitos Buzz in People's Ears: A West African Tale*. Illustrated by Leo & Diane Dillon. Dial Books for Young Readers, 1975.

Abolafia, Yossi. *My Three Uncles*. Illustrated by Yossi Abolafia. Greenwillow, 1985.

Ackerman, Karen. *Song and Dance Man*. Illustrated by Stephen Gammell. Alfred A. Knopf, 1988.

Ada, Alma Flor. *The Gold Coin*. Illustrated by Neil Waldman. Atheneum, 1991.

_____. *The Rooster Who Went to His Uncle's Wedding: A Latin American Folktale*. Illustrated by Kathleen Kuchera. Putnam, 1993.

Adler, David. *A Picture Book of Passover*. Illustrated by Linda Heller. Holiday House, 1982.

_____. *The Purple Turkey & Other Thanksgiving Riddles*. Illustrated by Marylin Hafner. Holiday House, 1986.

Adoff, Arnold. *Chocolate Dreams*. Illustrated by Turi MacCombie. Lothrop, Lee & Shepard, 1989.

_____. *Eats: Poems*. Illustrated by Susan Russo. Lothrop, Lee & Shepard, 1979.

147

_____. *Greens: Poetry.* Illustrated by Betsy Lewin. Lothrop, Lee & Shepard, 1988.

Aesop. *The Hare and the Tortoise.* Illustrated by Paul Galdone. McGraw-Hill, 1962.

Ahlberg, Janet and Allan Ahlberg. *The Baby's Catalogue.* Illustrated by Janet & Allan Ahlberg. Little, Brown, 1982.

Alda, Arlene. *Matthew and His Dad.* Illustrated by Arlene Alda. Little Simon, 1983.

Alderson, Sue. *Ida and the Wool Smugglers.* Illustrated by Ann Blades. Margaret K. McElderry, 1988.

Alexander, Ellen. *Llama and the Great Flood: A Folktale from Peru.* Illustrated by Ellen Alexander. Thomas Y. Crowell, 1989.

Alexander, Lloyd. *The Fortune-Tellers.* Illustrated by Trina Schart Hyman. Dutton Children's Books, 1992.

Alexander, Martha. *Blackboard Bear.* Illustrated by Martha Alexander. Dial Books for Young Readers, 1988.

_____. *Nobody Asked Me If I Wanted a Baby Sister.* Illustrated by Martha Alexander. Dial Books for Young Readers, 1971.

_____. *When the New Baby Comes I'm Moving Out.* Illustrated by Martha Alexander. Dial Books for Young Readers, 1979.

Alexander, Sally. *Mom Can't See Me.* Illustrated by George Ancona. Macmillan, 1990.

Aliki. *Manners.* Illustrated by Aliki. Greenwillow, 1990.

Allen, Linda. *Mrs. Simkin's Bed.* Illustrated by Loretta Lustig. William Morrow, 1976.

Allington, Richard L. and Kathleen Cowles. *Touching.* Illustrated by Yoshi Miyake. Raintree Childrens Books, 1980.

Ancona, George and Mary Beth. *Handtalk Zoo.* Illustrated by George Ancona. Four Winds Press, 1989.

Andersen, Hans Christian. *The Princess and the Pea.* Illustrated by Paul Galdone. Clarion, 1979.

_____. *The Ugly Duckling: A Tale from Hans Christian Andersen.* Illustrated by Lorinda Bryan Cauley. Harcourt Brace Jovanovich, 1979.

Andrews, Jan. *Very Last First Time.* Illustrated by Ian Wallace. Atheneum, 1986.

Anno, Mitsumasa. *Anno's Britain.* Illustrated by Mitsumasa Anno. Philomel, 1982.

Arnold, Caroline. *Guide Dog Puppy Grows Up.* Illustrated by Richard Hewett. Harcourt Brace Jovanovich, 1991.

Arnold, Tedd. *Green Wilma.* Illustrated by Tedd Arnold. Dial Books for Young Readers, 1993.

Aruego, Jose. *Crocodile's Tale: A Philippine Folk Story.* Illustrated by Jose Aruego and Ariane Dewey. Scribner, 1972.

Asch, Frank. *Bread and Honey.* Illustrated by Frank Asch. Parents Magazine Press, 1982.

_____. *Just Like Daddy.* Illustrated by Frank Asch. Simon & Schuster, 1984.

_____. *Popcorn.* Illustrated by Frank Asch. Parents Magazine Press, 1979.

_____. *Sand Cake.* Illustrated by Frank Asch. Parents Magazine Press, 1979.

_____. *Skyfire.* Illustrated by Frank Asch. Little, Brown, 1984.

_____. *Turtle Tale.* Illustrated by Frank Asch. Dial, 1978.

_____. *Yellow, Yellow.* Illustrated by Mark Alan Stamaty. McGraw-Hill, 1971.

Ata, Te. *Baby Rattlesnake.* Illustrated by Veg Reisberg. Children's Book Press, 1989.

Aylesworth, Jim. *Hanna's Hog.* Illustrated by Glen Rounds. Atheneum, 1988.

_____. *Hush Up!* Illustrated by Glen Rounds. Holt, Rinehart & Winston, 1980.

_____. *Old Black Fly.* Illustrated by Stephen Gammell. Henry Holt, 1992.

Azarian, Mary. *A Farmer's Alphabet.* Illustrated by Mary Azarian. David R. Godine, 1981.

Bahr, Robert. *Blizzard at the Zoo.* Illustrated by Consuelo Joerns. Lothrop, Lee & Shepard, 1982.

Baker, Keith. *Hide & Snake.* Illustrated by Keith Baker. Harcourt Brace Jovanovich, 1991.

Balian, Lorna. *The Aminal.* Illustrated by Lorna Balian. Humbug Books, 1987.

_____. *A Garden for a Groundhog.* Illustrated by Lorna Balian. Humbug Books, 1985.

_____. *Leprechauns Never Lie.* Illustrated by Lorna Balian. Humbug Books, 1981.

_____. *Sometimes It's Turkey, Sometimes It's Feathers.* Illustrated by Lorna Balian. Humbug Books, 1973.

Barnhart, Peter. *The Wounded Duck.* Illustrated by Adrienne Adams. Scribner, 1979.

Barrett, Judith. *Cloudy with a Chance of Meatballs.* Illustrated by Ron Barrett. Atheneum, 1978.

_____. *A Snake Is Totally Tail.* Illustrated by Lonni S. Johnson. Aladdin Books, 1987.

Barton, Byron. *The Little Red Hen.* Illustrated by Byron Barton. HarperCollins, 1993.

Bartone, Elisa. *Peppe, the Lamplighter.* Illustrated by Ted Lewin. Lothrop, Lee & Shepard, 1993.

Bate, Lucy. *How Georgina Drove the Car Very Carefully from Boston to New York.* Illustrated by Tamar Taylor. Crown, 1989.

Bauer, Caroline Feller. *Midnight Snowman.* Illustrated by Katherine Stock. Atheneum Children's Books, 1987.

_____. *My Mom Travels a Lot.* Illustrated by Nancy Winslow Parker. Puffin, 1985.

_____ (ed.). *Snowy Day: Stories and Poems.* Illustrated by Margot Tomes. Lippincott, 1986.

Belpre, Pura. *Perez & Martina: A Puerto Rican Folktale.* Illustrated by Carlos Sanchez. Viking, 1991.

Bemelmans, Ludwig. *Madeline.* Illustrated by Ludwig Bemelmans. Viking, 1985.

Bennett, Jill. *Teeny Tiny.* Illustrated by Tomie DePaola. Putnam, 1986.

Berenstain, Stan and Janice Berenstain. *Bears' Picnic.* Illustrated by Stan and Jan Berenstain. Beginner Books, 1966.

_____. *The Berenstain Bears Forget Their Manners.* Illustrated by Stan and Jan Berenstain. Random House Books for Young Readers, 1985.

Bergman, Donna. *Timmy Green's Blue Lake.* Illustrated by Ib Ohlsson. William Morrow, 1992.

Berman, Linda. *The Good-Bye Painting.* Illustrated by Mark Hannon. Human Science Press, 1982.

Birdseye, Tom. *Airmail to the Moon.* Illustrated by Stephen Gammell. Holiday House, 1988.

Blaine, Marge. *The Terrible Thing That Happened at Our House.* Illustrated by John C. Wallner. Four Winds Press, 1986.

Blake, Quentin. *All Join In.* Illustrated by Quentin Blake. Little, Brown, 1991.

Blegvad, Lenore (comp.). *This Little Pig-a-Wig, and Other Rhymes About Pigs.* Illustrated by Erik Blegvad. Atheneum, 1978.

Blood, Charles L. *The Goat in the Rug.* Illustrated by Nancy Winslow Parker. Four Winds Press, 1980.

Blos, Joan W. *Old Henry.* Illustrated by Stephen Gammell. William Morrow, 1987.

Bond, Felicia. *Four Valentines in a Rainstorm.* Illustrated by Felicia Bond. Crowell Junior Books, 1986.

_____. *Poinsettia & Her Family.* Illustrated by Felicia Bond. Harper & Row, 1981.

_____. *Poinsettia and the Firefighters.* Illustrated by Felicia Bond. Thomas Y. Crowell, 1984.

Bowman, Margret and Nicholas Millhouse. *Blue Footed Booby: Bird of the Galapagos.* Illustrated by Margret Bowman. Walker & Company, 1986.

Brandenberg, Franz. *Aunt Nina and Her Nephews and Nieces.* Illustrated by Aliki. Greenwillow, 1983.

_____. *Aunt Nina, Good Night.* Illustrated by Aliki. Greenwillow, 1989.

_____. *Aunt Nina's Visit.* Illustrated by Aliki. Greenwillow, 1984.

_____. *A Picnic, Hurrah!* Illustrated by Aliki. Greenwillow, 1978.

Brett, Jan. *First Dog.* Illustrated by Jan Brett. Harcourt Brace Jovanovich, 1988.

_____. *The Mitten: A Ukrainian Folktale.* Illustrated by Jan Brett. Putnam, 1989.

_____. *Trouble with Trolls.* Illustrated by Jan Brett. Putnam, 1992.

_____. *The Twelve Days of Christmas.* Illustrated by Jan Brett. Putnam, 1986.

Bridwell, Norman. *Clifford the Big Red Dog.* Illustrated by Norman Bridwell. Scholastic, 1988.

_____. *Clifford's Good Deeds.* Illustrated by Norman Bridwell. Scholastic, 1985.

Briggs, Raymond. *The Snowman.* Illustrated by Raymond Briggs. Random House, 1978.

Bright, Robert. *My Red Umbrella.* Illustrated by Robert Bright. William Morrow, 1985.

Brown, Craig. *City Sounds.* Illustrated by Craig Brown. Greenwillow, 1992.

Brown, Marc Tolon. *Arthur Babysits.* Illustrated by Marc Tolon Brown. Little, Brown, 1992.

_____. *Arthur's April Fool.* Illustrated by Marc Tolon Brown. Little, Brown, 1985.

_____. *Arthur's Nose.* Illustrated by Marc Tolon Brown. Little, Brown, 1986.

_____. *Finger Rhymes.* Illustrated by Marc Tolon Brown. Dutton, 1980.

_____. *Hand Rhymes.* Illustrated by Marc Tolon Brown. Dutton, 1985.

_____. *Party Rhymes.* Illustrated by Marc Tolon Brown. Dutton, 1988.

_____. *Play Rhymes.* Illustrated by Marc Tolon Brown. Dutton, 1987.

_____. *Your First Garden Book.* Illustrated by Marc Tolon Brown. Little, Brown, 1981.

_____ and Stephen Krensky. *Perfect Pigs: An Introduction to Manners.* Illustrated by Marc Tolon Brown and Stephen Krensky. Little, Brown, 1983.

Brown, Marcia. *Dick Whittington and His Cat.* Illustrated by Marcia Brown. Scribner, 1950.

_____. *Stone Soup: An Old Tale.* Illustrated by Marcia Brown. Scribner, 1947.

Brown, Margaret Wise. *Big Red Barn.* Illustrated by Felicia Bond. Harper & Row, 1989.

_____. *Red Light, Green Light.* Illustrated by Leonard Weisgard. Scholastic, 1992.

Brown, Ruth. *The Big Sneeze.* Illustrated by Ruth Brown. Lothrop, Lee & Shepard, 1985.

_____. *A Dark, Dark Tale.* Illustrated by Ruth Brown. Dial Books for Young Readers, 1981.

_____. *If at First You Do Not See.* Illustrated by Ruth Brown. Henry Holt, 1983.

Browne, Anthony. *Piggybook.* Illustrated by Anthony Browne. Knopf Books for Young Readers, 1986.

Bruchac, Joseph and Jonathan London. *Thirteen Moons on Turtle's Back: A Native American Year of Moons.* Illustrated by Thomas Locker. Philomel, 1992.

Brustlein, Janice. *Little Bear's New Year's Party.* Illustrated by Marianna. Lothrop, Lee & Shepard, 1973.

Buckley, Helen. *Grandfather and I.* Illustrated by Jan Ormerod. Lothrop, Lee & Shepard, 1994.

_____. *Grandmother and I.* Illustrated by Jan Ormerod. Lothrop, Lee & Shepard, 1994.

Bunting, Eve. *How Many Days to America? A Thanksgiving Story.* Illustrated by Beth Peck. Clarion Books, 1988.

_____. *The Mother's Day Mice.* Illustrated by Jan Brett. Clarion Books, 1986.

_____. *A Perfect Father's Day.* Illustrated by Susan Meddaugh. Clarion Books, 1991.

_____. *St. Patrick's Day in the Morning.* Illustrated by Jan Brett. Clarion Books, 1983.

_____. *A Turkey for Thanksgiving.* Illustrated by Diane de Groat. Clarion Books, 1991.

Burton, Virginia Lee. *Katie and the Big Snow.* Illustrated by Virginia Lee Burton. Houghton Mifflin, 1943.

Byars, Betsy Cromer. *Go and Hush the Baby.* Illustrated by Emily A. McCully. Viking, 1971.

Byers, Rinda M. *Mycca's Baby.* Illustrated by David Tamura. Orchard, 1990.

Caines, Jeannette. *Just Us Women.* Illustrated by Pat Cummings. Harper & Row, 1982.

Calhoun, Mary. *The Battle of Reuben Robin & Kite Uncle John.* Illustrated by Janet McCaffrey. William Morrow, 1973.

Calmenson, Stephanie. *Hotter Than a Hot Dog!* Illustrated by Elivia. Little, Brown, 1994.

Caple, Kathy. *The Biggest Nose.* Illustrated by Kathy Caple. Houghton Mifflin, 1985.

————. *The Purse.* Illustrated by Kathy Caple. Houghton Mifflin, 1986.

Carle, Eric. *Eric Carle's Dragons, Dragons and Other Creatures That Never Were.* Illustrated by Eric Carle. Philomel, 1991.

————. *The Mixed-Up Chameleon.* Illustrated by Eric Carle. Thomas Y. Crowell, 1984.

————. *The Very Hungry Caterpillar.* Illustrated by Eric Carle. Philomel, 1981.

————. *Walter the Baker.* Illustrated by Eric Carle. Alfred A. Knopf, 1972.

Carlson, Nancy. *I Like Me!* Illustrated by Nancy Carlson. Viking Kestrel, 1988.

Carlstrom, Nancy White. *Goodbye Geese.* Illustrated by Ed Young. Philomel, 1991.

————. *Northern Lullaby.* Illustrated by Leo and Diane Dillon. Philomel, 1992.

————. *Wild, Wild Sunflower Child, Anna.* Illustrated by Jerry Pinkney. Macmillan, 1987.

Carson, Jo. *You Hold Me and I'll Hold You.* Illustrated by Bruce Degen. Macmillan, 1992.

Castaneda, Omar S. *Abuela's Weave.* Illustrated by Enrique O. Sanchez. Lothrop, Lee & Shepard, 1993.

Catalanotto, Peter. *Dylan's Day Out.* Illustrated by Peter Catalanotto. Orchard, 1989.

Cauley, Lorinda Bryan. *The Cock, the Mouse, and the Little Red Hen.* Illustrated by Lorinda Bryan Cauley. Putnam, 1982.

————. *Old MacDonald Had a Farm.* Illustrated by Lorinda Bryan Cauley. Putnam, 1989.

————. *Pease Porridge Hot: A Mother Goose Cookbook.* Illustrated by Lorinda Bryan Cauley. Putnam, 1977.

Cazet, Denys. *Mud Baths for Everyone.* Illustrated by Denys Cazet. Bradbury, 1981.

Cech, John. *My Grandmother's Journey.* Illustrated by Sharon McGinley-Nally. Bradbury, 1991.

Cendrars, Blaise. *Shadow.* Illustrated by Marcia Brown. Scribner, 1982.

Chall, Marsha W. *Up North at the Cabin.* Illustrated by Marsha W. Chall. Lothrop, Lee & Shepard, 1992.

Charlip, Remy, Mary Beth and George Ancona. *Handtalk Birthday: A Number & Story Book in Sign Language.* Illustrated by George Ancona. Four Winds Press, 1987.

Cherry Lynne. *The Great Kapok Tree: A Tale of the Amazon Rainforest.* Illustrated by Lynne Cherry. Harcourt Brace Jovanovich, 1990.

Child, Lydia Maria Francis. *Over the River and Through the Woods.* Illustrated by Nadine Bernard Westcott. HarperCollins, 1993.

Christelow, Eileen. *Five Little Monkeys Jumping on the Bed.* Illustrated by Eileen Christelow. Clarion Books, 1989.

————. *Five Little Monkeys Sitting in a Tree.* Illustrated by Eileen Christelow. Clarion Books, 1991.

————. *Jerome the Baby-Sitter.* Illustrated by Eileen Christelow. Clarion Books, 1987.

Clifton, Lucille. *Everett Anderson's Nine-Months-Long.* Illustrated by Ann Grifalconi. Henry Holt, 1978.

Coatsworth, Elizabeth. *Under the Green Willow.* Illustrated by Janina Domanska. Greenwillow, 1984.

Cohen, Miriam. *See You Tomorrow, Charles.* Illustrated by Lillian Hoban. Greenwillow, 1983.

Cole, Babette. *The Smelly Book.* Illustrated by Babette Cole. Simon & Schuster, 1988.

_____. *The Trouble with Gran.* Illustrated by Babette Cole. Putnam, 1987.

Cole, Brock. *No More Baths.* Illustrated by Brock Cole. Doubleday, 1980.

Cole, Joanna. *Bony-Legs.* Illustrated by Dirk Zimmer. Four Winds Press, 1983.

_____. *A Chick Hatches.* Illustrated by Jerome Wexler. William Morrow, 1976.

_____. *Golly Gump Swallowed a Fly.* Illustrated by Bari Weissman. Parents Magazine Press, 1982.

Cole, William *What's Good for a Three-Year-Old?* Illustrated by Lillian Hoban. Holt, Rinehart & Winston, 1974.

_____ (ed). *A Zooful of Animals.* Illustrated by Lynn Munsinger. Houghton Mifflin, 1992.

Cooney, Barbara. *Chanticleer and the Fox.* Illustrated by Barbara Cooney. Thomas Y. Crowell, 1958.

_____. *Snow-White and Rose-Red.* Illustrated by Barbara Cooney. Delacorte, 1991.

Cooney, Nancy Evans. *The Blanket That Had to Go.* Illustrated by Diane Dawson. Putnam, 1981.

Craft, Ruth. *Carrie Hepple's Garden.* Illustrated by Irene Haas. Margaret K. McElderry, 1979.

_____. *The Winter Bear.* Illustrated by Erik Blegvad. Atheneum, 1975.

Crews, Donald. *Bigmama's.* Illustrated by Donald Crews. Greenwillow, 1991.

Cummings, Pat. *Jimmy Lee Did It.* Illustrated by Pat Cummings. Lothrop, Lee & Shepard, 1985.

Cushman, Doug. *Possum Stew.* Illustrated by Doug Cushman. Dutton, 1990.

Cutchins, Judy and Ginny Johnston. *Scoots, the Bog Turtle.* Illustrated by Frances Smith. Atheneum, 1989.

Cutler, Jane. *Darcy and Gran Don't Like Babies.* Illustrated by Susanna Ryan. Scholastic, 1993.

Dabcovich, Lydia. *Sleepy Bear.* Illustrated by Lydia Dabcovich. Dutton Children's Books, 1982.

Daly, Niki. *Not So Fast Songololo.* Illustrated by Niki Daly. Atheneum, 1986.

Daugherty, James Henry. *The Picnic: A Frolic in Two Colors and Three Parts.* Illustrated by James Henry Daugherty. Viking, 1957.

Davis, Maggie S. *The Best Way to Ripton.* Illustrated by Stephen Gammell. Holiday House, 1982.

Deedy, Carmen A. *Agatha's Feather Bed: Not Just Another Wild Goose Story.* Illustrated by Laura L. Seeley. Peachtree Publications, 1991.

Degen, Bruce. *Jamberry.* Illustrated by Bruce Degen. HarperCollins, 1983.

De La Mare, Walter. *Molly Whuppie.* Illustrated by Errol Le Cain. Farrar, Straus & Giroux, 1983.

Delton, Judy. *A Walk on a Snowy Night*. Illustrated by Ruth Rosner. Harper-Collins Children's Books, 1982.

Demarest, Chris. *No Peas for Nellie!* Illustrated by Chris Demarest. Macmillan, 1988.

Demi. *The Artist and the Architect*. Illustrated by Demi. Henry Holt, 1991.

_____. *Dragon Kites and Dragonflies: A Collection of Chinese Nursery Rhymes*. Illustrated by Demi. Harcourt Brace Jovanovich, 1986.

_____. *The Empty Pot*. Illustrated by Demi. Henry Holt, 1990.

_____. *The Magic Boat*. Illustrated by Demi. Henry Holt, 1990.

DePaola, Tomie. *Bill and Pete*. Illustrated by Tomie DePaola. Putnam, 1978.

_____. *Bill and Pete Go Down the Nile*. Illustrated by Tomie DePaola. Putnam, 1987.

_____. *Charlie Needs a Cloak*. Illustrated by Tomie DePaola. Simon & Schuster, 1992.

_____. *The Clown of God: An Old Story*. Illustrated by Tomie DePaola. Harcourt Brace Jovanovich, 1978.

_____. *Fin M'Coul, the Giant of Knockmany Hill*. Illustrated by Tomie DePaola. Holiday House, 1981.

_____. *Four Stories for Four Seasons*. Illustrated by Tomie DePaola. Simon & Schuster, 1987.

_____. *Jamie O'Rourke and the Big Potato: An Irish Folktale*. Illustrated by Tomie DePaola. Putnam, 1992.

_____. *The Legend of the Bluebonnet: An Old Tale of Texas*. Illustrated by Tomie DePaola. Putnam, 1983.

_____. *The Legend of the Indian Paintbrush*. Illustrated by Tomie DePaola. Putnam, 1989.

_____. *Marianna May & Nursery*. Illustrated by Tomie DePaola. Holiday House, 1983.

_____. *Nana Upstairs & Nana Downstairs*. Illustrated by Tomie DePaola. Putnam, 1973.

_____. *Now One Foot, Now the Other*. Illustrated by Tomie DePaola. Putnam, 1981.

_____. *Strega Nona*. Illustrated by Tomie DePaola. Simon & Schuster, 1979.

_____. *Strega Nona's Magic Lesson*. Illustrated by Tomie DePaola. Harcourt Brace Jovanovich, 1982.

_____ (ed.). *Tomie DePaola's Book of Poems*. Illustrated by Tomie DePaola. Putnam, 1988.

_____. *The Walking Coat*. Illustrated by Tomie DePaola. Prentice-Hall, 1987.

_____. *Watch Out for the Chicken Feet in Your Soup*. Illustrated by Tomie DePaola. Simon & Schuster, 1974.

DeRegniers, Beatrice Schenk. *May I Bring a Friend?* Illustrated by Beni Montresor. Atheneum, 1964.

_____. *Red Riding Hood*. Illustrated by Edward Gorey. Aladdin, 1990.

_____ (ed.). *Sing a Song of Popcorn*. Illustrated by 9 Caldecott Medal artists. Scholastic, 1988.

_____. *Waiting for Mama*. Illustrated by Victoria De Larrea. Clarion Books, 1984.

Dionetti, Michelle. *Coal Mine Peaches.* Illustrated by Anita Riggio. Orchard, 1991.

DiSalvo-Ryan, DyAnne. *Uncle Willie and the Soup Kitchen.* Illustrated by DyAnne DiSalvo-Ryan. Morrow Junior, 1991.

Domanska, Janina. *What Do You See?* Illustrated by Janina Domanska. Macmillan, 1974.

Dorros, Arthur. *Abuela.* Illustrated by Elisa Kleven. Dutton Children's Books, 1991.

————. *Tonight Is Carnaval.* Illustrated by Club de Madres Virgen del Carmen of Lima, Peru. Dutton Children's Books, 1991.

Douglass, Barbara. *The Chocolate Chip Cookie Contest.* Illustrated by Eric Jon Nones. Lothrop, Lee & Shepard, 1985.

————. *Good as New!* Illustrated by Patience Brewster. Lothrop, Lee & Shepard, 1982.

Downing, Julie. *White Snow-Blue Feather.* Illustrated by Julie Downing. Bradbury Press, 1989.

Drescher, Joan. *Your Family, My Family.* Illustrated by Joan Drescher. Walker & Company, 1980.

Drucker, Malka. *Grandma's Latkes.* Illustrated by Eve Chwast. Harcourt Brace Jovanovich, 1992.

Dubanevich, Arlene. *Pigs in Hiding.* Illustrated by Arlene Dubanevich. Four Winds Press, 1983.

Duff, Maggie. *Dancing Turtle.* Illustrated by Maria Horvath. Macmillan, 1981.

Dunbar, Joyce. *A Cake for Barney.* Illustrated by Emilie Boon. Orchard, 1988.

————. *I Want a Blue Banana.* Illustrated by James Dunbar. Houghton Mifflin, 1991.

Dunham, Meredith. *Picnic: How Do You Say It?* Illustrated by Meredith Dunham. Lothrop, Lee & Shepard, 1987.

Dunn, Judy. *The Little Duck.* Illustrated by Phoebe Dunn. Random House, 1976.

————. *The Little Goat.* Illustrated by Phoebe Dunn. Random House, 1979.

Dunrea, Olivier. *The Broody Hen.* Illustrated by Olivier Dunrea. Doubleday, 1992.

Duntze, Dorothee. *The Twelve Days of Christmas.* Illustrated by Dorothee Duntze. North-South Books, 1992.

Edwards, Richard. *The Word Party.* Illustrated by John Lawrence. Delacorte, 1992.

Ehlert, Lois. *Eating the Alphabet: Fruits and Vegetables from A to Z.* Illustrated by Lois Ehlert. Harcourt Brace Jovanovich, 1989.

————. *Growing Vegetable Soup.* Illustrated by Lois Ehlert. Harcourt Brace Jovanovich, 1987.

————. *Moon Rope/Un Lazo a la Luna: A Peruvian Folktale.* Illustrated by Lois Ehlert. Harcourt Brace Jovanovich, 1992.

————. *Planting a Rainbow.* Illustrated by Lois Ehlert. Harcourt Brace Jovanovich, 1988.

Ekoomiak, Normee. *Arctic Memories.* Illustrated by Normee Ekoomiak. Henry Holt, 1988.

Elkin, Benjamin. *The Wisest Man in the World: A Legend of Ancient Israel.* Illustrated by Anita Lobel. Parents Magazine Press, 1968.

Emberley, Barbara. *Drummer Hoff.* Illustrated by Ed Emberley. Simon & Schuster, 1987.

Emberley, Ed. *Ed Emberley's Big Purple Drawing Book.* Illustrated by Ed Emberley. Little, Brown, 1981.

_____. *Green Says Go.* Illustrated by Ed Emberley. Little, Brown, 1972.

Engvick, William (ed.). *Lullabies and Night Songs.* Illustrated by Maurice Sendak. Harper & Row, 1965.

Ericksson, Jennifer. *No Milk!* Illustrated by Ora Eitan. William Morrow, 1993.

Ernst, Lisa Campbell. *When Bluebell Sang.* Illustrated by Lisa Campbell Ernst. Bradbury, 1989.

_____. *Zinnia and Dot.* Illustrated by Lisa Campbell Ernst. Viking, 1992.

Ets, Marie Hall. *Gilberto and the Wind.* Illustrated by Marie Hall Ets. Viking, 1963.

Everett, Gwen. *Li'l Sis and Uncle Willie: A Story Based on the Life and Paintings of William H. Johnson.* Illustrated by William H. Johnson. Rizzoli, 1991.

Everitt, Betsy. *Mean Soup.* Illustrated by Betsy Everitt. Harcourt Brace Jovanovich, 1992.

Farber, Norma. *As I Was Crossing Boston Common.* Illustrated by Arnold Lobel. Dutton Children's Books, 1991.

Feelings, Muriel. *Jambo Means Hello: Swahili Alphabet Book.* Illustrated by Tom Feelings. Dial Books for Young Readers, 1981.

_____. *Moja Means One: Swahili Counting Book.* Illustrated by Tom Feelings. Dial Books for Young Readers, 1971.

Firman, Peter. *Chicken Stew.* Illustrated by Peter Firman. Merrimack Book Service, 1982.

Flack, Marjorie. *The Story About Ping.* Illustrated by Kurt Wiese. Viking, 1933.

Fleischman, Sid. *The Scarebird.* Illustrated by Peter Sis. Greenwillow, 1988.

Fleming, Denise. *Lunch!* Illustrated by Denise Fleming. Henry Holt, 1993.

Florian, Douglas. *Turtle Day.* Illustrated by Douglas Florian. Thomas Y. Crowell, 1989.

Flournoy, Valerie. *The Patchwork Quilt.* Illustrated by Jerry Pinkney. Dial Books for Young Readers, 1985.

Fonteyn, Dame Margot. *Swan Lake.* Illustrated by Trina Schart Hyman. Harcourt Brace Jovanovich, 1988.

Forest, Heather. *The Woman Who Flummoxed the Fairies: An Old Tale from Scotland.* Illustrated by Susan Gaber. Harcourt Brace Jovanovich, 1990.

Fowler, Susi L. *I'll See You When the Moon Is Full.* Illustrated by Jim Fowler. Greenwillow, 1994.

Freeman, Don. *Quiet! There's a Canary in the Library.* Illustrated by Don Freeman. Childrens Press, 1969.

Freschet, Berniece. *The Ants Go Marching.* Illustrated by Stefan Marti. Scribner, 1973.

_____. *Black Bear Baby.* Illustrated by Jim Arnosky. Putnam, 1981.

_____. *Turtle Pond.* Illustrated by Donald Carrick. Scribner, 1971.

_____. *The Watersnake.* Illustrated by Susanne Suba. Scribner, 1979.

_____. *Wood Duck Baby.* Illustrated by Jim Arnosky. Putnam, 1983.

Friedman, Ina R. *How My Parents Learned to Eat.* Illustrated by Allen Say. Houghton Mifflin, 1984.

Friskey, Margaret. *Seven Diving Ducks.* Illustrated by Jean Morey. Childrens Press, 1965.

Fritz, Jean. *The Man Who Loved Books.* Illustrated by Trina Schart Hyman. Putnam, 1981.

_____. *Why Don't You Get a Horse, Sam Adams?* Illustrated by Trina Schart Hyman. Coward-McCann, 1982.

_____. *Will You Sign Here, John Hancock?* Illustrated by Trina Schart Hyman, Coward-McCann, 1982.

Frost, Erica. *I Can Read About Good Manners.* Illustrated by Erica Frost. Troll Associates, 1975.

Frost, Robert. *Stopping by Woods on a Snowy Evening.* Illustrated by Susan Jeffers. Dutton, 1978.

Gackenback, Dick. *Poppy the Panda.* Illustrated by Dick Gackenback. Houghton Mifflin, 1987.

Gaeddert, Lou Ann. *Noisy Nancy Nora.* Illustrated by Lou Ann Gaeddert. Doubleday, 1965.

Galdone, Paul. *The Amazing Pig: An Old Hungarian Tale.* Illustrated by Paul Galdone. Clarion Books, 1981.

_____. *The Gingerbread Boy.* Illustrated by Paul Galdone. Seabury, 1975.

_____. *The Greedy Old Fat Man: An American Folk Tale.* Illustrated by Paul Galdone. Clarion Books, 1983.

_____. *Henny Penny.* Illustrated by Paul Galdone. Clarion Books, 1968.

_____. *Jack and the Beanstalk.* Illustrated by Paul Galdone. Clarion Books, 1982.

_____. *King of the Cats: A Ghost Story.* Illustrated by Paul Galdone. Clarion Books, 1980.

_____. *Little Bo-Peep.* Illustrated by Paul Galdone. Clarion Books, 1986.

_____. *The Little Red Hen.* Illustrated by Paul Galdone. Clarion Books, 1979.

_____. *Little Red Riding Hood.* Illustrated by Paul Galdone. McGraw-Hill, 1974.

_____. *Little Tuppen.* Illustrated by Paul Galdone. Clarion Books, 1979.

_____. *The Magic Porridge Pot.* Illustrated by Paul Galdone. Clarion Books, 1979.

_____. *The Monkey and the Crocodile: A Jataka Tale from India.* Illustrated by Paul Galdone. Clarion Books, 1969.

_____. *The Three Billy Goats Gruff.* Illustrated by Paul Galdone. Clarion Books, 1973.

_____. *The Three Little Pigs.* Illustrated by Paul Galdone. Clarion Books, 1970.

_____. *What's in Fox's Sack? An Old English Tale.* Illustrated by Paul Galdone. Clarion Books, 1982.

Gammell, Stephen. *Git Along, Old Scudder.* Illustrated by Stephen Gammell. Lothrop, Lee & Shepard, 1983.

_____. *Once Upon MacDonald's Farm.* Illustrated by Stephen Gammell. Four Winds Press, 1984.

Gardener, Beau. *Look Again . . . & Again, & Again, & Again Book.* Illustrated by Beau Gardener. Lothrop, Lee & Shepard, 1983.

Gauch, Patricia Lee. *Christina Katerina and the Time She Quit the Family.* Illustrated by Elize Primavera. Putnam, 1987.

_____. *On to Widecomb Fair.* Illustrated by Trina Schart Hyman. Putnam, 1978.

Geisert, Arthur. *Oink.* Illustrated by Arthur Geisert. Houghton Mifflin, 1991.

Gellman, Ellie. *It's Rosh-Hashanah!* Illustrated by Katherine J. Kahn. Kar-Ben Copies, 1985.

George, William T. *Box Turtle at Long Pond.* Illustrated by Lindsay Barrett George. Greenwillow Books, 1989.

_____. *Christmas at Long Pond.* Illustrated by Lindsay Barrett George. Greenwillow Books, 1992.

Gerson, Mary-Joan. *Why the Sky Is Far Away: A Nigerian Folktale.* Illustrated by Carla Golembe. Little, Brown, 1992.

Gibbons, Gail. *Farming.* Illustrated by Gail Gibbons. Holiday House, 1988.

_____. *Happy Birthday!* Illustrated by Gail Gibbons. Holiday House, 1986.

_____. *The Milk Makers.* Illustrated by Gail Gibbons. Macmillan, 1985.

Giblin, James Cross. *From Hand to Mouth: Or, How We Invented Knives, Forks, Spoons & Chopsticks, & The Table Manners to Go with Them.* Crowell Junior Books, 1987.

Ginsburg, Mirra. *The Chick and the Duckling.* Illustrated by Jose Aruego and Ariane Dewey. Macmillan, 1972.

_____. *The Chinese Mirror.* Illustrated by Margot Zemach. Harcourt Brace Jovanovich, 1988.

_____. *Good Morning, Chick.* Illustrated by Byron Barton. Greenwillow, 1980.

_____. *The Three Kittens.* Illustrated by Mirra Ginsburg. David McKay, n.d.

Glazer, Tom. *Do Your Ears Hang Low?: 50 More Musical Fingerplays.* Illustrated by Mila Lazarevich. Doubleday, 1980.

_____. *Eye Winker, Tom Tinker, Chin Chopper, Fifty Musical Fingerplays.* Illustrated by Ron Himler. Doubleday, 1973.

Goble, Paul. *The Gift of the Sacred Dog.* Illustrated by Paul Goble. Bradbury, 1980.

_____. *The Girl Who Loved Wild Horses.* Illustrated by Paul Goble. Bradbury, 1978.

_____. *Iktomi and the Buffalo Skull: A Plains Indian Story.* Illustrated by Paul Goble. Orchard Books, 1991.

Goldin, Augusta. *Ducks Don't Get Wet.* Illustrated by Leonard Kessler. HarperCollins, 1989.

Goldin, Barbara Diamond. *Cakes and Miracles: A Purim Tale.* Illustrated by Erika Weihs. Viking, 1991.

_____. *Just Enough Is Plenty: A Hanukkah Tale.* Illustrated by Seymour Chwast. Viking Penguin, 1988.

_____. *The World's Birthday: A Rosh Hashanah Story.* Illustrated by Jeanette Winter. Harcourt Brace Jovanovich, 1990.

Goode, Diane. *Where's Our Mama?* Illustrated by Diane Goode. Dutton Children's Books, 1991.

Gordon, Gaelyn. *Duckat.* Illustrated by Gaelyn Gordon. Scholastic, 1992.

Gordon, Margaret. *Wilberforce Goes on a Picnic.* Illustrated by Margaret Gordon. William Morrow, 1982.

————. *Wilberforce Goes to a Party.* Illustrated by Margaret Gordon. Viking Kestrel, 1985.

Green, Carol. *The Thirteen Days of Halloween.* Illustrated by Carol Green. Childrens Press, 1983.

Green, Phyllis. *Bagdad Ate It.* Illustrated by Joel Schick. Franklin Watts, 1980.

————. *Uncle Roland, the Perfect Guest.* Illustrated by Marybeth Farrell. Four Winds Press, 1983.

Greenberg, Barbara. *The Bravest Babysitter.* Illustrated by Diane Paterson. Dial Books for Young Readers, 1977.

Greenberg, David. *Slugs.* Illustrated by Victoria Chess. Little, Brown, 1983.

Greenberg, Polly. *Oh Lord, I Wish I Was a Buzzard.* Illustrated by Aliki. Macmillan, 1968.

Greenfield, Eloise. *First Pink Light.* Illustrated by Jan S. Gilchrist. Writers & Readers Publishing, 1991.

————. *Grandpa's Face.* Illustrated by Floyd Cooper. Philomel, 1988.

————. *She Come Bringing That Little Baby Girl.* Illustrated by John Steptoe. Lippincott, 1974.

Gregory, Valiska. *Babysitting for Benjamin.* Illustrated by Lynn Munsinger. Little, Brown, 1993.

Gretz, Susanna. *Roger Takes Charge!* Illustrated by Susanna Gretz. Dial, 1987.

———— and Alison Sage. *Teddybear's Cookbook.* Illustrated by Susanna Gretz. Doubleday, 1978.

Grifalconi, Ann. *Darkness and the Butterfly.* Illustrated by Ann Grifalconi. Little, Brown, 1987.

————. *The Village of Round and Square Houses.* Illustrated by Ann Grifalconi. Little, Brown, 1986.

Griffith, Helen V. *Georgia Music.* Illustrated by James Stevenson. Greenwillow, 1987.

————. *Grandaddy's Place.* Illustrated by James Stevenson. Greenwillow, 1987.

Grimm, Jacob and Wilhelm Grimm. *Rapunzel.* Illustrated by Michael Hague. Creative Education, 1986.

————. *Rapunzel.* Illustrated by Carol Heyer. Ideals, 1992.

————. *Sleeping Beauty.* Illustrated by Trina Schart Hyman. Little, Brown, 1983.

————. *Snow White.* Illustrated by Trina Schart Hyman. Little, Brown, 1979.

————. *Snow White & the Seven Dwarfs.* Illustrated by Nancy Ekholm Burkert. Farrar, Straus & Giroux, 1972.

————. *Snow White & the Seven Dwarfs.* Illustrated by Chihiro Iwasaki. Picture Book Studio, 1991.

Grimm, Wilhelm. *Dear Mili.* Illustrated by Maurice Sendak. Farrar, Straus & Giroux, 1988.

Groner, Judyth & Madeine Wikler. *Let's Build a Sukkah.* Illustrated by Katherine J. Kahn. Kar-Ben Copies, 1986.

Guiberson, Brenda Z. *Spoonbill Swamp.* Illustrated by Megan Lloyd. Henry Holt, 1992.

Gundersheimer, Karen. *Happy Winter*. Illustrated by Karen Gundersheimer. Harper & Row, 1982.

Had Gadya. *One Little Goat: A Passover Song*. Illustrated by Marilyn Hirsh. Holiday House, 1979.

Hague, Kathleen. *The Man Who Kept House*. Illustrated by Michael Hague. Harcourt Brace Jovanovich, 1981.

Hale, Sarah Josepha. *Mary Had a Little Lamb*. Illustrated by Tomie DePaola. Holiday House, 1984.

_____. *Mary Had a Little Lamb*. Illustrated by Bruce McMillan. Scholastic, 1990.

Haley, Gail E. *Jack & the Bean Tree*. Illustrated by Gail E. Haley. Crown Books for Young Readers, 1986.

_____. *A Story, a Story: An African Tale*. Illustrated by Gail E. Haley. Atheneum, 1970.

Hall, Donald. *Ox-Cart Man*. Illustrated by Barbara Cooney. Viking, 1979.

Hancock, Sibyl. *Esteban and the Ghost*. Illustrated by Dirk Zimmer. Dial Books for Young Readers, 1983.

Harper, Wilhelmina. *The Gunniwolf*. Illustrated by William Weisner. Dutton, 1967.

Hart, Jane (ed.). *Singing Bee! A Collection of Favorite Children's Songs*. Illustrated by Anita Lobel. Lothrop, Lee & Shepard, 1989.

Hartley, Deborah. *Up North in Winter*. Illustrated by Lydia Dabcovich. Dutton Children's Books, 1986.

Hasely, Dennis. *The Old Banjo*. Illustrated by Stephen Gammell. Aladdin, 1990.

Hawkins, Colin and Jacqui Hawkins. *I Know an Old Lady Who Swallowed a Fly*. Illustrated by Jacqui and Colin Hawkins. Putnam, 1987.

Hayes, Geoffrey. *Patrick and His Grandpa*. Illustrated by Geoffrey Hayes. Random House, 1986.

Hayes, Sarah. *Clap Your Hands: Finger Rhymes*. Illustrated by Toni Goffe. Lothrop, Lee & Shepard, 1988.

Hazen, Barbara Shook. *Even if I Did Something Awful?* Illustrated by Nancy Kincade. Atheneum Children's Books, 1981.

_____. *Tight Times*. Illustrated by Trina Schart Hyman. Viking, 1979.

Heath, Amy. *Sofie's Role*. Illustrated by Sheila Hamanaka. Four Winds Press, 1992.

Heilbroner, Joan. *Robert the Rose Horse*. Illustrated by Joan Heilbroner. Beginner Books, 1962.

Heine, Helme. *The Pigs' Wedding*. Illustrated by Helme Heine. Margaret K. McElderry, 1986.

Henkes, Kevin. *Chrysanthemum*. Illustrated by Kevin Henkes. Greenwillow, 1991.

_____. *Grandpa & Bo*. Illustrated by Kevin Henkes. Greenwillow Books, 1986.

_____. *Julius, the Baby of the World*. Illustrated by Kevin Henkes. Greenwillow, 1990.

_____. *A Weekend with Wendell*. Illustrated by Kevin Henkes. Greenwillow, 1986.

Henriod, Lorraine. *Grandma's Wheelchair*. Illustrated by Lorraine Henriod. Albert Whitman, 1982.

Hepworth, Catherine. *Antics! An Alphabetical Anthology*. Illustrated by Catherine Hepworth, Putnam, 1992.

Herriot, James. *Bonny's Big Day*. Illustrated by Ruth Brown. St. Martin's Press, 1987.

_____. *Moses the Kitten*. Illustrated by Peter Barrett. St. Martin's Press, 1984.

Hest, Amy. *The Crack-of-Dawn Walkers*. Illustrated by Amy Schwartz. Macmillan, 1984.

_____. *Fancy Aunt Jess*. Illustrated by Amy Schwartz. Morrow Junior, 1990.

_____. *The Mommy Exchange*. Illustrated by DyAnne DiSalvo-Ryan. Four Winds Press, 1988.

_____. *The Purple Coat*. Illustrated by Amy Schwartz. Four Winds Press, 1986.

Hill, Eric. *Spot's First Easter*. Illustrated by Eric Hill. Putnam, 1988.

_____. *Spot's First Picnic*. Illustrated by Eric Hill. Putnam, 1987.

Hillert, Margaret. *The Yellow Boat*. Illustrated by Margaret Hillert. Modern Curriculum Press, 1966.

Hines, Anna Grossnickle. *Daddy Makes the Best Spaghetti*. Illustrated by Anna Grossnickle Hines. Clarion Books, 1986.

_____. *Mean Old Uncle Jack*. Illustrated by Anna Grossnickel Hines. Clarion Books, 1990.

Hirschi, Ron. *Harvest Song*. Illustrated by Deborah Haeffele. Cobblehill, 1991.

_____. *Who Lives In . . . Alligator Swamp?* Illustrated by Galen Burrell. Dodd, Mead, 1987.

Hirsch, Marilyn. *I Love Hanukkah*. Illustrated by Marilyn Hirsch. Holiday House, 1984.

_____. *I Love Passover*. Illustrated by Marilyn Hirsch. Holiday House, 1985.

Hoban, Lillian. *Turtle Spring*. Illustrated by Lillian Hoban. Dell, 1992.

Hoban, Russell. *A Baby Sister for Frances*. Illustrated by Lillian Hoban. HarperCollins, 1964.

_____. *Bread and Jam for Frances*. Illustrated by Lillian Hoban. HarperCollins, 1965.

_____. *Dinner at Alberta's*. Illustrated by James Marshall. Thomas Y. Crowell, 1975.

_____. *Egg Thoughts, and Other Frances Songs*. Illustrated by Lillian Hoban. Harper & Row, 1972.

Hoban, Tana. *Is It Red? Is It Yellow? Is It Blue? An Adventure in Color*. Illustrated by Tana Hoban. Greenwillow, 1978.

_____. *Is It Rough? Is It Smooth? Is It Shiny?* Illustrated by Tana Hoban. Greenwillow, 1984.

_____. *Look Again!* Illustrated by Tana Hoban. Macmillan, 1971.

_____. *Take Another Look*. Illustrated by Tana Hoban. Greenwillow, 1981.

Hodges, Margaret. *The Kitchen Knight: A Tale of King Arthur*. Illustrated by Trina Schart Hyman. Holiday House, 1990.

_____. *Saint George and the Dragon: A Golden Legend*. Illustrated by Trina Schart Hyman. Little, Brown, 1984.

_____. *The Voice of the Great Bell*. Illustrated by Ed Young. Little, Brown, 1989.

Hoffman, E. T. A. *The Nutcracker*. Illustrated by Lisbeth Zwerger. Picture Book Studio, 1987.

Hogrogian, Nonny. *Carrot Cake.* Illustrated by Nonny Hogrogian. Greenwillow, 1977.

––––––––. *One Fine Day.* Illustrated by Nonny Hogrogian. Macmillan, 1971.

Hoopes, Lyn L. *Wing-A-Ding.* Illustrated by Stephen Gammell. Little, Brown, 1990.

Hopkins, Lee Bennett (ed.). *Happy Birthday: Poems.* Illustrated by Hilary Knight. Simon & Schuster Books for Young Readers, 1991.

–––––––– (ed.). *Merrily Comes Our Harvest In: Poems for Thanksgiving.* Illustrated by Ben Schecter. Harcourt Brace Jovanovich, 1978.

Hort, Lenny. *The Fool and the Fish: A Tale from Russia.* Illustrated by Gennady Spirin. Dial Books for Young Readers, 1990.

Houston, Gloria. *My Great-Aunt Arizona.* Illustrated by Susan C. Lamb. Harper-Collins, 1992.

Howard, Elizabeth Fitzgerald. *Aunt Flossie's Hats (and Crab Cakes Later).* Illustrated by James Ransome. Clarion Books, 1991.

Huck, Charlotte S. *Princess Furball.* Illustrated by Anita Lobel. Greenwillow, 1989.

Hughes, Shirley. *Alfie Gives a Hand.* Illustrated by Shirley Hughes. William Morrow, 1986.

––––––––. *An Evening at Alfie's.* Illustrated by Shirley Huhes. Lothrop, Lee & Shepard, 1985.

––––––––. *George, the Baby-Sitter.* Illustrated by Shirley Hughes. Prentice-Hall, 1975.

Hurd, Edith Thacher. *I Dance in My Red Pajamas.* Illustrated by Emily Arnold McCully. Harper & Row, 1982.

––––––––. *No Funny Business.* Illustrated by Clement Hurd. Harper & Row, 1962.

––––––––. *Under the Lemon Tree.* Illustrated by Clement Hurd. Little, Brown, 1980.

Hurd, Thacher. *Mama Don't Allow: Starring Miles and the Swamp Band.* Illustrated by Thacher Hurd. Harper & Row, 1984.

Hutchins, Pat. *The Doorbell Rang.* Illustrated by Pat Hutchins. Greenwillow, 1986.

––––––––. *Happy Birthday, Sam.* Illustrated by Pat Hutchins. Greenwillow, 1978.

––––––––. *Rosie's Walk.* Illustrated by Pat Hutchins. Macmillan, 1968.

––––––––. *Titch.* Illustrated by Pat Hutchins. Macmillan, 1971.

––––––––. *The Wind Blew.* Illustrated by Pat Hutchins. Macmillan, 1974.

––––––––. *You'll Soon Grow into Them, Titch.* Illustrated by Pat Hutchins. Greenwillow, 1983.

Hyman, Trina Schart Hyman. *Little Red Riding Hood.* Illustrated by Trina Schart Hyman. Holiday House, 1983.

––––––––. *Self Portrait: Trina Schart Hyman.* Illustrated by Trina Schart Hyman. HarperCollins, 1989.

Inkpen, Mick. *Blue Balloon.* Illustrated by Mick Inkpen. Little, Brown, 1990.

Ipcar, Dahlov. *Brown Cow Farm: A Counting Book.* Illustrated by Dahlov Ipcar. Doubleday, 1959.

Isadora, Rachel. *At the Crossroads.* Illustrated by Rachel Isadora. Greenwillow, 1991.

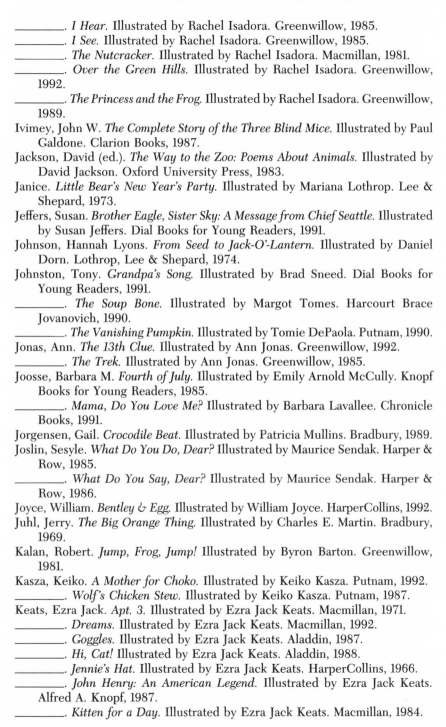

_____. *I Hear*. Illustrated by Rachel Isadora. Greenwillow, 1985.

_____. *I See*. Illustrated by Rachel Isadora. Greenwillow, 1985.

_____. *The Nutcracker*. Illustrated by Rachel Isadora. Macmillan, 1981.

_____. *Over the Green Hills*. Illustrated by Rachel Isadora. Greenwillow, 1992.

_____. *The Princess and the Frog*. Illustrated by Rachel Isadora. Greenwillow, 1989.

Ivimey, John W. *The Complete Story of the Three Blind Mice*. Illustrated by Paul Galdone. Clarion Books, 1987.

Jackson, David (ed.). *The Way to the Zoo: Poems About Animals*. Illustrated by David Jackson. Oxford University Press, 1983.

Janice. *Little Bear's New Year's Party*. Illustrated by Mariana Lothrop. Lee & Shepard, 1973.

Jeffers, Susan. *Brother Eagle, Sister Sky: A Message from Chief Seattle*. Illustrated by Susan Jeffers. Dial Books for Young Readers, 1991.

Johnson, Hannah Lyons. *From Seed to Jack-O'-Lantern*. Illustrated by Daniel Dorn. Lothrop, Lee & Shepard, 1974.

Johnston, Tony. *Grandpa's Song*. Illustrated by Brad Sneed. Dial Books for Young Readers, 1991.

_____. *The Soup Bone*. Illustrated by Margot Tomes. Harcourt Brace Jovanovich, 1990.

_____. *The Vanishing Pumpkin*. Illustrated by Tomie DePaola. Putnam, 1990.

Jonas, Ann. *The 13th Clue*. Illustrated by Ann Jonas. Greenwillow, 1992.

_____. *The Trek*. Illustrated by Ann Jonas. Greenwillow, 1985.

Joosse, Barbara M. *Fourth of July*. Illustrated by Emily Arnold McCully. Knopf Books for Young Readers, 1985.

_____. *Mama, Do You Love Me?* Illustrated by Barbara Lavallee. Chronicle Books, 1991.

Jorgensen, Gail. *Crocodile Beat*. Illustrated by Patricia Mullins. Bradbury, 1989.

Joslin, Sesyle. *What Do You Do, Dear?* Illustrated by Maurice Sendak. Harper & Row, 1985.

_____. *What Do You Say, Dear?* Illustrated by Maurice Sendak. Harper & Row, 1986.

Joyce, William. *Bentley & Egg*. Illustrated by William Joyce. HarperCollins, 1992.

Juhl, Jerry. *The Big Orange Thing*. Illustrated by Charles E. Martin. Bradbury, 1969.

Kalan, Robert. *Jump, Frog, Jump!* Illustrated by Byron Barton. Greenwillow, 1981.

Kasza, Keiko. *A Mother for Choko*. Illustrated by Keiko Kasza. Putnam, 1992.

_____. *Wolf's Chicken Stew*. Illustrated by Keiko Kasza. Putnam, 1987.

Keats, Ezra Jack. *Apt. 3*. Illustrated by Ezra Jack Keats. Macmillan, 1971.

_____. *Dreams*. Illustrated by Ezra Jack Keats. Macmillan, 1992.

_____. *Goggles*. Illustrated by Ezra Jack Keats. Aladdin, 1987.

_____. *Hi, Cat!* Illustrated by Ezra Jack Keats. Aladdin, 1988.

_____. *Jennie's Hat*. Illustrated by Ezra Jack Keats. HarperCollins, 1966.

_____. *John Henry: An American Legend*. Illustrated by Ezra Jack Keats. Alfred A. Knopf, 1987.

_____. *Kitten for a Day*. Illustrated by Ezra Jack Keats. Macmillan, 1984.

_____. *A Letter to Amy.* Illustrated by Ezra Jack Keats. HarperCollins, 1968.

_____. *The Little Drummer Boy.* Illustrated by Ezra Jack Keats. Aladdin, 1987.

_____. *Louie.* Illustrated by Ezra Jack Keats. Greenwillow, 1983.

_____. *Maggie and the Pirate.* Illustrated by Ezra Jack Keats. Four Winds Press, 1979.

_____. *My Dog Is Lost.* Illustrated by Ezra Jack Keats. Thomas Y. Crowell, 1960.

_____. *Pet Show!* Illustrated by Ezra Jack Keats. Aladdin, 1972.

_____. *Peter's Chair.* Illustrated by Ezra Jack Keats. HarperCollins, 1967.

_____. *Regards to the Man in the Moon.* Illustrated by Ezra Jack Keats. Macmillan, 1987.

_____. *Skates.* Illustrated by Ezra Jack Keats. Four Winds Press, 1973.

_____. *The Snowy Day.* Illustrated by Ezra Jack Keats. Viking, 1962.

_____. *The Trip.* Illustrated by Ezra Jack Keats. William Morrow, 1987.

_____. *Whistle for Willie.* Illustrated by Ezra Jack Keats. Viking, 1964.

Keller, Holly. *Furry.* Illustrated by Holly Keller. Greenwillow, 1992.

_____. *Henry's Fourth of July.* Illustrated by Holly Keller. Greenwillow, 1985.

_____. *What Alvin Wanted.* Illustrated by Holly Keller. Greenwillow, 1990.

Keller, Irene. *The Thingumajig Book of Manners.* Illustrated by Dick Keller. Ideals Publishing, 1989.

Kellogg, Steven. *Chicken Little.* Illustrated by Steven Kellogg. William Morrow, 1985.

_____. *Jack and the Beanstalk.* Illustrated by Steven Kellogg. Morrow Junior Books, 1991.

_____. *Much Bigger Than Martin.* Illustrated by Steven Kellogg. Dial Books for Young Readers, 1976.

_____. *The Mysterious Tadpole.* Illustrated by Steven Kellogg. Dial Books for Young Readers, 1977.

_____. *The Mystery of the Missing Red Mitten.* Illustrated by Steven Kellogg. Dial Books for Young Readers, 1974.

_____. *Pecos Bill: A Tall Tale.* Illustrated by Steven Kellogg. William Morrow, 1986.

Kennedy, Jimmy. *Teddy Bear's Picnic.* Illustrated by Alexandra Day. Green Tiger Press, 1983.

_____. *Teddy Bear's Picnic.* Illustrated by Alexandra Day. Green Tiger Press, 1983.

_____. *Teddy Bear's Picnic.* Illustrated by Michael Hague. Henry Holt, 1992.

_____. *Teddy Bear's Picnic.* Illustrated by Prue Theobalds. Bedrick Blackie, 1987.

Kennedy, X. J. and Dorothy M. Kennedy (eds.). *Talking Like the Rain: A First Book of Poems.* Illustrated by Jane Dyer. Little, Brown, 1992.

Kent, Jack. *The Caterpillar and the Polliwog.* Illustrated by Jack Kent. Simon & Schuster Books for Young Readers, 1985.

_____. *The Fat Cat: A Danish Folktale.* Illustrated by Jack Kent. Scholastic, 1971.

_____. *Jack Kent's Twelve Days of Christmas.* Illustrated by Jack Kent. Parents Magazine Press, 1973.

_____. *Little Peep.* Illustrated by Jack Kent. Simon & Schuster, 1989.

_____. *Round Robin.* Illustrated by Jack Kent. Simon & Schuster Books for Young Readers, 1989.

_____. *Socks for Supper.* Illustrated by Jack Kent. Parents Magazine Press, 1978.

Kessler, Leonard. *Mr. Pine's Purple House.* Illustrated by Leonard Kessler. Grosset & Dunlap, 1965.

Khalsa, Dayal Kaur. *Cowboy Dreams.* Illustrated by Dayal Kaur Khalsa. Clarkson N. Potter, 1990.

_____. *How Pizza Came to Queens.* Illustrated by Dayal Kaur Khalsa. Clarkson N. Potter, 1989.

Kimmel, Eric A. *Bearhead: A Russian Folktale.* Illustrated by Charles Mikolaycak. Holiday House, 1991.

_____. *The Chanukkah Guest.* Illustrated by Giora Carmi. Holiday House, 1990.

_____. *Charlie Drives the Stage.* Illustrated by Glen Rounds. Holiday House, 1989.

_____. *Four Dollars and Fifty Cents.* Illustrated by Glen Rounds. Holiday House, 1990.

_____. *Herschel and the Hanukkah Goblins.* Illustrated by Trina Schart Hyman. Holiday House, 1989.

Kirstein, Lincoln. *Puss in Boots.* Illustrated by Alain Vaes. Little, Brown, 1992.

Kitamura, Satoshi. *When Sheep Cannot Sleep.* Illustrated by Satoshi Kitamura. Farrar, Straus & Giroux, 1986.

Klein, David J. *Irwin the Sock.* Illustrated by David J. Klein. Raintree, 1987.

Kleven, Elisa. *The Lion and the Little Red Bird.* Illustrated by Elisa Kleven. Dutton Children's Books, 1989.

Knutson, Barbara. *How the Guinea Fowl Got Her Spots: A Swahili Tale of Friendship.* Illustrated by Barbara Knutson. Carolrhoda, 1990.

Koller, Jackie F. *Fish Fry Tonight.* Illustrated by Catherine O'Neill. Crown Books for Young Readers, 1992.

Kovalski, Maryann. *Jingle Bells.* Illustrated by Maryann Kovalski. Little, Brown, 1988.

_____. *The Wheels on the Bus.* Illustrated by Maryann Kovalski. Little, Brown, 1987.

Kowalczyk, Carolyn. *Purple Is Part of the Rainbow.* Illustrated by Gene Sharp. Childrens Press, 1988.

Kraus, Robert. *Whose Mouse Are You?* Illustrated by Jose Aruego. Macmillan, 1970.

Krauss, Ruth. *The Carrot Seed.* Illustrated by Crockett Johnson. Harper & Row, 1989.

_____. *A Hole Is to Dig: A First Book of First Definitions.* Illustrated by Maurice Sendak. Harper & Row, 1989.

Kroll, Steven. *Happy Father's Day.* Illustrated by Marylin Hafner. Holiday House, 1988.

_____. *Happy Mother's Day.* Illustrated by Marylin Hafner. Holiday House, 1985.

_____. *It's Groundhog Day!* Illustrated by Jeni Bassett. Holiday House, 1987.

————. *Mary McClean and the St. Patrick's Day Parade.* Illustrated by Michael Dooling. Scholastic, 1991.

————. *One Tough Turkey: A Thanksgiving Story.* Illustrated by John Wallner. Holiday House, 1982.

Kroll, Virginia L. *Masai and I.* Illustrated by Nancy Carpenter. Four Winds Press, 1992.

Krull, Kathleen (ed.). *Gonna Sing My Head Off! American Folk Songs for Children.* Illustrated by Allen Garns. Alfred A. Knopf, 1992.

Kudrna, C. Imbior. *To Bathe a Boa.* Illustrated by C. Imbior Kudrna. Carolrhoda Books, 1986.

Lammorisse, Albert. *The Red Balloon.* Illustrated by Albert Lammorisse. Doubleday, 1957.

Langstaff, John M. *Frog Went a-Courtin'.* Illustrated by Feodor Rojankovsky. Harcourt Brace Jovanovich, 1955.

Lasker, Joe. *Lentil Soup.* Illustrated by Joe Lasker. Albert Whitman, 1977.

Lathrop, Dorothy Pulis. *Who Goes There?* Illustrated by Dorothy Pulis Lathrop. Macmillan, 1935.

Lavies, Bianca. *Lily Pad Pond.* Illustrated by Bianca Lavies. Dutton, 1989.

Leaf, Margaret. *The Eyes of the Dragon.* Illustrated by Ed Young. Lothrop, Lee & Shepard, 1987.

Leaf, Munro. *The Story of Ferdinand.* Illustrated by Robert Lawson. Viking, 1936.

————. *Wee Gillis.* Illustrated by Robert Lawson. Viking, 1938.

Lear, Edward. *The Owl and the Pussycat.* Illustrated by Jan Brett. Putnam, 1991.

————. *The Owl and the Pussycat.* Illustrated by Lorinda Bryan Cauley. Putnam, 1986.

————. *The Owl and the Pussycat.* Illustrated by Janet Stevens. Holiday House, 1983.

Lee, Jeanne M. *Silent Lotus.* Illustrated by Jeanne M. Lee. Farrar, Straus & Giroux, 1991.

Leodhas, Sorche Nic. *Always Room for One More.* Illustrated by Nonny Hogrogian. Henry Holt, 1965.

Lerner, Sharon. *Orange Is a Color.* Illustrated by Sharon Lerner. Lerner, 1970.

Lester, Alison. *Clive Eats Alligators.* Illustrated by Alison Lester. Houghton Mifflin, 1986.

Levinson, Riki. *I Go with My Family to Grandma's.* Illustrated by Diane Goode. Dutton, 1986.

————. *Watch the Stars Come Out.* Illustrated by Diane Goode. Dutton, 1985.

Lewin, Betsy. *Cat Count.* Illustrated by Betsy Lewin. Putnam, 1981.

Lewin, Hugh. *Jafta's Father.* Illustrated by Lisa Kopper. Lerner Publications, 1983.

————. *Jafta's Mother.* Illustrated by Lisa Kopper. Lerner Publications, 1983.

Lewin, Ted. *Amazon Boy.* Illustrated by Ted Lewin. Macmillan, 1993.

Lewis, Kim. *Emma's Lamb.* Illustrated by Kim Lewis. Macmillan, 1991.

Lewison, Wendy Cheyette. *Going to Sleep on the Farm.* Illustrated by Juan Wijngaard. Dial Books for Young Readers, 1992.

Lillegard, Dee. *I Can Be a Baker.* Childrens Press, 1986.

Lindbergh, Reeve. *Benjamin's Barn*. Illustrated by Susan Jeffers. Dial Books for Young Readers, 1990.

————. *The Day the Goose Got Loose*. Illustrated by Steven Kellogg. Dial Books for Young Readers, 1990.

Lindgren, Barbro. *Sam's Cookie*. Illustrated by Eva Eriksson. Morrow Junior, 1982.

————. *The Wild Baby*. Illustrated by Eva Eriksson. Greenwillow, 1981.

Lionni, Leo. *Little Blue and Little Yellow*. Illustrated by Leo Lionni. Astor-Honor, 1959.

Livingston, Myra Cohn. *Birthday Poems*. Illustrated by Margot Tomes. Holiday House, 1989.

———— (ed.). *Cat Poems*. Illustrated by Trina Schart Hyman. Holiday House, 1987.

———— (ed.). *Christmas Poems*. Illustrated by Trina Schart Hyman. Holiday House, 1984.

———— (ed.). *Halloween Poems*. Illustrated by Stephen Gammell. Holiday House, 1989.

———— (ed.). *Poems for Brothers, Poems for Sisters*. Illustrated by Jean Zallinger. Holiday House, 1991.

———— (ed.). *Poems for Fathers*. Illustrated by Robert Casilla. Holiday House, 1989.

———— (ed.). *Poems for Mothers*. Illustrated by Deborah Kogan Ray. Holiday House, 1988.

———— (ed.). *Thanksgiving Poems*. Illustrated by Stephen Gammell. Holiday House, 1985.

Lobel, Anita. *Alison's Zinnia*. Illustrated by Anita Lobel. Greenwillow, 1990.

————. *The Dwarf Giant*. Illustrated by Anita Lobel. Greenwillow, 1991.

————. *King Rooster, Queen Hen*. Illustrated by Anita Lobel. Greenwillow, 1975.

————. *The Pancake*. Illustrated by Anita Lobel. Dell, 1992.

————. *The Straw Maid*. Illustrated by Anita Lobel. Greenwillow, 1983.

————. *Troll Music*. Illustrated by Anita Lobel. Harper & Row, 1986.

Lobel, Arnold. *The Book of Pigericks: Pig Limericks*. Illustrated by Arnold Lobel. HarperCollins, 1983.

————. *Days with Frog and Toad*. Illustrated by Arnold Lobel. HarperCollins, 1979.

————. *Fables*. Illustrated by Arnold Lobel. HarperCollins, 1980.

————. *Frog and Toad All Year*. Illustrated by Arnold Lobel. HarperCollins, 1976.

————. *Frog and Toad Are Friends*. Illustrated by Arnold Lobel. HarperCollins, 1985.

————. *Frog and Toad Together*. Illustrated by Arnold Lobel. HarperCollins, 1972.

————. *Holiday for Mr. Muster*. Illustrated by Arnold Lobel. HarperCollins, 1963.

————. *How the Rooster Saved the Day*. Illustrated by Anita Lobel. Greenwillow, 1977.

————. *The Man Who Took the Indoors Out*. Illustrated by Arnold Lobel. Harper & Row, 1974.

————. *Ming Lo Moves the Mountain*. Illustrated by Arnold Lobel. Green-willow, 1982.

————. *Mouse Soup*. Illustrated by Arnold Lobel. Harper & Row, 1977.

————. *Mouse Tales*. Illustrated by Arnold Lobel. HarperCollins, 1972.

————. *On Market Street*. Illustrated by Anita Lobel. Greenwillow, 1981.

————. *Owl at Home*. Illustrated by Arnold Lobel. HarperCollins, 1975.

———— (ed.). *Random House Book of Mother Goose: A Treasury of 306 Timeless Nursery Tales*. Illustrated by Arnold Lobel. Random House, 1986.

————. *The Rose in My Garden*. Illustrated by Anita Lobel. Greenwillow, 1984.

————. *A Treeful of Pigs*. Illustrated by Anita Lobel. Greenwillow, 1979.

————. *The Turnaround Wind*. Illustrated by Arnold Lobel. HarperCollins, 1988.

————. *Uncle Elephant*. Illustrated by Arnold Lobel. Harper & Row, 1981.

————. *Whiskers & Rhymes*. Illustrated by Arnold Lobel. Greenwillow, 1985.

————. *Zoo for Mister Muster*. Illustrated by Arnold Lobel. HarperCollins, 1962.

Locker, Thomas. *The Land of Gray Wolf*. Illustrated by Thomas Locker. Dial, 1991.

Lomas Garza, Carmen. *Family Pictures*. Illustrated by Carmen Lomas Garza. Children's Book Press, 1990.

London, Jonathan. *Froggy Gets Dressed*. Illustrated by Frank Remkiewicz. Viking Children's Books, 1992.

Longfellow, Henry Wadsworth. *Hiawatha*. Illustrated by Susan Jeffers. Dial Books for Young Readers, 1983.

Lord, John Vernon. *The Giant Jam Sandwich*. Illustrated by John Vernon Lord. Houghton Mifflin, 1973.

Lottridge, Celia B. *The Name of the Tree: A Bantu Folktale*. Illustrated by Ian Wallace. Margaret K. McElderry Books, 1989.

Louie, Ai-Ling. *Yeh-Shen: A Cinderella Story from China*. Illustrated by Ed Young. Philomel, 1982.

Lyon, George Ella. *Come a Tide*. Illustrated by Stephen Gammell. Orchard, 1990.

————. *A Regular Rolling Noah*. Illustrated by Stephen Gammell. Bradbury, 1986.

Macaulay, David. *Black and White*. Illustrated by David Macaulay. Houghton Mifflin, 1990.

MacClintock, Dorcas. *Red Pandas: A Natural History*. Illustrated by Ellan Young. Scribner's Young Readers, 1988.

McCloskey, Robert. *Blueberries for Sal*. Illustrated by Robert McCloskey. Viking, 1948.

————. *Make Way for Ducklings*. Illustrated by Robert McCloskey. Viking, 1941.

————. *Time of Wonder*. Illustrated by Robert McCloskey. Viking, 1957.

McCully, Emily Arnold. *First Snow*. Illustrated by Emily Arnold McCully. HarperCollins Childrens Books, 1985.

————. *Mirette on the High Wire*. Illustrated by Emily Arnold McCully. Putnam, 1992.

————. *New Baby*. Illustrated by Emily Arnold McCully. HarperCollins, 1988.

————. *Picnic.* Illustrated by Emily Arnold McCully. HarperCollins, 1984.

————. *Speak Up, Blanche!* Illustrated by Emily Arnold McCully. Harper-Collins, 1991.

McDermott, Gerald. *Anansi the Spider: A Tale from the Ashanti.* Illustrated by Gerald McDermott. Henry Holt, 1972.

————. *Zomo the Rabbit: A Trickster Tale from West Africa.* Illustrated by Gerald McDermott. Harcourt Brace Jovanovich, 1992.

McDonald, Megan. *The Great Pumpkin Switch.* Illustrated by Ted Lewin. Orchard, 1991.

————. *Whoo-oo Is It?* Illustrated by S. D. Schindler. Orchard, 1992.

McGovern, Ann. *Too Much Noise.* Illustrated by Simms Taback. Houghton Mifflin, 1967.

MacLachlan, Patricia. *Seven Kisses in a Row.* Illustrated by Maria P. Marella. HarperCollins, 1983.

McMillan, Bruce. *Counting Wildflowers.* Illustrated by Bruce McMillan. Lothrop, Lee & Shepard, 1986.

————. *Growing Colors.* Illustrated by Bruce McMillan. Lothrop, Lee & Shepard, 1988.

————. *Here a Chick, There a Chick.* Illustrated by Bruce McMillan. Lothrop, Lee & Shepard, 1983.

McPhail, David M. *Alligators Are Awful (and They Have Terrible Manners, Too!).* Illustrated by David M. McPhail. Doubleday, 1980.

————. *Farm Boy's Year.* Illustrated by David M. McPhail. Atheneum, 1992.

————. *Grandfather's Cake.* Illustrated by David M. McPhail. Scribner, 1979.

————. *Pig Pig Goes to Camp.* Illustrated by David M. McPhail. Dutton Children's Books, 1983.

————. *Pig Pig Grows Up.* Illustrated by David M. McPhail. Dutton, 1980.

————. *Pig Pig Rides.* Illustrated by David M. McPhail. Dutton, 1982.

————. *Where Can an Elephant Hide?* Illustrated by David M. McPhail. Doubleday, 1979.

Maestro, Betsy and Giulio Maestro. *Lambs for Dinner.* Illustrated by Betsy and Giulio Maestro. Crown, 1978.

————. *Snow Day.* Illustrated by Giulio Maestro. Scholastic, 1989.

Mahy, Margaret. *The Seven Chinese Brothers.* Illustrated by Jean and Mou-Sien Tseng. Scholastic, 1990.

Malone, Whitney (ed.). *The Red Carpet.* Illustrated by Rex Parkin. Aladdin, 1993.

Maris, Ron. *Better Move On, Frog!* Illustrated by Ron Maris. Franklin Watts, 1982.

————. *In My Garden.* Illustrated by Ron Maris. Greenwillow, 1988.

Marshall, Edward. *Space Case.* Illustrated by James Marshall. Dial Books for Young Readers, 1980.

Marshall, James. *Hansel and Gretel.* Illustrated by James Marshall. Dial Books for Young Readers, 1990.

————. *Red Riding Hood.* Illustrated by James Marshall. Dial Books for Young Readers, 1987.

Martin, Bill Jr. *Brown Bear, Brown Bear, What Do You See?* Illustrated by Eric Carle. Henry Holt, 1983.

_____. *Polar Bear, Polar Bear, What Do You Hear?* Illustrated by Eric Carle. Henry Holt, 1991.

_____ and John Archambault. *Barn Dance!* Illustrated by Ted Rand. Henry Holt, 1986.

_____. *The Ghost-Eye Tree.* Illustrated by Ted Rand. Henry Holt, 1985.

_____. *Knots on a Counting Rope.* Illustrated by Ted Rand. Henry Holt, 1987.

_____. *White Dynamite & Curly Kidd.* Illustrated by Ted Rand. Henry Holt, 1986.

_____ and Peggy Brogan. *Bill Martin, Jr.'s Treasure Chest of Poetry.* D L M Teaching Resources, 1986.

Martin, Charles E. *For Rent.* Illustrated by Charles E. Martin. Greenwillow, 1986.

Martin, Rafe. *The Rough-Face Girl.* Illustrated by David Shannon. Putnam, 1992.

_____. *Will's Mammoth.* Illustrated by Stephen Gammell. Putnam, 1989.

Marzollo, Jean. *Pretend You're a Cat.* Illustrated by Jerry Pinkney. Dial Books for Young Readers, 1990.

Mayer, Mercer. *A Boy, a Dog, a Frog, and a Friend.* Illustrated by Mercer Mayer. Dial Books for Young Readers, 1978.

_____. *A Boy, a Dog, and a Frog.* Illustrated by Mercer Mayer. Dial Books for Young Readers, 1985.

_____. *Frog Goes to Dinner.* Illustrated by Mercer Mayer. Dial Books for Young Readers, 1977.

_____. *Frog on His Own.* Illustrated by Mercer Mayer. Dial Books for Young Readers, 1973.

_____. *Frog, Where Are You?* Illustrated by Mercer Mayer. Dial Books for Young Readers, 1969.

_____. *There's an Alligator Under My Bed.* Illustrated by Mercer Mayer. Dial Books for Young Readers, 1987.

_____ and Marianna Mayer. *One Frog Too Many.* Illustrated by Mercer Mayer. Dial Books for Young Readers, 1985.

Meddaugh, Susan. *Martha Speaks.* Illustrated by Susan Meddaugh. Houghton Mifflin, 1992.

_____. *Tree of Birds.* Illustrated by Susan Meddaugh. Houghton Mifflin, 1990.

Miller, Edna. *Mousekin's Golden House.* Illustrated by Edna Miller. Prentice-Hall, 1964.

Mills, Claudia. *A Visit to Amy-Claire.* Illustrated by Sheila Hamanaka. Macmillan, 1992.

Milne, A. A. *When We Were Very Young.* Illustrated by Ernest H. Shepard. Dutton, 1961.

_____. *Winnie-the-Pooh.* Illustrated by Ernest H. Shepard. Dutton, 1974.

Minarik, Elsa H. *Father Bear Comes Home.* Illustrated by Maurice Sendak. HarperCollins, 1959.

_____. *A Kiss for Little Bear.* Illustrated by Maurice Sendak. HarperCollins, 1968.

_____. *Little Bear.* Illustrated by Maurice Sendak. HarperCollins, 1957.

_____. *Little Bear's Friend.* Illustrated by Maurice Sendak. HarperCollins, 1960.

_____. *Little Bear's Visit.* Illustrated by Maurice Sendak. HarperCollins, 1961.

_____. *No Fighting, No Biting!* Illustrated by Maurice Sendak. HarperCollins, 1958.

Modell, Frank. *Goodbye Old Year, Hello New Year.* Illustrated by Frank Modell. Greenwillow, 1984.

_____. *Look Out, It's April Fools' Day.* Illustrated by Frank Modell. Greenwillow, 1985.

_____. *One Zillion Valentines.* Illustrated by Frank Modell. Greenwillow, 1981.

Mollel, Tololwa M. *The Orphan Boy: A Masai Story.* Illustrated by Paul Morin. Clarion Books, 1990.

Moncure, Jane B. *The Tasting Party.* Illustrated by Lois Axeman. Childrens Press, 1982.

_____. *What Was It Before It Was Orange Juice?* Illustrated by Susan Lexa. Child's World, 1985.

Monjo, F. N. *Indian Summer.* Illustrated by Anita Lobel. HarperCollins, 1968.

Moore, Clement C. *The Night Before Christmas.* Illustrated by Tomie DePaola. Holiday House, 1980.

_____. *The Night Before Christmas.* Illustrated by Michael Foreman. Viking Children's, 1988.

_____. *The Night Before Christmas.* Illustrated by Gyo Fujikawa. Putnam, 1961.

_____. *The Night Before Christmas.* Illustrated by Michael Hague. Henry Holt, 1981.

_____. *The Night Before Christmas.* Illustrated by Anita Lobel. Alfred A. Knopf, 1992.

_____. *The Night Before Christmas.* Illustrated by James Marshall. Scholastic, 1991.

_____. *The Night Before Christmas.* Illustrated by Tasha Tudor. Rand McNally, 1975.

_____. *A Visit from St. Nicholas.* Illustrated by Paul Galdone. McGraw-Hill, 1968.

Moore, Elaine. *Grandma's Promise.* Illustrated by Elise Primavera. Lothrop, Lee & Shepard, 1985.

Moore, Lilian. *Little Raccoon and No Trouble at All.* Illustrated by Gioia Fiammenghi. McGraw-Hill, 1972.

Moore, Sheila. *Samson Svenson's Baby.* Illustrated by Karen Ann Weinhaus. Harper & Row, 1983.

Mora, Pat. *A Birthday Basket for Tia.* Illustrated by Cecily Lang. Macmillan, 1992.

Morgan, Pierr. *The Turnip: An Old Russian Folktale.* Illustrated by Pierr Morgan. Philomel, 1990.

Morris, Ann. *Little Red Riding Hood Rebus Book.* Illustrated by Ljiljana Rylands. Orchard, 1987.

Morrison, Blake. *The Yellow House.* Illustrated by Helen Craig. Harcourt Brace Jovanovich, 1987.

Mosel, Arlene. *Tikki Tikki Tembo.* Illustrated by Blair Lent. Henry Holt, 1968.

Most, Bernard. *The Cow That Went Oink.* Illustrated by Bernard Most. Harcourt Brace Jovanovich, 1990.

_____. *My Very Own Octopus*. Illustrated by Diane D'Andrade. Voyager Books, 1991.

Mother Goose. *Baa Baa Black Sheep*. Illustrated by Moira Kemp. Dutton, 1991.

Murphy, Jill. *Five Minutes' Peace*. Illustrated by Jill Murphy. Putnam, 1986.

Mwenye Hadithi. *Crafty Chameleon*. Illustrated by Adrienne Kennaway. Little, Brown, 1987.

Neitzel, Shirley. *The Jacket I Wear in the Snow*. Illustrated by Shirley Neitzel. Greenwillow, 1989.

Nelson, Esther. *The Funny Songbook*. Illustrated by Joyce Behr. Sterling Publications, 1984.

_____. *The Silly Songbook*. Illustrated by Joyce Behr. Sterling Publications, 1981.

Newton, Laura. *Me and My Aunts*. Illustrated by Robin Oz. Albert Whitman, 1986.

Noble, Trinka Hakes. *The Day Jimmy's Boat Ate the Wash*. Illustrated by Steven Kellogg. Dial Books for Young Readers, 1980.

_____. *Jimmy's Boa and the Big Splash Birthday Bash*. Illustrated by Steven Kellogg. Dial Books for Young Readers, 1989.

_____. *Jimmy's Boa Bounces Back*. Illustrated by Steven Kellogg. Dial Books for Young Readers, 1984.

Nodset, Joan L. *Who Took the Farmer's Hat?* Illustrated by Fritz Siebel. HarperCollins, 1963.

Numeroff, Laura Joffe. *If You Give a Mouse a Cookie*. Illustrated by Felicia Bond. Harper & Row, 1985.

_____ and Alice Numeroff Richter. *Emily's Bunch*. Illustrated by Laura Joffe Numeroff. Macmillan, 1978.

Nussbaumer, Paul and Mares Nussbaumer. *Away in a Manger: A Story of the Nativity*. Illustrated by Paul Nussbaumer. Harcourt Brace Jovanovich, 1965.

O'Donnell, Elizabeth L. *I Can't Get My Turtle to Move*. Illustrated by Maxie Chambliss. Morrow Junior Books, 1989.

O'Neill, Mary Le Duc. *Hailstones and Halibut Bones: Adventures in Color*. Illustrated by John Wallner. Doubleday, 1989.

Opie, Peter and Iona Opia (eds.). *I Saw Esau: The Schoolchild's Pocket Book*. Illustrated by Maurice Sendak. Candlewick Press, 1992.

_____ (eds.). *The Oxford Dictionary of Nursery Rhymes*. Oxford University Press, 1951.

Oppenheim, Joanne. *Mrs. Peloki's Snake*. Illustrated by Joyce Audy Dos Santos. Dodd, Mead, 1980.

Oppenheim, Shulamith Levey. *Waiting for Noah*. Illustrated by Lillian Hoban. Harper & Row, 1990.

Ormerod, Jan. *101 Things to Do with a Baby*. Illustrated by Jan Ormerod. Lothrop, Lee & Shepard, 1984.

_____. *The Story of Chicken Licken*. Illustrated by Jan Ormerod. Lothrop, Lee & Shepard, 1986.

Osofsky, Audrey. *Dreamcatcher*. Illustrated by Ed Young. Orchard Books, 1992.

Oughton, Jerrie. *How the Stars Fell into the Sky: A Navajo Legend*. Illustrated by Lisa Desimini. Houghton Mifflin, 1992.

Oxenbury, Helen. *The Birthday Party*. Illustrated by Helen Oxenbury. Dial Books for Young Readers, 1983.

Palmer, S. *Blue Whales.* Rourke Corporation, 1988.

Parish, Peggy. *Amelia Bedelia and the Surprise Shower.* Illustrated by Fritz Siebel. HarperCollins, 1966.

Parker, Nancy Winslow. *Love, from Aunt Betty.* Illustrated by Nancy Winslow Parker. Dodd, Mead, 1983.

_____. *Love, from Uncle Clyde.* Illustrated by Nancy Winslow Parker. Dodd, Mead, 1977.

Parnall, Peter. *Winter Barn.* Illustrated by Peter Parnall. Macmillan, 1986.

Patron, Susan. *Burgoo Stew.* Illustrated by Mike Shenon. Orchard, 1991.

Pearson, Susan. *Happy Birthday, Grampie.* Illustrated by Ron Himler. Dial Books for Young Readers, 1987.

Pearson, Tracey Campbell. *Old MacDonald Had a Farm.* Illustrated by Tracey Campbell Pearson. Dial Books for Young Readers, 1984.

_____. *Sing a Song of Sixpence.* Illustrated by Tracey Campbell Pearson. Dial Books for Young Readers, 1985.

_____. *We Wish You a Merry Christmas: A Traditional Christmas Carol.* Illustrated by Tracey Campbell Pearson. Dial Books for Young Readers, 1983.

Peek, Merle. *Mary Wore Her Red Dress, & Henry Wore His Green Sneakers.* Illustrated by Merle Peek. Houghton Mifflin, 1985.

Pellowski, Anne. *The Story Vine: A Source Book of Unusual and Easy-to-Tell Stories from Around the World.* Illustrated by Lynn Sweat. Collier Macmillan, 1984.

Perrault, Charles. *Cinderella; Or, The Little Glass Slipper.* Illustrated by Marcia Brown. Scribner, 1954.

Pflomm, Phyllis Noe. *Chalk in Hand: The Draw and Tell Book.* Illustrated by Phyllis Noe Pflomm. Scarecrow, 1986.

Pilkey, Dav. *When Cats Dream.* Illustrated by Dav Pilkey. Orchard, 1992.

Pinkwater, Daniel Manus. *Aunt Lulu.* Illustrated by Daniel Manus Pinkwater. Macmillan, 1988.

_____. *Big Orange Splot.* Illustrated by Daniel Manus Pinkwater. Hastings House, 1992.

Polacco, Patricia. *Chicken Sunday.* Illustrated by Patricia Polacco. Philomel, 1992.

_____. *The Keeping Quilt.* Illustrated by Patricia Polacco. Simon & Schuster, 1988.

_____. *Mrs. Katz & Tush.* Illustrated by Patricia Polacco. Bantam, 1992.

_____. *Picnic at Mudsock Meadow.* Illustrated by Patricia Polacco. Putnam, 1992.

_____. *Rechenka's Eggs.* Illustrated by Patricia Polacco. Philomel, 1988.

_____. *Thunder Cake.* Illustrated by Patricia Polacco. Philomel, 1990.

_____. *Uncle Vova's Tree.* Illustrated by Patricia Polacco. Philomel, 1989.

Polushkin, Maria. *The Little Hen and the Giant.* Illustrated by Maria Polushkin. Harper & Row, 1977.

_____. *Mother, Mother, I Want Another.* Illustrated by Diane Dawson. Crown Books for Young Readers, 1988.

Pomerantz, Charlotte. *The Half-Birthday Party.* Illustrated by DyAnne DiSalvo-Ryan. Clarion Books, 1984.

_____. *One Duck, Another Duck.* Illustrated by Jose Aruego and Ariane Dewey. Greenwillow, 1984.

_____. *The Piggy in the Puddle*. Illustrated by James Marshall. Macmillan, 1974.

Porte-Thomas, Barbara Ann. *Harry Gets an Uncle*. Illustrated by Yossi Abolafia. Greenwillow, 1991.

Poulet, Virginia. *Blue Bug and the Bullies*. Illustrated by Don Meighan. Childrens Press, 1971.

_____. *Blue Bug Finds a Friend*. Illustrated by Mary Maloney and Stan Fleming. Childrens Press, 1977.

_____. *Blue Bug Goes to School*. Illustrated by Peggy P. Anderson. Childrens Press, 1985.

_____. *Blue Bug Goes to the Library*. Illustrated by Peggy P. Anderson. Childrens Press, 1979.

_____. *Blue Bug to the Rescue*. Childrens Press, 1976.

_____. *Blue Bug's Circus*. Illustrated by Mary Maloney and Stan Fleming. Childrens Press, 1977.

_____. *Blue Bug's Surprise*. Illustrated by Mary Maloney and Stan Fleming. Childrens Press, 1977.

_____. *Blue Bug's Vegetable Garden*. Illustrated by Donald Charles. Childrens Press, 1973.

Prelutsky, Jack. *Circus!* Illustrated by Arnold Lobel. Aladdin, 1989.

_____. *It's Halloween*. Illustrated by Marylin Hafner. Greenwillow, 1977.

_____. *It's Snowing! It's Snowing!* Illustrated by Jeanne Titherington. Greenwillow, 1984.

_____. *It's Thanksgiving*. Illustrated by Marylin Hafner. Greenwillow, 1982.

_____ (ed.). *The Random House Book of Poetry*. Illustrated by Arnold Lobel. Random House, 1983.

_____ (ed.). *Read-Aloud Rhymes for the Very Young*. Illustrated by Marc Tolon Brown. Alfred A. Knopf, 1986.

_____ (ed.). *Tyrannosaurus Was a Beast*. Illustrated by Arnold Lobel. Greenwillow, 1988.

Provensen, Martin and Alice Provensen. *The Glorious Flight: Across the Channel with Louis Bleriot, July 25, 1909*. Illustrated by Alice and Martin Provensen. Viking, 1983.

Quackenbush, Robert M. *I Don't Want to Go, I Don't Know How to Act*. Illustrated by Robert M. Quackenbush. Lippincott, 1983.

_____. *Old MacDonald Had a Farm*. Illustrated by Robert M. Quackenbush. Lippincott, 1972.

_____. *She'll Be Comin' Round the Mountain*. Illustrated by Robert Quackenbush. Lippincott, 1973.

Quigley, Lillian Fox. *The Blind Men and the Elephant: An Old Tale from the Land of India*. Illustrated by Janice Holland. Scribner, 1959.

Rabe, Berniece. *The Balancing Girl*. Illustrated by Lillian Hoban. Dutton, 1981.

Raffi. *Five Little Ducks*. Illustrated by Jose Aruego and Ariane Dewey. Crown, 1989.

_____. *The Raffi Everything Grows Songbook*. Crown, 1989.

_____. *The Raffi Singable Songbook: a Collection of 51 Songs from Raffi's First Three Records for Young Children*. Illustrated by Joyce Yamamoto. Crown Books for Young Readers, 1988.

_____. *The 2nd Raffi Songbook: 42 Songs from Raffi's Albums Baby Beluga, Risa and Shine and One Light, One Sun.* Illustrated by Joyce Yamamoto. Crown, 1987.

Raposo, Joe and Jeffrey Moss. *The Sesame Street Song Book.* Illustrated by Loretta Trezzo. Simon & Schuster, 1971.

Raschka, Chris. *Charlie Parker Played Be-Bop.* Illustrated by Chris Raschka. Orchard, 1992.

Rayner, Mary. *Garth Pig and the Ice Cream Lady.* Illustrated by Mary Rayner. Atheneum, 1978.

_____. *Mr. & Mrs. Pig's Evening Out.* Illustrated by Mary Rayner. Atheneum, 1976.

Remkiewicz, Frank. *The Last Time I Saw Harris.* Illustrated by Frank Remkiewicz. Lothrop, Lee & Shepard, 1991.

Rey, Hans Augusto. *Curious George.* Illustrated by Hans Augusto Rey. Houghton Mifflin, 1973.

_____. *Curious George Flies a Kite.* Illustrated by Hans Augusto Rey. Houghton Mifflin, 1973.

_____. *Curious George Gets a Medal.* Illustrated by Hans Augusto Rey. Houghton Mifflin, 1957.

_____. *Curious George Learns the Alphabet.* Illustrated by Hans Augusto Rey. Houghton Mifflin, 1963.

_____. *Curious George Rides a Bike.* Illustrated by Hans Augusto Rey. Houghton Mifflin, 1952.

_____. *Curious George Takes a Job.* Illustrated by Hans Augusto Rey. Houghton Mifflin, 1973.

_____ and Margaret Rey. *Curious George Goes to the Hospital.* Illustrated by Hans Augusto Rey and Margaret Rey. Houghton Mifflin, 1973.

Rey, Margaret. *Curious George Goes to the Circus.* Houghton Mifflin, 1984.

_____ (ed.). *Curious George Visits the Zoo.* Houghton Mifflin, 1985.

Riley, James Whitcomb. *The Gobble-uns'll Git You Ef You Don't Watch Out!* Illustrated by Joel Schick. Lippincott, 1975.

Robart, Rose. *The Cake That Mack Ate.* Illustrated by Maryann Kovalski. Little, Brown, 1991.

Robbins, Ruth. *Baboushka and the Three Kings.* Illustrated by Nicolas Sidjakov. Houghton Mifflin, 1960.

Robertus, Polly. *The Dog Who Had Kittens.* Illustrated by Janet Stevens. Holiday House, 1992.

Roche, A. K. *The Clever Turtle.* Illustrated by A. K. Roche. Prentice-Hall, 1969.

Rockwell, Anne. *First Comes Spring.* Illustrated by Anne Rockwell. Thomas Y. Crowell, 1985.

_____. *Mother Goose Cookie-Candy Book.* Illustrated by Anne Rockwell. Random House, 1983.

_____ and Harlow Rockwell. *Happy Birthday to Me.* Illustrated by Anne and Harlow Rockwell. Macmillan, 1981.

_____. *How My Garden Grew.* Illustrated by Anne and Harlow Rockwell. Macmillan, 1982.

Rogasky, Barbara. *Rapunzel.* Illustrated by Trina Schart Hyman. Holiday House, 1982.

_____. *The Water of Life: A Tale from the Brothers Grimm.* Illustrated by Trina Schart Hyman. Holiday House, 1986.

Root, Phyllis. *The Old Red Rocking Chair.* Illustrated by John Sandford. Arcade, 1992.

_____. *Soup for Supper.* Illustrated by Sue Truesdell. Harper & Row, 1986.

Rose, Agatha. *Hide and Seek in the Yellow House.* Illustrated by Kate Spohn. Viking, 1992.

Rose, David S. *It Hardly Seems Like Halloween.* Illustrated by David S. Rose. Lothrop, Lee & Shepard, 1983.

Rosen, Michael. *We're Going on a Bear Hunt.* Illustrated by Helen Oxenbury. Margaret K. McElderry, 1989.

Rosen, Michael J. *Elijah's Angel: A Story for Chanukah and Christmas.* Illustrated by Aminah Brenda Lynn Robinson. Harcourt Brace Jovanovich, 1992.

Rosenberg, Liz. *Monster Mama.* Illustrated by Stephen Gammell. Philomel, 1993.

Ross, Tony. *Jack and the Beanstalk.* Illustrated by Tony Ross. Delacorte, 1980.

Roth, Susan L. *The Story of Light.* Illustrated by Susan Roth. Morrow Junior Books, 1990.

Rounds, Glen. *Cowboys.* Illustrated by Glen Rounds. Holiday House, 1991.

_____. *I Know an Old Lady Who Swallowed a Fly.* Illustrated by Glen Rounds. Holiday House, 1990.

_____. *Old MacDonald Had a Farm.* Illustrated by Glen Rounds. Holiday House, 1989.

_____. *The Three Billy Goats Gruff.* Illustrated by Glen Rounds. Holiday House, 1993.

_____. *Three Little Pigs and the Big Bad Wolf.* Illustrated by Glen Rounds. Holiday House, 1992.

Roy, Ron. *Three Ducks Went Wandering.* Illustrated by Paul Galdone. Clarion Books, 1979.

Ruffins, Reynold. *My Brother Never Feeds the Cat.* Illustrated by Reynold Ruffins. Scribner, 1979.

Ruschak, Lynette. *Snack Attack: A Tasty Pop-Up Book.* Illustrated by David A. Carter. Simon & Schuster, 1990.

Russo, Marisabina. *A Visit to Oma.* Illustrated by Marisabina Russo. Greenwillow, 1991.

_____. *Waiting for Hannah.* Illustrated by Marisabina Russo. Greenwillow, 1989.

Ruthstrom, Dorotha. *The Big Kite Contest.* Illustrated by Lillian Hoban. Pantheon, 1980.

Rylant, Cynthia. *Birthday Presents.* Illustrated by Sucie Stevenson. Orchard, 1987.

_____. *The Relatives Came.* Illustrated by Stephen Gammell. Bradbury, 1985.

_____. *This Year's Garden.* Illustrated by Mary Szilagyi. Bradbury, 1984.

Sadler, Marilyn. *Elizabeth and Larry.* Illustrated by Roger Bollen. Simon & Schuster, 1992.

Salus, Naomi Panush. *My Daddy's Mustache.* Illustrated by Tomie DePaola. Doubleday, 1979.

Saunders, Susan. *A Sniff in Time.* Illustrated by Michael Mariano. Atheneum, 1982.

Say, Allen. *Tree of Cranes.* Illustrated by Allen Say. Houghton Mifflin, 1991.

Scamell, Ragnhild. *Solo Plus One.* Illustrated by Elizabeth Martland. Little, Brown, 1992.

Scarry, Richard. *Richard Scarry's Please and Thank You Book.* Illustrated by Richard Scarry. Random House Books for Young Readers, 1973.

Scheller, Melanie. *My Grandfather's Hat.* Illustrated by Keiko Narahashi. Margaret K. McElderry, 1992.

Schimmel, Nancy. *Just Enough to Make a Story: A Sourcebook for Storytelling.* Sisters' Choice Press, 1978.

Schneider, Rex. *Wide-Mouthed Frog.* Illustrated by Rex Schneider. Stemmer House, 1980.

Schoenherr, John. *The Barn.* Illustrated by John Schoenherr. Little, Brown, 1968.

Schram, Peninnah. *The Big Sukkah.* Illustrated by Jacqueline Kahane. Kar-Ben Copies, 1986.

Schubert, Dieter and Ingrid Schubert. *There's a Crocodile Under My Bed!* Illustrated by Dieter and Ingrid Schubert. McGraw-Hill, 1980.

Schwartz, Alvin. *And the Green Grass Grew All Around: Folk Poetry from Everyone.* Illustrated by Sue Truesdell. HarperCollins, 1992.

Schwartz, Amy. *Bea and Mr. Jones.* Illustrated by Amy Schwartz. Bradbury, 1982.

_____. *Her Majesty, Aunt Essie.* Illustrated by Amy Schwartz. Bradbury, 1984.

_____. *Oma and Bobo.* Illustrated by Amy Schwartz. Bradbury, 1987.

Scieszka, Jon. *The Frog Prince Continued. . . .* Illustrated by Steve Johnson. Viking, 1991.

_____. *The True Story of the Three Little Pigs.* Illustrated by Lane Smith. Viking Kestrel, 1989.

Scott, Ann Herbert. *On Mother's Lap.* Illustrated by Glo Coalson. Clarion Books, 1992.

_____. *One Cowboy: A Cowpuncher's Counting Book.* Illustrated by Lynn Sweat. Greenwillow, 1990.

Seeger, Pete and Charles Seeger. *The Foolish Frog.* Illustrated by Miloslav Jagr. Macmillan, 1973.

Selkowe, Valerie M. *Spring Green.* Illustrated by Jeni Bassett. Lothrop, Lee & Shepard, 1985.

Selsam, Millicent. *Egg to Chick.* Illustrated by Barbara Wolff. Harper & Row, 1970.

_____. *Let's Get Turtles.* Illustrated by Arnold Lobel. Harper & Row, 1965.

Sendak, Maurice. *Alligators All Around: An Alphabet.* Illustrated by Maurice Sendak. HarperCollins, 1962.

_____. *Chicken Soup with Rice: A Book of Months.* Illustrated by Maurice Sendak. HarperCollins, 1962.

_____. *Higglety Pigglety Pop! Or, There Must Be More to Life.* Illustrated by Maurice Sendak. HarperCollins, 1967.

_____. *In the Night Kitchen.* Illustrated by Maurice Sendak. HarperCollins, 1970.

_____. *Maurice Sendak's Really Rosie.* Illustrated by Maurice Sendak. Harper-Collins, 1986.

————. *One Was Johnny: A Counting Book.* Illustrated by Maurice Sendak. HarperCollins, 1962.

————. *Outside Over There.* Illustrated by Maurice Sendak. Harper & Row, 1981.

————. *Pierre: A Cautionary Tale in Five Chapters and a Prologue.* Illustrated by Maurice Sendak. HarperCollins, 1962.

————. *Seven Little Monsters.* Illustrated by Maurice Sendak. HarperCollins, 1977.

————. *The Sign on Rosie's Door.* Illustrated by Maurice Sendak. Harper-Collins, 1960.

————. *Where the Wild Things Are.* Illustrated by Maurice Sendak. Harper-Collins, 1988.

Serfozo, Mary. *Who Said Red?* Illustrated by Keiko Narahashi. Macmillan, 1988.

Seuling, Barbara. *The Teeny Tiny Woman: An Old English Ghost Tale.* Illustrated by Barbara Seuling. Viking, 1976.

Seuss, Dr. *Green Eggs & Ham.* Illustrated by Dr. Seuss. Random House Books for Young Readers, 1960.

Shannon, George. *Lizard's Song.* Illustrated by Jose Aruego and Ariane Dewey. Greenwillow, 1981.

Sharmat, Marjorie W. *Hooray for Father's Day.* Illustrated by John Wallner. Holiday House, 1987.

————. *I'm Terrific!* Illustrated by Kay Chorao. Holiday House, 1977.

Sharmat, Mitchell. *Gregory the Terrible Eater.* Illustrated by Jose Aruego and Ariane Dewey. Four Winds Press, 1980.

Sharon, Lois & Bram. *Sharon, Lois & Bram's Mother Goose Songs, Finger Rhymes, Tickling Verses, Games & More.* Illustrated by Maryann Kovalski. Little, Brown, 1986.

Shaw, Nancy E. *Sheep in a Jeep.* Illustrated by Margot Apple. Houghton Mifflin, 1986.

————. *Sheep in a Shop.* Illustrated by Margot Apple. Houghton Mifflin, 1991.

————. *Sheep on a Ship.* Illustrated by Margot Apple. Houghton Mifflin, 1989.

————. *Sheep Out to Eat.* Illustrated by Margot Apple. Houghton Mifflin, 1992.

Shetterly, Susan Hand. *Raven's Light: A Myth from the People of the Northwest Coast.* Illustrated by Robert Shetterly. Atheneum, 1991.

Shub, Elizabeth. *Clever Kate.* Illustrated by Anita Lobel. Macmillan, 1973.

Shulevitz, Uri. *Hanukkah Money.* Illustrated by Uri Shulevitz. Greenwillow, 1978.

Shute, Linda. *Clever Tom and the Leprechaun.* Illustrated by Linda Shute. Lothrop, Lee & Shepard, 1988.

Sierra, Judy. *The Flannel Board Storytelling Book.* H. W. Wilson, 1987.

———— and Robert Kaminski. *Multicultural Folktales: Stories to Tell Young Children.* Oryx, 1991.

Silverman, Erica. *The Big Pumpkin.* Illustrated by S. D. Schindler. Macmillan, 1992.

Simmie, Lois. *Auntie's Knitting a Baby.* Illustrated by Anne Simmie. Orchard, 1988.

Singer, Marilyn. *Turtle in July.* Illustrated by Jerry Pinkney. Macmillan, 1989.

Smith, Lane. *Glasses: Who Needs 'Em?* Illustrated by Lane Smith. Viking, 1991.

Sneeve, Virginia Driving Hawk (ed.). *Dancing Teepees: Poems of American Indian Youth.* Illustrated by Stephen Gammell. Holiday House, 1989.

Spier, Peter. *Crash! Bang! Boom!* Illustrated by Peter Spier. Doubleday, 1986.

————. *The Erie Canal.* Illustrated by Peter Spier. Doubleday, 1990.

————. *Gobble, Growl, Grunt.* Illustrated by Peter Spier. Doubleday, 1971.

————. *London Bridge Is Falling Down!* Illustrated by Peter Spier. Doubleday, 1967.

————. *Oh, Were They Ever Happy!* Illustrated by Peter Spier. Doubleday, 1978.

Spinelli, Eileen. *Somebody Loves You, Mr. Hatch.* Illustrated by Paul Yalowitz. Macmillan, 1992.

Stangl, Jean. *Paper Stories.* Fearon Teacher Aids, 1982.

Steig, William. *Spinky Sulks.* Illustrated by William Steig. Farrar, Straus & Giroux, 1988.

————. *Sylvester and the Magic Pebble.* Illustrated by William Steig. Simon & Schuster, 1969.

————. *Yellow and Pink.* Illustrated by William Steig. Farrar, Straus & Giroux, 1984.

Steptoe, John. *The Story of Jumping Mouse: A Native American Legend.* Illustrated by John Steptoe. Lothrop, Lee & Shepard, 1984.

Stevens, Janet. *The Three Billy Goats Gruff.* Illustrated by Janet Stevens. Harcourt Brace Jovanovich, 1987.

————. *The Tortoise and the Hare: An Aesop Fable.* Illustrated by Janet Stevens. Holiday House, 1984.

Stevenson, James. *Brrr!* Illustrated by James Stevenson. Greenwillow, 1991.

————. *"Could Be Worse!"* Illustrated by James Stevenson. Greenwillow, 1977.

————. *The Great Big Especially Beautiful Easter Egg.* Illustrated by James Stevenson. Greenwillow, 1983.

————. *Monty.* Illustrated by James Stevenson. Greenwillow, 1979.

————. *The Sea View Hotel.* Illustrated by James Stevenson. Greenwillow, 1978.

————. *Worse Than Willy!* Illustrated by James Stevenson. Greenwillow, 1984.

————. *Yuck!* Illustrated by James Stevenson. Greenwillow, 1984.

Stevenson, Robert Louis. *My Shadow.* Illustrated by Ted Rand. Putnam, 1990.

Stinson, Kathy. *Red Is Best.* Illustrated by Robin B. Lewis. Annick Press, 1992.

Stobbs, William. *Jack and the Beanstalk.* Illustrated by William Stobbs. Delacorte, 1966.

————. *There's a Hole in My Bucket.* Illustrated by William Stobbs. Oxford University Press, 1981.

Stover, Jo Ann. *If Everybody Did.* Illustrated by Jo Ann Stover. Bob Jones Press, 1989.

Tafuri, Nancy. *Have You Seen My Duckling?* Illustrated by Nancy Tafuri. Greenwillow, 1984.

————. *Spots, Feathers and Curly Tails.* Illustrated by Nancy Tafuri. Greenwillow, 1988.

Tarcov, Edith H. *The Frog Prince.* Illustrated by James Marshall. Scholastic, 1987.

Tashjian, Virginia A. *Juba This and Juba That: Story Hour Stretches for Large or Small Groups.* Illustrated by Victoria De Larrea. Little, Brown, 1969.

Teague, Mark. *The Field Beyond the Outfield*. Illustrated by Mark Teague. Scholastic, 1992.

Teal, Val. *The Little Woman Wanted Noise*. Illustrated by Robert Lawson. Rand McNally, 1943.

Tejima, Keizaburo. *The Bear's Autumn*. Illustrated by Keizaburo Tejima. Green Tiger Press, 1991.

Thayer, Mike. *In the Middle of the Puddle*. Illustrated by Bruce Degen. Harper-Collins, 1988.

Thiele, Colin. *Farmer Schulz's Ducks*. Illustrated by Mary Milton. HarperCollins, 1988.

Thompson, Susan L. *One More Thing, Dad*. Illustrated by Dora Leder. Albert Whitman, 1980.

Threadgall, Colin. *The Proud Rooster & the Fox*. Illustrated by Colin Threadgall. Tambourine Books, 1992.

Titherington, Jeanne. *Pumpkin, Pumpkin*. Illustrated by Jeanne Titherington. Greenwillow, 1986.

Tresselt, Alvin R. *White Snow, Bright Snow*. Illustrated by Roger Duvoisin. Lothrop, Lee & Shepard, 1988.

Trivizas, Eugene. *The Three Little Wolves and the Big Bad Pig*. Illustrated by Helen Oxenbury. Margaret K. McElderry, 1993.

Ungerer, Tomi. *Crictor*. Illustrated by Tomi Ungerer. Harper & Row, 1958.

_____. *No Kiss for Mother*. Illustrated by Tomi Ungerer. Delacorte, 1991.

Untermeyer, Louis (ed.). *The Golden Treasury of Poetry*. Illustrated by Joan Walsh Anglund. Golden Press, 1959.

Vagin, Vladimir and Frank Asch. *Here Comes the Cat!* Illustrated by Vladimir Vagin and Frank Asch. Scholastic, 1988.

Van Allsburg, Chris. *Ben's Dream*. Illustrated by Chris Van Allsburg. Houghton Mifflin, 1982.

_____. *The Garden of Abdul Gasazi*. Illustrated by Chris Van Allsburg. Houghton Mifflin, 1979.

_____. *Jumanji*. Illustrated by Chris Van Allsburg. Houghton Mifflin, 1981.

_____. *Just a Dream*. Illustrated by Chris Van Allsburg. Houghton Mifflin, 1990.

_____. *The Mysteries of Harris Burdick*. Illustrated by Chris Van Allsburg. Houghton Mifflin, 1984.

_____. *Polar Express*. Illustrated by Chris Van Allsburg. Houghton Mifflin, 1985.

_____. *The Stranger*. Illustrated by Chris Van Allsburg. Houghton Mifflin, 1986.

_____. *Two Bad Ants*. Illustrated by Chris Van Allsburg. Houghton Mifflin, 1988.

_____. *The Widow's Broom*. Illustrated by Chris Van Allsburg. Houghton Mifflin, 1992.

_____. *The Wreck of the Zephyr*. Illustrated by Chris Van Allsburg. Houghton Mifflin, 1983.

_____. *The Wretched Stone*. Illustrated by Chris Van Allsburg. Houghton Mifflin, 1991.

_____. *The Z Was Zapped: A Play in Twenty-Six Acts.* Illustrated by Chris Van Allsburg. Houghton Mifflin, 1987.

Van Der Beek, Deborah. *Alice's Blue Cloth.* Illustrated by Deborah Van Der Beek. Putnam, 1989.

Van Laan, Nancy. *The Legend of El Dorado: A Latin American Tale.* Illustrated by Beatriz Vidal. Alfred A. Knopf, 1991.

Van Woerkom, Dorothy. *Alexandra the Rock Eater: An Old Rumanian Tale.* Illustrated by Rosekrans Hoffman. Alfred A. Knopf, 1978.

Vaughan, Marcia. *Wombat Stew.* Illustrated by Pamela Lofts. Silver Burdett, 1986.

_____ and Patricia Mullins. *The Sea-Breeze Hotel.* Illustrated by Marcia Vaughan and Patricia Mullins. HarperCollins Children's Books, 1992.

Vincent, Gabrielle. *Ernest & Celestine's Picnic.* Illustrated by Gabrielle Vincent. Greenwillow, 1982.

_____. *Feel Better, Ernest!* Illustrated by Gabrielle Vincent. Greenwillow, 1988.

_____. *Smile, Ernest & Celestine.* Illustrated by Gabrielle Vincent. Greenwillow, 1982.

Viorst, Judith. *Alexander and the Terrible, Horrible, No Good, Very Bad Day.* Illustrated by Ray Cruz. Atheneum, 1972.

_____. *The Good-Bye Book.* Illustrated by Kay Chorao. Atheneum, 1988.

Waddell, Martin. *Farmer Duck.* Illustrated by Helen Oxenbury. Candlewick Press, 1992.

Wadsworth, Olive A. *Over in the Meadow.* Illustrated by Ezra Jack Keats. Scholastic, 1985.

Waggoner, Karen. *The Lemonade Babysitter.* Illustrated by Karen Waggoner. Little, Brown, 1992.

Wagner, Karen. *Chocolate Chip Cookies.* Illustrated by Leah P. Priess. Henry Holt, 1990.

Wallace, Brooks B. *Argyle.* Illustrated by John Sandford. Boyds Mills Press, 1992.

Walsh, Ellen Stoll. *Mouse Count.* Illustrated by Ellen Stoll Walsh. Harcourt Brace Jovanovich, 1991.

Walter, Mildred Pitts. *My Mama Needs Me.* Illustrated by Pat Cummings. Lothrop, Lee & Shepard, 1983.

Wang, Rosalind C. *The Fourth Question: A Chinese Tale.* Illustrated by Ju-Hong Chen. Holiday House, 1991.

Warren, Jean. *"Cut & Tell" Scissors Stories for Winter.* Totline Press, 1984.

Wasmuth, Eleanor. *The Picnic Basket.* Illustrated by Eleanor Wasmuth. Grosset & Dunlap, 1983.

Watanabe, Shigeo. *What a Good Lunch!* Illustrated by Shigeo Watanabe. Philomel, 1991.

Waters, Kate and Slovenz-Low Waters. *Lion Dancer: Ernie Wan's Chinese New Year.* Illustrated by Martha Cooper. Scholastic, 1990.

Watson, Clyde. *Valentine Foxes.* Illustrated by Wendy Watson. Orchard, 1989.

Watson, Wendy. *Thanksgiving at Our House.* Illustrated by Wendy Watson. Clarion Books, 1991.

Weiss, Nicki. *If You're Happy and You Know It.* Illustrated by Nicki Weiss. Greenwillow, 1987.

_____. *On a Hot, Hot Day.* Illustrated by Nicki Weiss. Putnam, 1992.

Wellington, Monica. *Mr. Cookie Baker.* Illustrated by Monica Wellington. Dutton Children's Books, 1992.

Wells, Rosemary. *Fritz and the Mess Fairy.* Illustrated by Rosemary Wells. Dial Books for Young Readers, 1991.

_____. *Hazel's Amazing Mother.* Illustrated by Rosemary Wells. Dial Books for Young Readers, 1985.

_____. *A Lion for Lewis.* Illustrated by Rosemary Wells. Dial Books for Young Readers, 1982.

_____. *Max's Birthday.* Illustrated by Rosemary Wells. Dial Books for Young Readers, 1985.

_____. *Max's Chocolate Chicken.* Illustrated by Rosemary Wells. Dial Books for Young Readers, 1989.

_____. *Max's Christmas.* Illustrated by Rosemary Wells. Dial Books for Young Readers, 1986.

_____. *Max's Dragon Shirt.* Illustrated by Rosemary Wells. Dial Books for Young Readers, 1991.

_____. *Peabody.* Illustrated by Rosemary Wells. Dial Books for Young Readers, 1983.

_____. *Shy Charles.* Illustrated by Rosemary Wells. Dial Books for Young Readers, 1988.

_____. *Stanley & Rhoda.* Illustrated by Rosemary Wells. Dial Books for Young Readers, 1985.

Westcott, Nadine Bernard. *I Know an Old Lady Who Swallowed a Fly.* Illustrated by Nadine Bernard Westcott. Little, Brown, 1980.

_____. *The Lady with the Alligator Purse.* Illustrated by Nadine Bernard Westcott. Little, Brown, 1988.

_____. *Peanut Butter and Jelly: A Play Rhyme.* Illustrated by Nadine Bernard Westcott. Dutton, 1987.

_____. *Skip to My Lou.* Illustrated by Nadine Bernard Westcott. Little, Brown, 1989.

_____. *There's a Hole in My Bucket.* Illustrated by Nadine Bernard Westcott. HarperCollins, 1990.

Wheeler, Cindy. *Marmalade's Yellow Leaf.* Illustrated by Cindy Wheeler. Alfred A. Knopf, 1982.

Wickstrom, Sylvie. *Turkey on the Loose!* Illustrated by Sylvie Wickstrom. Dial Books for Young Readers, 1990.

Widman, Christine. *The Lemon Drop Jar.* Illustrated by Christa Kieffer. Macmillan, 1992.

Wiesner, David. *June 29, 1999.* Illustrated by David Wiesner. Clarion, 1992.

_____. *Tuesday.* Illustrated by David Wiesner. Clarion, 1991.

Wild, Margaret. *Let the Celebrations Begin!* Illustrated by Julie Vivas. Orchard, 1991.

Wilde, Oscar. *The Selfish Giant.* Illustrated by Lisbeth Zwerger. Picture Book Studio, 1984.

Wildsmith, Brian. *Brian Wildsmith's the Twelve Days of Christmas.* Illustrated by Brian Wildsmith. Franklin Watts, 1972.

_____. *Daisy.* Illustrated by Brian Wildsmith. Pantheon, 1984.

_____. *Goat's Trail.* Illustrated by Brian Wildsmith. Alfred A. Knopf, 1986.

_____. *The Hunter & His Dog.* Illustrated by Brian Wildsmith. Oxford University Press, 1979.

_____. *Python's Party.* Illustrated by Brian Wildsmith. Oxford University Press, 1987.

Willard, Nancy. *The High Rise Glorious Skittle Skat Roarious Sky Pie Angel Food Cake.* Illustrated by Richard J. Watson. Harcourt Brace Jovanovich, 1990.

_____. *A Visit to William Blake's Inn: Poems for Innocent and Experienced Travelers.* Illustrated by Alice and Martin Provensen. Harcourt Brace Jovanovich, 1981.

Williams, Barbara. *Albert's Toothache.* Illustrated by Kay Chorao. Dutton, 1974.

_____. *Jeremy Isn't Hungry.* Illustrated by Martha Alexander. Dutton, 1978.

_____. *Kevin's Grandma.* Illustrated by Kay Chorao. Dutton, 1975.

Williams, Garth. *The Chicken Book.* Illustrated by Garth Williams. Delacorte, 1970.

_____. *Rabbits' Wedding.* Illustrated by Garth Williams. HarperCollins, 1958.

Williams, Jay. *Everyone Knows What a Dragon Looks Like.* Illustrated by Mercer Mayer. Four Winds Press, 1976.

Williams, Karen Lynn. *When Africa Was Home.* Illustrated by Floyd Cooper. Orchard, 1991.

Williams, Vera. *"More! More! More!" Said the Baby: 3 Love Stories.* Illustrated by Vera Williams. Greenwillow, 1990.

_____. *Music, Music for Everyone.* Illustrated by Vera Williams. Greenwillow, 1984.

_____. *Something Special for Me.* Illustrated by Vera Williams. Greenwillow, 1983.

Winter, Jeanette. *Klara's New World.* Illustrated by Jeanette Winter. Alfred A. Knopf, 1992.

Winthrop, Elizabeth. *Bear & Mrs. Duck.* Illustrated by Patience Brewster. Holiday House, 1990.

_____. *I Think He Likes Me.* Illustrated by Denise Saldutti. Harper & Row, 1980.

Wisniewski, David. *Rain Player.* Illustrated by David Wisniewski. Clarion Books, 1991.

Wold, Joanne. *Tell Them My Name Is Amanda.* Illustrated by Joanne Wold. Albert Whitman, 1977.

Wolf, Janet. *The Rosy Fat Magenta Radish.* Illustrated by Janet Wolf. Little, Brown, 1990.

Wolff, Ashley. *Stella & Roy.* Illustrated by Ashley Wolff. Dutton Children's Books, 1993.

_____. *A Year of Birds.* Illustrated by Ashley Wolff. Dodd, Mead, 1984.

Wolff, Robert Jay. *Hello Yellow.* Illustrated by Robert Jay Wolff. Scribner, 1968.

Wood, Audrey. *Elbert's Bad Word.* Illustrated by Audrey and Don Wood. Harcourt Brace Jovanovich, 1988.

_____. *Heckedy Peg.* Illustrated by Don Wood. Harcourt Brace Jovanovich, 1987.

_____. *King Bidgood's in the Bathtub.* Illustrated by Don Wood. Harcourt Brace Jovanovich, 1985.

Wood, Don and Audrey Wood. *Piggies.* Illustrated by Don Wood. Harcourt Brace Jovanovich, 1991.

Woodruff, Elvira. *The Wing Shop.* Illustrated by Stephen Gammell. Holiday House, 1991.

Yacowitz, Caryn. *The Jade Stone: A Chinese Folktale.* Illustrated by Ju-Hong Chen. Holiday House, 1992.

Yarbrough, Camille. *Cornrows.* Illustrated by Carole Byard. Coward, McCann & Geoghegan, 1979.

Yee, Paul. *Roses Sing on New Snow: A Delicious Tale.* Illustrated by Harvey Chan. Macmillan Children's Books, 1992.

Yen, Clara. *Why Rat Comes First: A Story of the Chinese Zodiac.* Illustrated by Hideo C. Yoshida. Children's Book Press, 1991.

Yolen, Jane. *The Emperor and the Kite.* Illustrated by Ed Young. Philomel, 1988.

_____. *Grandad Bill's Song.* Illustrated by Melissa Bay Mathis. Philomel, 1994.

_____. *No Bath Tonight.* Illustrated by Nancy Winslow Parker. Thomas Y. Crowell, 1978.

_____. *Owl Moon.* Illustrated by John Schoenherr. Philomel, 1987.

_____. *Picnic with Piggins.* Illustrated by Jane Dyer. Harcourt Brace Jovanovich, 1988.

_____. *Piggins.* Illustrated by Jane Dyer. Harcourt Brace Jovanovich, 1987.

_____. *Sky Dogs.* Illustrated by Barry Moser. Harcourt Brace Jovanovich, 1990.

_____. *The Three Bears Rhyme Book.* Illustrated by Jane Dyer. Harcourt Brace Jovanovich, 1987.

Yorinks, Arthur. *Company's Coming.* Illustrated by David Small. Crown, 1988.

_____. *Hey, Al.* Illustrated by Richard Egielski. Farrar, Straus & Giroux, 1986.

Young, Ed. *High on a Hill: A Book of Chinese Riddles.* Illustrated by Ed Young. Philomel, 1980.

_____. *Lon Po Po: A Red Riding Hood Story from China.* Illustrated by Ed Young. Philomel, 1989.

_____. *Moon Mother: A Native American Creation Tale.* Illustrated by Ed Young. HarperCollins, 1993.

_____. *Seven Blind Mice.* Illustrated by Ed Young. Philomel, 1992.

Young, James. *A Million Chameleons.* Illustrated by James Young. Little, Brown, 1990.

Zacharias, Thomas. *Where Is the Green Parrot?* Illustrated by Thomas Zacharias. Doubleday, 1990.

Zemach, Harve. *Nail Soup, a Swedish Folk Tale.* Illustrated by Margot Zemach. Follett, 1964.

_____ and Kaethe Zemach. *The Princess and Froggie.* Illustrated by Margot Zemach. Farrar, Straus & Giroux, 1975.

Zemach, Margot. *It Could Always Be Worse.* Illustrated by Margot Zemach. Farrar, Straus & Giroux, 1990.

_____. *The Little Red Hen: An Old Story.* Illustrated by Margot Zemach. Farrar, Straus & Giroux, 1983.

_____. *The Three Little Pigs: An Old Story.* Illustrated by Margot Zemach. Farrar, Straus & Giroux, 1989.

Ziefert, Harriet. *Bear All Year.* Illustrated by Arnold Lobel. Harper & Row, 1986.

_____. *Bear Gets Dressed.* Illustrated by Arnold Lobel. Harper & Row, 1986.

_____. *Bear Goes Shopping.* Illustrated by Arnold Lobel. Harper & Row, 1986.

————. *Bear's Busy Morning.* Illustrated by Arnold Lobel. Harper & Row, 1986.

————. *Happy Birthday, Grandpa!* Illustrated by Sidney Levitt. Harper & Row, 1988.

————. *A New Coat for Anna.* Illustrated by Anita Lobel. Alfred A. Knopf, 1986.

Ziegler, Sandra. *A Visit to the Bakery.* Illustrated by Pilot Productions Staff. Childrens Press, 1987.

Zimelman, Nathan. *The Great Adventures of Wo Ti.* Illustrated by Julie Downing. Macmillan, 1992.

Zion, Gene. *Harry and the Lady Next Door.* Illustrated by Margaret B. Graham. HarperCollins, 1978.

————. *Harry by the Sea.* Illustrated by Margaret B. Graham. HarperCollins, 1965.

————. *Harry the Dirty Dog.* Illustrated by Margaret B. Graham. HarperCollins, 1956.

————. *No Roses for Harry.* Illustrated by Margaret B. Graham. HarperCollins, 1958.

————. *Really Spring?* Illustrated by Margaret Bloy. Harper & Row, 1956.

————. *The Summer Snowman.* Illustrated by Margaret Bloy. Harper & Row, 1955.

Zola, Meguido. *Only the Best.* Illustrated by Valerie Littlewood. Franklin Watts, 1981.

Zolotow, Charlotte. *If You Listen.* Illustrated by Marc Simont. HarperCollins, 1980.

————. *Mr. Rabbit and the Lovely Present.* Illustrated by Maurice Sendak. Harper & Row, 1962.

————. *My Grandson Lew.* Illustrated by William Pene Du Bois. Harper & Row, 1974.

————. *Summer Is....* Illustrated by Ruth L. Bornstein. Crowell Junior Books, 1983.

————. *William's Doll.* Illustrated by William Pene Du Bois. Harper & Row, 1972.

Filmstrips, 16mm Films & Videocassettes

Aardema, Verna. *Why Mosquitoes Buzz in People's Ears.* Illustrated by Leo and Diane Dillon. Weston Woods, n.d. (10 min., 16mm film/videocassette)

Aesop. *The Tortoise and the Hare.* Illustrated by Janet Stevens. Listening Library, n.d. (7:50 min., filmstrip)

Asbjornsen, P. C. and J. E. Moe. *The Three Billy Goats Gruff.* Illustrated by Marcia Brown. Weston Woods, n.d. (4 min., filmstrip; 6 min., videocassette)

Berenstain, Stan and Jan Berenstain. *Bear's Picnic.* Illustrated by Stan and Jan Berenstain. Random House Educational Media, 1974. (5:40 min., filmstrip)

Bishop, Clare. *The Five Chinese Brothers.* Illustrated by Kurt Wiese. Weston Woods, n.d. (10 min., filmstrip/16mm film/videocassette)

Bond, Felicia. *The Halloween Performance.* Illustrated by Felicia Bond. Spoken Arts, n.d. (3:30 min., filmstrip)

_____. *Mary Betty Lizzie McNutt's Birthday.* Illustrated by Felicia Bond. Spoken Arts, n.d., (3:30 min., filmstrip)

Bridwell, Norman. *Clifford the Small Red Puppy.* Illustrated by Norman Bridwell. Listening Library, n.d. (5:02 min., filmstrip)

Brown, Marc Tolon. *Arthur's Thanksgiving.* Illustrated by Marc Tolon Brown. Random House/Miller-Brody, 1983. (8:44 min., filmstrip)

Brown, Marcia. *Shadow.* Illustrated by Marcia Brown. Weston Woods, n.d. (9 min., filmstrip)

_____. *Stone Soup.* Illustrated by Marcia Brown. Weston Woods, n.d. (11 min., filmstrip/16mm film/videocassette)

Burgess, Gelett. *The Goops.* Illustrated by Gelett Burgess. Listening Library, n.d. (9 min., filmstrip)

Carlson, Nancy. *I Like Me.* Illustrated by Nancy Carlson. Weston Woods, n.d. (4 min. filmstrip)

Daly, Niki. *Not So Fast, Songololo.* Illustrated by Niki Daly. Weston Woods, n.d. (8 min., 16mm film/videocassette)

Daugherty, James. *Andy and the Lion.* Illustrated by James Daugherty. Weston Woods, n.d. (7 min., filmstrip; 10 min., 16mm film/videocassette)

DePaola, Tomie. *Charlie Needs a Cloak.* Illustrated by Tomie DePaola. Weston Woods, n.d. (6 min., filmstrip; 8 min., 16mm film/videocassette)

_____. *The Legend of the Bluebonnett: An Old Tale of Texas.* Illustrated by Tomie DePaola. Listening Library, n.d. (9 min., filmstrip)

_____. *The Legend of the Indian Paintbrush.* Illustrated by Tomie DePaola. Listening Library, n.d. (8:45 min., filmstrip)

_____. *Sing, Pierrot, Sing.* Illustrated by Tomie DePaola. Random House, 1984. (6:40 min., filmstrip)

_____. *Strega Nona.* Illustrated by Tomie DePaola. Weston Woods, n.d. (9 min., 16mm film/videocassette)

DeRegniers, Beatrice Schenk. *May I Bring a Friend?* Illustrated by Beni Montresor. Weston Woods, n.d. (7 min., filmstrip)

Emberley, Barbara. *Drummer Hoff.* Illustrated by Ed Emberley. Weston Woods, n.d. (4 min., filmstrip; 6 min., 16mm film/videocassette)

Farms in the Fall. Journal Films, 1976. (9 min., filmstrip)

Flack, Marjorie. *The Story About Ping.* Illustrated by Kurt Wiese. Weston Woods, n.d. (10 min., filmstrip/16mm film/videocassette)

Freeman, Don. *A Rainbow of My Own.* Illustrated by Don Freeman. Live Oak Media, 1987. (5 min., videocassette)

Galdone, Paul. *The Gingerbread Boy.* Illustrated by Paul Galdone. Listening Library, n.d. (10 min., filmstrip)

_____. *King of the Cats.* Illustrated by Paul Galdone. Weston Woods, n.d. (6 min., filmstrip; 5 min., 16mm film/videocassette)

_____. *The Little Red Hen.* Illustrated by Paul Galdone. Weston Woods, n.d. (8 min., filmstrip/videocassette)

_____. *The Magic Porridge Pot.* Illustrated by Paul Galdone. Listening Library, n.d. (5:50 min., filmstrip)

_____. *The Three Little Pigs.* Illustrated by Paul Galdone. Listening Library, n.d. (filmstrip)

Haley, Gail E. *A Story, a Story.* Illustrated by Gail E. Haley. Weston Woods, n.d. (10 min., filmstrip/16mm film/videocassette)

Heine, Helme. *The Most Wonderful Egg in the World.* Illustrated by Helme Heine. Weston Woods, n.d. (6 min., 16mm film/videocassette)

_____. *The Pigs' Wedding.* Illustrated by Helme Heine. Weston Woods, n.d. (8 min., filmstrip; 7 min., 16mm/videocassette)

Hodges, Margaret. *Saint George and the Dragon.* Illustrated by Trina Schart Hyman. Listening Library, n.d. (12 min., filmstrip/videocassette)

Hutchins, Pat. *Rosie's Walk.* Illustrated by Pat Hutchins. Weston Woods, n.d. (3 min., filmstrip; 5 min., 16mm film/videocassette)

_____. *Surprise Party.* Illustrated by Pat Hutchins. Weston Woods, 1977. (6 min., filmstrip)

Hyman, Trina Schart. *Little Red Riding Hood.* Illustrated by Trina Schart Hyman. Listening Library, 1984. (13 min., filmstrip)

Johnson, Crockett. *Harold and the Purple Crayon.* Illustrated by Crockett Johnson. Weston Woods, n.d. (7 min., filmstrip; 8 min., 16mm film/videocassette)

Keats, Ezra Jack. *Apt. 3.* Illustrated by Ezra Jack Keats. Weston Woods, n.d. (8 min., filmstrip/16mm film/videocassette)

_____. *Goggles.* Illustrated by Ezra Jack Keats. Weston Woods, n.d. (6 min., filmstrip/16mm film/videocassette)

_____. *Peter's Chair.* Illustrated by Ezra Jack Keats. Weston Woods, n.d. (4 min., filmstrip; 6 min., 16mm film/videocassette)

_____. *The Snowy Day.* Illustrated by Ezra Jack Keats. Weston Woods, n.d. (6 min., filmstrip/16mm film/videocassette)

_____. *Whistle for Willie.* Illustrated by Ezra Jack Keats. Weston Woods, n.d. (5 min., filmstrip; 6 min., 16mm film/videocassette)

La Fontaine, Jean De. *The Hare and the Tortoise.* Illustrated by Brian Wildsmith. Weston Woods, n.d. (4 min., filmstrip)

Ladybug, Ladybug, Winter Is Coming. Coronet Films & Video, 1976. (9:30 min., 16mm film/videocassette)

Langstaff, John. *Frog Went a-Courtin'.* Illustrated by Feodor Rojankovsky. Weston Woods, n.d. (12 min., 16mm film/videocassette)

Leaf, Munro. *Ferdinand the Bull.* Illustrated by Robert Lawson. Walt Disney Educational Media, 1968. (8 min., 16mm film)

_____. *The Story of Ferdinand.* Illustrated by Robert Lawson. Live Oak Media, 1985. (9 min., filmstrip)

Levinson, Riki. *Watch the Stars Come Out.* Illustrated by Diane Goode. Random House, 1986. (7:41 min., filmstrip)

Lionni, Leo. *Little Blue and Little Yellow.* Illustrated by Leo Lionni. Contemporary Films, 1962. (10 min., 16mm film)

Lobel, Arnold. *Cookies* (from *Frog and Toad Together*). Illustrated by Arnold Lobel. Churchill Films, 1987. (videocassette)

————. *Fables.* Illustrated by Arnold Lobel. Random House, 1981. (filmstrip)

————. *The Garden* (from *Frog and Toad Together*). Illustrated by Arnold Lobel. Churchill Films, 1987. (videocassette)

————. *On Market Street.* Illustrated by Anita Lobel. Miller-Brody, 1982. (13 min., filmstrip)

————. *Spring* (from *Frog and Toad Together*). Illustrated by Arnold Lobel. Newbery Award Records, 1976. (5:40 min., filmstrip)

————. *A Treeful of Pigs.* Illustrated by Anita Lobel. Educational Enrichment Materials, 1980. (filmstrip)

Lyon, George Ella. *A Regular Rolling Noah.* Illustrated by Stephen Gammell. Random House, 1988. (7:22 min., filmstrip)

McCloskey, Robert. *Blueberries for Sal.* Illustrated by Robert McCloskey. Weston Woods, n.d. (9 min., filmstrip/16mm film/videocassette)

————. *Make Way for Ducklings.* Illustrated by Robert McCloskey. Weston Woods, n.d. (11 min., filmstrip/16mm film/videocassette)

McCully, Emily Arnold. *Picnic.* Illustrated by Emily Arnold McCully. Weston Woods, n.d. (4 min., filmstrip; 10 min., 16mm film/videocassette)

McDermott, Gerald. *Arrow to the Sun.* Illustrated by Gerald McDermott. Weston Woods, n.d. (9 min., filmstrip)

McPhail, David M. *Alligators Are Awful (and They Have Terrible Manners, Too!).* Illustrated by David M. McPhail. Spoken Arts, 1982. (3:50 min., filmstrip)

Marshall, James. *Goldilocks and the Three Bears.* Illustrated by James Marshall. Weston Woods, n.d. (8 min., 16mm film/videocassette)

————. *The Three Little Pigs.* Illustrated by James Marshall. Weston Woods, n.d. (9 min., filmstrip; 8 min., 16mm film/videocassette)

Mayer, Mercer. *A Boy, a Dog and a Frog.* Illustrated by live action. Phoenix BFA Films & Video, 1967. (9 min., 16mm film/videocassette)

————. *Frog Goes to Dinner.* Illustrated by Mercer Mayer. Phoenix Films, n.d. (12 min., 16mm film)

Miller, Edna. *Mousekin's Golden House.* Illustrated by Edna Miller. Prentice-Hall, 1964. (filmstrip)

Mosel, Arlene. *Tikki Tikki Tembo.* Illustrated by Blaire Lent. Weston Woods, n.d. (8 min., filmstrip; 9 min., 16mm film/videocassette)

Rayner, Mary. *Mr. & Mrs. Pig's Evening Out.* Illustrated by Mary Rayner. Weston Woods, n.d. (9 min., filmstrip)

Reyher, Rebecca. *My Mother Is the Most Beautiful Woman in the World.* Illustrated by Ruth Gannett. Filmic Archives, 1968. (9 min., 16mm film)

Rylant, Cynthia. *The Relatives Came.* Illustrated by Stephen Gammell. Listening Library, n.d. (8 min., filmstrip/videocassette)

————. *This Year's Garden.* Illustrated by Mary Szilagyi. Random House, 1986. (5:12 min., filmstrip)

Seeger, Pete and Charles Seeger. *The Foolish Frog.* Illustrated by Miloslav Jagr. Weston Woods, n.d. (8 min., filmstrip/16mm film/videocassette)

Sendak, Maurice. *In the Night Kitchen.* Illustrated by Maurice Sendak. Weston Woods, n.d. (6 min., filmstrip/16mm film/videocassette)

_____. *Where the Wild Things Are.* Illustrated by Maurice Sendak. Weston Woods, n.d. (5 min., filmstrip; 8 min., 16mm film/videocassette)

Seuss, Dr. *Dr. Seuss: Green Eggs and Ham.* Illustrated by Dr. Seuss. BFA Educational Media, 1973. (9 min., 16mm film)

Spier, Peter. *Oh, Were They Ever Happy!* Illustrated by Peter Spier. Listening Library, n.d. (4 min., filmstrip)

Steig, William. *Sylvester and the Magic Pebble.* Illustrated by William Steig. Weston Woods, n.d. (10 min., 16mm film/videocassette)

Tafuri, Nancy. *Have You Seen My Duckling?* Illustrated by Nancy Tafuri. Random House/Miller-Brody, 1985. (4:50 min., filmstrip)

Tolstoi, Aleksei Nikolaevich. *The Great Big Enormous Turnip.* Illustrated by Helen Oxenbury. Weston Woods, 1972. (filmstrip)

Vagin, Vladimir and Frank Asch. *Here Comes the Cat!* Illustrated by Vladimir Vagin and Frank Asch. Weston Woods, n.d. (7 min., filmstrip; 6 min., 16mm film/videocassette)

Van Allsburg, Chris. *The Garden of Abdul Gasazi.* Illustrated by Chris Van Allsburg. Listening Library, n.d. (8 min., videocassette)

_____. *Polar Express.* Illustrated by Chris Van Allsburg. Random House/Miller-Brody, 1988. (12 min., filmstrip)

Vincent, Gabrielle. *Ernest & Celestine's Picnic.* Illustrated by Gabrielle Vincent. Weston Woods, n.d. (5 mins., filmstrip)

Ward, Lynd. *The Biggest Bear.* Illustrated by Lynd Ward. Weston Woods, n.d. (7 min., filmstrip)

Wells, Rosemary. *Morris's Disappearing Bag.* Illustrated by Rosemary Wells. Weston Woods, n.d. (6 min., filmstrip/16mm film/videocassette)

Westcott, Nadine Bernard. *I Know an Old Lady Who Swallowed a Fly.* Illustrated by Nadine Bernard Westcott. Listening Library, n.d. (9:30 min., filmstrip)

Williams, Vera. *A Chair for My Mother.* Illustrated by Vera Williams. Random House/Miller-Brody, 1983. (8 min., filmstrip)

Wood, Audrey. *Heckedy Peg.* Illustrated by Don Wood. Random House/Educational Enrichment Materials, n.d. (10 min., filmstrip)

Yolen, Jane. *Owl Moon.* Illustrated by John Schoenherr. Weston Woods, n.d. (8 min., filmstrip/16mm film/videocassette)

Zion, Harry. *Harry the Dirty Dog.* Illustrated by Margaret B. Graham. Miller-Brody, n.d. (7:21 min., filmstrip)

Zolotow, Charlotte. *My Grandson Lew.* Illustrated by Charlotte Zolotow. Barr Films, 1976. (13 min., 16mm film)

Audio Cassettes,
Compact Discs & Records

Beech, Sandra. *Sidewalk Shuffle.* Kids Records, 1974. (Record)

Bishop, Heather. *Purple People Eater.* Mother of Pearl Records, 1980. (Audiocassette)

Brodey, Kim and Jerry Brodey. *Simple Magic.* Kids Records, 1984. (Audiocassette)

Chenille Sisters. *Chenille Sisters 1-2-3 Kids.* Red House Records, 1989. (Audiocassette)

A Children's Celebration of Show Tunes. Music for Little People, 1992. (Compact Disc)

Diamond, Charlotte. *10 Carrot Diamond: Songs and Stories.* CAPAC, 1985. (Audiocassette)

Fiedler, Arthur and the Boston Pops. *Fiedler's Favorites for Children.* RCA/Ariola, 1986. (Audiocassette)

Greg & Steve. *Kidding Around with Greg & Steve.* Youngheart Records, 1985. (Audiocassette)

_____. *On the Move with Greg & Steve.* Youngheart Records, 1983. (Audiocassette)

_____. *We All Live Together, Vol. 2.* Youngheart Records, 1978. (Audiocassette)

_____. *We All Live Together, Vol. 3.* Youngheart Records, 1979. (Audiocassette)

_____. *We All Live Together, Vol. 4.* Youngheart Records, 1980. (Audiocassette)

Jenkins, Ella. *Jambo and Other Call-&-Response Songs & Chants.* Folkways, 1974. (Audiocassette)

McGrath, Bob. *If You're Happy and You Know It—Sing Along with Bob #1.* Western Publishing, 1985. (Audiocassette)

Murray, Anne. *There's a Hippo in My Tub.* Capitol Records, 1977. (Audiocassette)

Palmer, Hap. *Hap Palmer's Sally the Swinging Snake.* Educational Activities, Inc., 1987. (Audiocassette)

Penner, Fred. *Fred Penner's Place.* Oak Street Music, 1988. (Audiocassette)

_____. *Special Delivery.* Shoreline, 1983. (Audiocassette)

Peter, Paul & Mary. *Peter, Paul & Mommy.* Warner Communications, 1969. (Audiocassette)

Powell, Ruth I. *Move Over, Mother Goose! Finger Plays, Action Verses, & Funny Rhymes.* Gryphon House, 1987. (Audiocassette)

Raffi. *The Corner Grocery Store.* Troubadour Records, 1979. (Audiocassette)

_____. *One Light, One Sun.* Troubadour Records, 1985. (Audiocassette)

_____. *Raffi: Baby Beluga.* Troubadour Records, 1980. (Audiocassette)

_____. *Raffi: Everything Grows.* Troubadour Records, 1987. (Audiocassette)

_____. *Raffi: More Singable Songs.* Troubadour Records, 1977. (Audiocassette)

_____. *Raffi: Rise and Shine.* Troubadour Records, 1982. (Audiocassette)

_____. *Raffi: Singable Songs for the Very Young.* Troubadour Records, 1976. (Audiocassette)

Scruggs, Joe. *Late Last Night.* Educational Graphics Press, 1984. (Audiocassette)

Sharon, Lois & Bram. *One Elephant.* Elephant Records, 1978. (Audiocassette)

_____. *Sharon, Lois & Bram: In the Schoolyard.* Elephant Records, 1980. (Audiocassette)

_____. *Sing A to Z.* Elephant Records, 1990. (Audiocassette)

_____. *Singing 'n Swinging.* Elephant Records, 1980. (Audiocassette)

Stewart, Georgiana. *Folk Dance Fun: Simple Folk Songs and Dances.* Kimbo Educational, 1984. (Record)

Wise, Joe. *Pockets: Songs for Little People.* G.I.A. Publications, 1978. (Audiocassette)

Professional Resources

Anderson, Paul S. *Storytelling with the Flannelboard: Book 1.* T. S. Denison, 1963.
    A flannel board bibliography, equipment list and storytelling bibliography
    for those wanting to begin telling stories with a flannel board.
_____. *Storytelling with the Flannelboard: Book 2.* T. S. Denison, 1970.
    Simple stories and patterns for making flannel figures.
Association for Library Service to Children. *Programming for 3–5 Year Olds,
    Revised Edition.* American Library Association, 1993.
    The philosophy of public library programming for children ages 3 to 5.
    Includes criteria for good library programming, time-tested procedures and
    information regarding personnel, facilities, costs, schedules and publicity.
_____. *Programming for Very Young Children, Revised Edition.* American
    Library Association, 1993.
    Criteria for programs, procedures for implementing them, a checklist for
    program planning, etc., are included. "Based on the belief that the library
    can become an important community resource for early childhood educa-
    tion."
Baker, Augusta and Ellin Greene. *Storytelling: Art & Technique.* R. R. Bowker,
    1987.
    Expanded and updated from the earlier edition; two added sections are
    on storytelling to infants and toddlers, and children as storytellers.
Bauer, Caroline Feller. *Caroline Feller Bauer's New Handbook for Storytellers.* Il-
    lustrated by Lynn Bredeson. American Library Association, 1993.
    Ideas for planning, publicizing and presenting story hour programs for all
    age groups. Helpful instructions for using a variety of presentation materials
    to add variety.
_____. *This Way to Books.* Illustrated by Lynn Gates. H. W. Wilson, 1983.
    Up-beat, inspirational, idea-filled—to get children involved with books
    through activities, poems, crafts, recipes, and more. Great for prodding your
    own imagination for lively story time ideas.
Carlson, Ann D. *Early Childhood Literature Sharing Programs in Libraries.*
    Library Professional Publications, 1985.
    Carlson's Columbia University School of Library Service doctoral disser-
    tation discusses research into the developmental stages of children from
    birth to age 3 and the benefits of library story hours.
Carlson, Bernice Wells. *Listen! and Help Tell the Story.* Illustrated by Burmah
    Burris. Abingdon, 1965.
    A truly varied collection of fingerplays, action verses and poems with
    sound effects to add variety, fun and participation to your story hours.
Champlin, Connie and Nancy Renfro. *Storytelling with Puppets.* American
    Library Association, 1985.
    Practical hints about storytelling with puppets, how to adapt stories to
    puppet presentation, useful patterns, innovative ideas for storytelling with
    puppets, etc.; includes a bibliography.

Cianciolo, Patricia J. *Picture Books for Children, 3rd Edition.* American Library Association, 1990.

A resource guide for "teachers of children from nursery school through junior high, for daycare..., for librarians..., for parents ... concerned with the selection of well-written, imaginatively illustrated picture books ... of interest to children."

Commire, Anne. *Something About the Author.* Gale Research, 1971+.

A 75+ volume series of biographical information about children's authors and illustrators; a photograph, reproductions of art from their books, candid evaluations of their work and quotes from book reviews; arranged chronologically.

Cromwell, Liz, Dixie Hibner and John R. Faitel. *Finger Frolics: Over 250 Fingerplays for Children from 3 Years.* Illustrated by Joan Lockwood, Partner, 1983.

Lots of fingerplays, some instructional as well as fun, in contemporary language. Spiral-bound paperback.

Cullum, Carolyn N. *Storytime Sourcebook: A Compendium of Ideas & Resources for Storytellers.* Neal-Schuman, 1990.

A comprehensive subject guide to preschool story time references to help locate appropriate crafts, fingerplays, stories, songs, etc.; 446 picture books, 351 filmstrips, 93 16mm films, 156 videocassettes; covers 100 topics; includes activities.

Cummings, Pat. *Talking with Artists: Conversations with... (14 Distinguished Picture Book Artists).* Bradbury, 1992.

Conversations with 14 distinguished picture book artists: Lane Smith, Leo and Diane Dillon, Lisa Campbell Ernst, Lois Ehlert, and more. Details of their childhood and working life as illustrators with "then" and "now" photos and "then" and "now" examples of their art.

Defty, Jeff. *Creative Fingerplays and Action Rhymes: An Index and Guide to Their Use.* Oryx, 1992.

"Describes how to choose and perform fingerplays and action rhymes and explains their importance as stimulus and entertainment." Includes 100 examples for preschool through second grade plus subject and first-line indexing of 3,000 rhymes in collections.

_____. *Teaching with Your Hands: A Developmental Guide and Index to Fingerplays and Action Rhymes.* Oryx, 1992.

Circle games, singing rhymes, dramatic play and movement, active verse and fingerplay. Really meant for primary-aged school children, but some useful ideas adaptable to preschool audiences.

Delamar, Gloria T. *Children's Counting-Out Rhymes, Fingerplays, Jump-Rope and Bounce-Ball Chants and Other Rhythms.* McFarland, 1983.

Hundreds of old and new fingerplays, holiday rhymes and chants, join-in rhythms, counting-out rhymes, jump-rope and bounce-ball chants, tongue-twisters, "staircase" tales, and narrative verses.

DeSalvo, Nancy N. *Beginning with Books: Library Programming for Infants, Toddlers and Preschoolers.* Shoe String, 1992.

Twenty-four structured book experience programs appropriate to the play level and stimulation needs of 0–5 year olds.

DeWit, Dorothy. *Children's Faces Looking Up: Program Building for the Storyteller*. American Library Association, 1979.

Six sample programs illustrate DeWit's approach to storytelling and library programming for children. DeWit defines a tellable tale, how to recognize quality material and outlines the evolution of storytelling.

Grayson, Marion. *Let's Do Fingerplays*. Robert B. Luce, 1962.

Two hundred rhymes and songs with fingerplay directions; lists sources, includes title and first line indexes; well designed and illustrated.

Green, Ellin. *Books, Babies, and Libraries; Serving Infants, Toddlers, Their Parents & Caregivers*. American Library Association, 1991.

An overview of major theories of early child development; a discussion of the roles of parents and librarians in fostering literacy; collection development; program planning and implementation; and evaluation of library services to early childhood.

Hayes, Sarah. *Stamp Your Feet: Action Rhymes*. Illustrated by Jan Ormerod. Lothrop, Lee & Shepard, 1988.

Twenty action rhymes suitable for preschool story hours.

Hunt, Mary Alice. *Multimedia Approach to Children's Literature: A Selective List of Films (& Videocassettes, Filmstrips & Recordings Based on Children's Books), 3rd Edition*. American Library Association, 1983.

A very selective collection of non-print materials arranged alphabetically by book title. Brief annotations include age levels, playing times, and comments on music or narration when particularly noteworthy.

Irving, Jan and Robin Currie. *Full Speed Ahead: Stories & Activities for Children on Transporation*. Libraries Unlimited, 1988.

Emphasizes skills development more than theme; more for self-contained classroom of preschool or primary grades but possibly some useful, adaptable ideas.

————. *Glad Rags: Stories & Activities Featuring Clothes for Children*. Illustrated by Tom Henrichsen. Libraries Unlimited, 1987.

Introduces quality picture book literature with extensions through a variety of enrichment activities. Includes activities, games and other literature sharing experiences with over 200 titles.

————. *Mudluscious: Stories & Activities Featuring Food for Preschool Children*. Illustrated by Robert B. Phillips. Libraries Unlimited, 1986.

Stories and activities about food, mostly geared to preschool classes in self-contained situations rather than once-a-week library story hours. Sometimes useful for that one more story or story-stretcher idea you need to round out a program.

————. *Raising the Roof*. Libraries Unlimited, 1990.

Books and programs about houses for preschool through grade 3. Oriented toward skills development; many activities require a longer time than available during library story hours but there are possible adaptations for your purposes.

Jones, Taffy. *Library Programs for Children*. McFarland, 1989.

Long and short programs for preschool through grade 4 on each of five topics: Bears, Mice, Dinosaurs, Bookworms, and Indians. Coordinating activities include: Story time, library skill time, games, crafts, music, etc.

Lamme, Linda Leonard et al. *Raising Readers: A Guide to Sharing Literature with Young Children.* Walker, 1980.
   For when parents ask how to prepare their children for reading. Practical advice, motivating readers, evaluating good literature, storytelling and more; divided into four age levels from infants to beginning readers.
Larrick, Nancy. *Let's Do a Poem! Introducing Poetry to Children Through Listening, Singing, Chanting, Impromptu Choral Reading, Body Movement, Dance and Dramatization; Including 98 Favorite Songs and Poems.* Delacorte, 1991.
   A good boost for those souls frightened by poetry in the past. Helpful ideas for sharing and having fun with poetry and children.
Lima, Carolyn W. and John A. Lima. *A to Zoo: Subject Access to Children's Picture Books; 4th Edition.* R. R. Bowker, 1993.
   A comprehensive subject guide to picture books for children. Full bibliographic information plus the subjects under which each title is listed. Invaluable for chasing down that one last story to round out a program.
Livo, Norma and Sandra Reitz. *Storytelling Folklore Sourcebook.* Libraries Unlimited, 1991.
   Livo discusses the importance of knowing another culture's folklore in order to be able to do justice to its stories.
MacDonald, Margaret Read. *Booksharing: 101 Programs to Use with Preschoolers.* Illustrated by Julie Liana MacDonald. Library Professional Publications, 1988.
   Excellent, practical advice on how to conduct preschool story times from a veteran children's librarian and storyteller. One hundred and one 45-minute programs for children ages 2.5 to 6, grouped by subject.
_____. *Twenty Tellable Tales: Audience Participation Folktales for the Beginning Storyteller.* Illustrated by Roxane Murphy. H. W. Wilson, 1986.
   How to select, shape, learn and tell each tale. Notes on tale origins, performance styles in other cultures, and how to summon audience participation. Stories are short, easy to remember, with repetitive verses.
McElmeel, Sharron L. *Bookpeople: A First Album.* Illustrated by Deborah L. McElmeel. Teacher Idea Press, 1990.
   Biographical information on picture book authors and illustrators including: Verna Aardema, Aliki, Frank Asch, Jim Aylesworth, Lorna Balian, Franz Brandenberg, Gail Haley, Trina Schart Hyman, James Marshall and more.
Miller, Teresa and Anne Pellowski. *Joining In: An Anthology of Audience Participation Stories and How to Tell Them.* Yellow Moon, 1988.
   A collection of stories and storytelling tips to encourage audience participation. Practical advice and some fun ideas to try.
Moore, Vardine. *Pre-School Story Hour, 2nd Edition.* Scarecrow, 1972.
   Basics on how to plan and conduct preschool story hours including music, activities, dance, fingerplays, story lists, room arrangement, parent involvement, and the history and importance of preschool story hours.
Nichols, Judy. *Storytimes for Two-Year-Olds.* Lora Sears. American Library Association, 1987.
   A step-by-step description of a typical toddler story hour with books, fingerplays, music, active dramatics; thirty-three programs in all.
Pellowski, Anne. *The Family Storytelling Handbook: How to use Stories, Anec-*

dotes, Rhymes, Handkerchiefs, Paper, and Other Objects to Enrich Your Family Traditions. Illustrated by Lynn Sweat. MacMillan, 1987.

Briefly outlines why, when, what and how to tell stories; but her main thrust is in encouraging storytellers to expand into fun, new, exciting methods of storytelling, with good stories as examples.

Peterson, Carolyn Sue and Brenny Hall. *Story Programs: A Source Book of Materials.* Scarecrow, 1980.

Ideas for library programming with toddlers, preschoolers and primary grade children. Storytelling using flannelboards, creative dramatics, and puppetry. Includes songs, poems, stories and puppet plays.

Raines, Shirley C. *More Story Stretchers: More Activities to Expand Children's Books.* Gryphon House, 1989.

Ninety books are extended with 450 different activities to integrate stories into the curriculum. However, the ideas are useful and adaptable for preschool story hours too. They open your mind to all sorts of possibilities.

_____ and Robert J. Canady. *Story Stretchers: Activities to Expand Children's Favorite Books.* Gryphon House, 1989.

Ninety books grouped into eighteen topics with specific story stretching ideas and activities. Largely aimed at classroom teachers but many ideas are adaptable to the library story hour setting.

Ring a Ring o' Roses: Stories, Games & Fingerplays for Preschool Children. Flint Public Library, Flint, Michigan, 1981.

A small paperback collection of 450+ fingerplays and action rhymes, organized into major headings and subheadings for ease of access; indispensable for story hour planners.

Sierra, Judy and Robert Kaminski. *Storytelling with Young Children.* Oryx, 1991.

How to share the enjoyment of language and literature with children ages two to seven. Complete story texts and proven techniques to involve children verbally, visually and kinesthetically. Includes traceable flannelboard figures.

Sitarz, Paula Gaj. *More Picture Book Story Hours: From Parties to Pets.* Libraries Unlimited, 1990.

Story hour programs designed to "bring children's literature of artistic and literary merit to four's and five's and have children view books and reading as pleasurable experiences."

_____. *Picture Book Story Hours: From Birthdays to Bears.* Libraries Unlimited, 1987.

Practical advice on selecting stories to use with four and five-year-olds, preparing for story hours plus twenty-two tried-and-true story hour programs outlined for immediate use.

Stangl, Jean. *Is Your Storytale Dragging?* Fearon Teaching Aids, 1988.

Storytelling extras such as tell & draw stories, paper folding, tearing or cutting, string boards, stories to eat, surprises, etc., to get your creative juices flowing and add pizzazz to your story hours.

Tashjian, Virginia. *With a Deep Sea Smile: Story Hour Stretches for Large and Small Groups.* Illustrated by Rosemary Wells. Little, Brown, 1974.

Companion volume to *Juba This and Juba That*—more chants, poetry, rhymes, fingerplays, riddles, songs, etc., and hints on how to stimulate participation.

Thomas, James L. *Play, Learn, & Grow: An Annotated Guide to the Best Books & Materials for Very Young Children.* R. R. Bowker, 1992.
An annotated guide including over 5,000 print and non-print titles.

Vonk, Idalee. *Storytelling with the Flannelboard; Book 3.* T. S. Denison, 1984.
More stories for flannel board telling. Companion to Books 1 & 2 by Paul Anderson, listed above.

Warren, Jean. *"Cut & Tell" Scissors Stories for Spring.* Totline, 1984.
Simple cut & tell stories using paper plates.

Wilson, Mary E. *Representing Children's Book Characters.* Illustrated by Diane Buchanan. Scarecrow, 1989.
Some interesting, unusual ideas for capturing the essence of a book character in costume and props. Chapters: Mother Goose, folktales, picture story books, fiction and biography. Though aimed at older readers, this may spur creative ideas of your own.

Ziskind, Sylvia. *Telling Stories to Children.* H. W. Wilson, 1976.
A basic introduction to storytelling with numerous examples; extensive bibliography of poetry, stories, drama, puppets, voice, speech, etc.

Author Index

Title Index